JEWISH GIRLS, JEWISH WOMEN, JEWISH WRITERS

"In the Country" by Grace Paley

A tantalizing fragment of family history reveals humor, tragedy, and the unmistakable tones of the Old Country, as a young girl hears little but learns much about her legacy.

"Grandma" by Laura Cunningham

When Grandma comes to live with her family, Lily expects a cookie-baking Bubbie—but instead finds herself struggling with an elegant, eccentric Grande Dame.

"Sephirot" by Dinah Berland

The mystic tradition of the Kabbalah is forbidden to Jewish women, but Sarah's grandfather teaches her that in America, freedom is more important than tradition.

"The Nose-Fixer" by Persis Knobbe

A young girl tries a home remedy for changing her hated profile—and reflects on her changing Jewishness too.

And 41 more outstanding pieces
in this wondrous collection

Nice Jewish Girls

MARLENE ADLER MARKS is managing editor of *The Jewish Journal of Greater Los Angeles*, and the author of a weekly syndicated newspaper column called "A Woman's Voice." She is a frequent contributor to *Hadassah* magazine and the op-ed page of the *Los Angeles Times*, and a popular speaker on issues relating to Jewish women.

Nice
Jewish
Girls

Growing Up in America

EDITED BY
MARLENE ADLER MARKS

A PLUME BOOK

PLUME
Published by the Penguin Group
Penguin Books USA Inc., 375 Hudson Street,
New York, New York 10014, U.S.A.
Penguin Books Ltd, 27 Wrights Lane,
London W8 5TZ, England
Penguin Books Australia Ltd, Ringwood,
Victoria, Australia
Penguin Books Canada Ltd, 10 Alcorn Avenue,
Toronto, Ontario, Canada M4V 3B2
Penguin Books (N.Z.) Ltd, 182–190 Wairau Road,
Auckland 10, New Zealand

Penguin Books Ltd, Registered Offices:
Harmondsworth, Middlesex, England

First published by Plume, an imprint of Dutton Signet,
a division of Penguin Books USA Inc.

First Printing, April, 1996
10 9 8 7 6 5 4

 REGISTERED TRADEMARK—MARCA REGISTRADA

LIBRARY OF CONGRESS CATALOGING-IN-PUBLICATION DATA
Nice Jewish girls : growing up in America / edited by Marlene Adler
Marks.
p. cm.
ISBN 0-452-27397-8
1. Jewish girls—United States—Literary collections. 2. Jewish
women—United States—Biography. 3. Jewish girls—United States—
Biography. 4. American literature—Jewish authors. 5. American
literature—Women authors.
PS508.J4N53 1996
810.8'09287'089924—dc20   95-39408
                                                              CIP

Printed in the United States of America
Set in Garamond Light

For Samantha
My own Jewish girl

ACKNOWLEDGMENTS

In the preparation for this book, my thanks and appreciation go to the hundreds of writers of Jewish stories whose submissions helped me shape the sense of what Jewish girlhood is all about. More personally, I have gained both insight and second sight from my gifted readers Tamara Leibman, Bonnie Trachtenberg, Ariel Gordon, and especially Sara Eve Roseman; Betsy Amster, my literary agent; Julia Moskin, my editor; and my dear teacher and friend, Marcia Cohn Spiegel.

Contents

Part Two
"With all your soul . . ."

Part Three
"With all your might . . ."

Part Four
"When you lie down, when you rise up . . ."

Introduction

"Know your place!" my mother used to tell me. It was my introduction to life as a Jewish girl. But where—or better what—was it? The elaborate rules defining "my place" were laid out for me on a daily basis. Some rules were based on common courtesy; others on self protection; still others on the hidden hierarchy of our community life. Don't talk back to your parents. Don't call a boy before he calls you. Don't buy the dress for a party until you get the invitation. Don't bring shame on the Jewish people. There were rules for making peace between warring friends, for who sits next to whom at family celebrations, and how to make and take criticism. In a tightly organized society, a Jewish girl learns early on to pay keen attention to the expectations of others, and to discern where she is in the community's pecking order.

This is an anthology about the "place" of the Jewish girl, and the experience known as coming of age; a time when she discovers who she is and why. The stories, memoirs, and poems gathered here pause to capture that special moment of youth when who you are is suddenly no longer negotiable, when history, legacy, personality, and inner awareness combine into a particular view of one's life. That moment can come as early as age five, and as late as under the marriage canopy. *Why* it comes is just as unpredictable as *when*: through a story told by Grandma, by confrontation with the Holocaust or a visit to the state of Israel, or by means of spiritual experience, whether listening to a prayer, lighting a candle or holding a ritual object. The mystery—and the beauty—is that it comes at all.

The title of this book, *Nice Jewish Girls*, is an expression of both respect and irony. It is loaded with expectations of what and who a "girl" should be. A "nice Jewish girl" is smart but not threateningly so, respectful of elders, brave, but not to the point of rebellion. More dutiful than religious. A "sheyna maidel," in Yiddish, is a pretty girl, and the word "pretty" itself indicates the moderation that so often guides a Jewish girl's life. A nice Jewish girl is not excessive; she lives within polite borders, her passions under control, aware of the rules. "Nice Jewish girl" is everything so many of us didn't want to be, but still, to a large extent, want our daughters to become.

Beyond how others think of her, just who is she to herself? In this book we learn that all along she has been watching and taking notes. The nice Jewish girl, it turns out, is the holder of family secrets, and the repository of family hopes and fears, the transmitter of the community's history and pain. The nice Jewish girl sees beyond the mythology into the truth of Grandma's real life, the secrets hidden in the ark, the costs of political radicalism and economic insecurity, the dark sexual neediness of men—Jewish and otherwise— and the burdens of history, including what the Holocaust has exacted from both survivors and victims alike. And now that she has at last been granted access to a Jewish education, she sees the wisdom of the past with that same clear eye and keen intelligence.

This book came together during the year my own daughter was preparing for her bat mitzvah. Watching the pleasure that she and her girlfriends took in learning their Torah portions, meeting with the rabbi and cantor and preparing for the big event, I could see clearly how much had changed in a relatively short period of time. Until Samantha's bat mitzvah, my mother had never before held the Torah; she was raised in a tradition which held women unclean to touch the sacred objects. But now she was up there on the bimah before the ark, joining my father in saying the opening blessings before the Torah reading, and passing the holy scrolls along from generation to generation.

As for me, I had been lucky enough to go to Hebrew school and often led my Junior Congregation each Saturday in prayers. And yet I could not avoid women's second-class status in the community and derailed my own bat mitzvah when I saw how meager it would be compared to my brother's bar mitzvah years down the road.

Samantha has none of the ambivalence of her mother or grandmother, and there is no reason she should. In a world full of opportunity, where women are rabbis and cantors and participate on all level of religious ceremony, she rushes to Jewish life without cynicism, recognizing Judaism as a strong central core of her being. I wanted this volume to speak to women across the generations about the love, yearning, and responsibility we all share, what is changing and what will remain the same.

Nearly 300 submissions were received for this book, in response to ads placed in Jewish newspapers, writers' publications, and Jewish internet forums across the country. My request was open-ended; for pieces about any aspect of female coming-of-age, so long as they had specific Jewish content. I've selected stories, memoirs, and poems which do not gloss over the pain of past discrimination so much as they offer a long-term view of where we're heading. While other anthologies have dwelled on the bitterness which marked Jewish women's second-class status, this volume moves into the future.

The question this volume poses is this: What is it that makes a young woman a Jew? The Jews are a people as much as a religion; they have a history, a culture, a code of ethics, a pride in purpose and a legacy of tragedy and triumph two thousand years old, any of which may influence an individual member of the group as much as the specific tenets of faith. Try to pin down what makes a person feel she or he is a Jew; some say the Ten Commandments, for others it's the eating of matzoh on Passover, and still others feel it in the Jewish mandate to repair the world. Peculiar among the world's faiths, Judaism can be as much an attitude toward life as a prescription of faith. We are iconoclasts, born to be suspicious of false gods and phony worship and reluctant to give up our skepticism.

For that reason, when the moment comes for declaring ourselves as Jews, God may not be mentioned at all. A Yiddish word like "chutzpah," used by an adult to describe a young girl's act of guts or grit, may define a girl for life. So too might a week spent watching a parent sitting on a low chair during shiva, the mourning ritual. Sometimes however, it's nothing more specific than the guarded way our family regards the "outside" world which makes us know that we are separate and distinct.

Even today, when so many are seeking "spirituality" and religious experience, a young girl coming of age in the Jewish world learns right away to distrust public pronouncements of religiosity, and to value intellect and rationality above all else. This discomfort makes sense against the bitter facts of history; Jews retain the knowledge that they have suffered for their beliefs and so keep the whys and hows of commitment buried from view. The legacy of a pariah nation means that many of us are uncomfortable describing the emotional or sensual aspects of our faith without recourse to cynicism or farce.

But as the stories and memoirs here reflect, today's young Jewish women writers are finally beginning to talk about what they know, things their parents and grandparents never admitted, including the role of the holy within our great tradition. And that's part of what made this volume such an exciting undertaking. American Jewish girls are heirs to the dramatic social revolutions of the last two decades, which are altering how they see themselves and the tradition that is being passed on to them. Their great pleasure in spirituality is not occurring in a vacuum. Full participation of Jews in American life is taken for granted now. American women's professional and social equality is no longer debatable and, finally, the rights to full participation of women in Jewish life and learning have been basically established in most denominations. With the breakdown of the ghetto and the ebbing of religious prejudice, American Jews are all Jews by choice. No one forces us today to don the mantle of our ancient beliefs. But those who do so often have the sense of stepping into open space, of moving into a tradition that is more than two thousand years old and yet being reborn every day. It is in the context of this dynamic era of change that this volume took shape.

The Parts here take their themes from a central Jewish prayer, the "V'ahavta." The word "v'ahavta" means "love," and the prayer, said aloud by every Bar and Bat Mitzvah child as part of the coming-of-age ceremony, defines the all-encompassing ways that the Jewish people show love for God: with all your heart, with all your soul, with all your might, and when you lie down and when you rise up.

Part One, "With all your heart," describes the first blush of contact with Jewish identity. In "Grinder," by Sharon Pomerantz, a young girl learns from her grandmother not only how to grind fish, but also some painful truths of life in the old country. Several stories cast a skeptical, often humorous eye on either the Jewish grandmother or a grandmother-like surrogate, including "Aunt Rose's Child," by Jane S. Fox.

Our young girls learn to take responsibility early and at great cost. In "Baby-Sitting," by Jane Bernstein, a young girl falls down on the job; Ilana Girard Singer examines her father's days as a Communist in "The Secret"; and in "Names," Jane Yolen tells a harrowing tale of food, the Holocaust, and survival. Finally, in "Theresa Weisberg's Wedding," we consider the hilarious consequences of an "intermarriage" between two Jews, one secular, one religious, proving that it's never too late to come of age.

Part Two, "With all your soul," is devoted to new spiritual territory. Here we find the sentimentality of a ritual object (a mother's "Kiddush Cup," by L. Schimel); several examinations of prayer (S. L. Wisenberg's "Shema, the First Prayer You Learn"); and memories of Hebrew school (Miriyam Glazer's memoir, "Watchman, What of the Night?"). Karen E. Bender's "Inside the Ark" transforms our sacred scrolls beyond physical recognition; and "Big White Pushka," by Karen Golden, is a flight of fancy on the act of charity.

In Part Three, "With all your might," the identity crisis of adolescence is faced, and with it the sobering responsibilities of Jewish history. Hard times and the immigrant experience come together in a mom-and-pop store in "Schmutz," by Sara Nuss-Galles; Carol V. Davis keeps history alive in "I dream of railway stations"; and in "The Discovery," by Belinda Cooper, a young journalist and her father travel to Germany, where she comes face to face with his past life.

Finally, in Part Four, "When you lie down, when you rise up," our young women take their Jewish identities out into the larger world. In "The Nose-Fixer," Persis Knobbe uses her ingenuity to try to alter nature; while in Alexandra J. Wall's "The Way 'We' Were," a young woman calls on Barbra Streisand to help her accept the physical facts of life. Mothers and daughters come to terms in Vivian Gornick's "That's Ridiculous" and Erica Jong's "Needlepoint"; while Letty Cottin Pogrebin explains why "I Don't Like to Write About My Father."

The lure of Israel is the focus of several stories (Jori Ranhand's "Desert Song," Dina Elenbogen's "The One Who Receives," and Allegra Goodman's "Onionskin"); while maintaining a Jewish identity in suburbia provides the background for several others, including Fern Kupfer's "Sleepwalking Through Suburbia."

As the stories and poems in this volume reflect, we are seeing the tradition through new eyes; finding as if for the first time what it means to touch a Torah, to say a prayer, to be part of a community; how the deaths of six million Jews in the Holocaust implicates itself in the lives of Jews living today in freedom, away from Israel. Most elementally, we see how the rituals and learning of Jewish life work themselves into the choices we make in love for parents, husbands, and family.

When the first wave of submissions came in, I expected an overwhelming number to be about food, or Jewish men, or the Jewish American Princess and the notorious Jewish mother. Nothing doing.

Instead, this book reveals a Jewish family altered almost completely beyond recognition; no Jewish mothers or princesses in sight. Among older writers there is still a focus on the dysfunctional Jewish family, and on the way the pain of making it financially in 20th century America was visited upon the children. But for the next generation, it just doesn't ring true. Gone for the younger writer is the smothering, shrewish Jewish mother—not one submission on chicken soup!—with her complaints that her children never call. The cast of characters of Jewish life is changing.

In its place, I found almost no Jewish family at all. Interestingly, for the younger writers, the Jewish mother hardly exists; when she does she is a vapor, lacking a true identity. She is a woman without a role, one who left her Jewishness behind when she left the ghetto, and who is often perceived as having actively discouraged the budding spiritual inclinations of her daughter.

If mother lacks power, the new icon of the Jewish family is Grandma, whose sufferings real and imagined have become a focus of Jewish female mythology. Grandma is the symbol of the bad/good Old World, the source of contemporary guilt. The blintzes she made, the challah she baked, the way her kitchen smelled, the way she braided her hair, the suffering she endured, the arthritis that nearly killed her, the floor she mopped, her thwarted ambition, the death of her children, the compromise of her dreams, and the way she fed a family of eight on $1.34 a week. Her self-sacrifice inevitably provided the basis of our own success, raising the question: are we worthy?

The question of worthiness is at the heart of the matter for women living in the relative safety of late 20th century America. Recognizing her story in our own, we look at our grandmother's lives first in bitterness and then in awe. Could we have withstood what she did? What if "it"—pogroms, discrimination, death camps, another Great Depression—happened again? Are we half the woman that she was? And so Grandma ultimately stands for the half-learned lessons of history, and the anxiety that our prized security is only temporarily ours, after all.

Finally, in our domestic cast of characters, the Jewish father is undergoing a makeover. While in no way rivaling Grandma, he is becoming empowered. No longer a nebbish, outweighed and outvoted by the Jewish mother, Father is now often imbued with wisdom. His tallit bag is a source of holiness, his efforts at preparing a daughter for religious ceremony hallowed and blessed. After decades of being portrayed as a buffoon, Father (and to some extent Grandfather) is being resurrected as a teacher and a source of wisdom, whether or not he ultimately falls short of providing all his daughter wants from him. In Father we see the Jewish girl's hunger for some concrete, continual contact with the tradition, and her disappointment at a connection which has been cut.

Inevitably in volumes by and about Jewish women, a certain question must be addressed: Will there ever be a female Philip Roth? Time and again I've been asked: Who are the women writers to equal the male writers of the Golden Era of Jewish American literature such as Saul Bellow, Norman Mailer, Joseph Heller, Herman Wouk? What woman writer will create counterparts for those archetypes of Jewish womanhood: Sophie Portnoy, Brenda Patimkin, and Marjorie Morningstar? The portrayal of Jewish girls and women in some Jewish literature has been fatally demeaning, influenc-

ing how scores of Jewish women come to think of themselves. By now generations of Jewish women writers have
wondered what to do to even the score.

There is no female "answer": Jewish women writers are no
longer (or perhaps only not yet) interested in literary revenge,
in not rebutting their symbolic annihilation at the hands of
our greatest male writers. Our Jewish women are too busy
exploring the tradition for themselves. What men think seems
almost an irrelevance. This has much to do with the success
of Jews in America. The stories written during the so-called
Jewish "Golden Age" captured the efforts of the first generation
of Jews to assimilate into American life. They were "coming-
of-age" stories on two levels; nominally about adolescent
boys leaving home but specifically about Jews moving out of
the ghetto and never coming back.

Today, assimilation is taken for granted, and the need to
run away, to destroy, to flee Judaism is no longer so apparent.
The Roths and the Mailers, in their frantic rejection of Judaism
now seem childish, and their penchant for throwing away the
wisdom of the ages seems questionable if not a tragic waste.
Why flee when there's no place to go?

In our more secure America at the end of the 20th century,
the obsession with "otherness"—and how Judaism looks
from the outside—is dying down, and an interest in who we
are seems to be rising up. The themes that concern our writers today as they come of age are less about the constraints
of the ghetto than nostalgia for its warmth; less about the
superstition and anti-intellectualism of early Jewish life, than
a longing for its implicit meaning. Today we hear the voices
of Jewish girls, angry and proud, confused and confirmed,
coming into their own.

Part One

"With all your heart . . ."

Jane Schulzinger Fox

Aunt Rose's Child

Aunt Rose was the toughest teacher at Oak Hills High. In 1942 there was talk of her joining the WACS, but instead she taught algebra, plane geometry, and trigonometry. Pictures in the high school annual show a tall, thin woman with hair pulled tightly back and none of those sausage rolls atop the forehead that slightly soften the faces of her more stylish contemporaries.

I have one picture of her on newsprint, fragile now though Aunt Rose kept it between glass. She stands next to David Ben-Gurion. The caption, accurate for the time, says "David Green." When he came to town, Aunt Rose was asked to take dictation for him, take notes at meetings, make coffee, run errands.

"She wanted to go after him," my mother told us. "She wanted to go off to Palestine. Not because of anything funny between her and Mr. Green. It was because he inspired her and she wanted to be part of all that. Of course, my father wouldn't let her go." My mother told us this in 1947, when David Ben-Gurion's picture was again in the city's papers.

"I would have gone," I said. "She could have been part of things."

"Don't be silly," my mother said. "She went to college instead." It had been a bribe to keep her home and made her the first in her family to get a college education.

With the other women Aunt Rose helped serve and clean up after meals. Fathers sat in the living room and discussed the war. Mothers shushed them. "The children shouldn't have to hear about things like that," they said.

When Aunt Rose took me out to lunch, she told me what the scientific method was: how you formed a hypothesis and tested it and how one counter example disproved any hypothesis or theory, however widespread, and meant you had to reformulate. I loved her for using words like *hypothesis* and *reformulate* with me.

"Is that what you do in math?" I asked.

"Math is something else," she said. "You'd use math to test your hypothesis. But the theories of math itself . . . those are beyond both of us."

"But you teach math," I objected.

"I teach it as a tool," she said. "I don't make new tools. I'm like your piano teacher, not like Bach."

When I won a science prize, my mother said, "You are your Aunt Rose's child." Then she brushed out my hair and put pink ribbons in it. For a while I entertained the romantic notion that I was indeed Aunt Rose's love child, but my looks favor my father, and in any case there are pictures of my mother pregnant with me, and Aunt Rose, very thin, beside her. I resolved to be her child in true spirit.

In 1947, at the age of thirty-five, Aunt Rose married a returning soldier she met in a photography shop. Aunt Rose and Uncle Eddie's wedding photo shows her still with her hair skinned back, but the ruffles at her throat are the first sign of the whimsy that marriage allowed in her life.

Their only child, Yankel, was the product of loving imagination. Shortly after her marriage Aunt Rose found a used towel on the wet floor of the bathroom. "Yankel did it," Uncle Eddie said, and so my imaginary cousin was born.

Aunt Rose continued to teach, and I survived the rigors of her courses. She talked to me about a career in science. "Your

math is good enough for that," she said. My majoring in
chemistry pleased Aunt Rose, but after I married Larry, I
stayed home to keep house. Aunt Rose's reaction surprised
me. "Children are more important," she said. "Your children
will be most important in your life."

After my daughter, Shana, was born, Aunt Rose would hold
her all afternoon, sometimes joking that Yankel would get
jealous. When Shana was about six, Aunt Rose began to take
her out to lunch. "Great-Aunt Rose treats me like a real person," Shana told me at age ten, and I knew that they were
talking about hypotheses and theories and scientific proofs.

Shana is like Aunt Rose in working after marriage and like
me in having children. Aunt Rose was pleased. "Times have
changed," she said. "Men help take care of the children just
as your Uncle Eddie helped with Yankel. Of course, Yankel
was such a handful he needed two parents looking after him."

My son-in-law, a photo archivist, wanted to see the photographs Aunt Rose and Uncle Eddie had taken over the
years. "She said, 'Yankel made Uncle Eddie laugh while he
was taking this one, and that's why it's blurry,' " Joel quoted.
"Who's Yankel? Why wouldn't you let me ask her?" he asked
Shana.

"Yankel's her imaginary son," Shana told him. "I'm not sure
she knows he's imaginary anymore."

But Aunt Rose was quite willing to tell Joel how Yankel
came into being. It was clear she did know he was imaginary.
His mischief ran more to lost maps on cross-country trips and
bills mislaid than it did to spilt milk, but all the same he was
that sort of imaginary child.

"And then he died during the war," Aunt Rose told Joel.

"The war?" Joel asked.

"World War II," Rose said.

"He must have been very young," Joel said.

"So many were," she said.

Shana wouldn't let Joel pursue this. "She didn't even marry
until after the war," she told him later. "Don't make her face
the fact that she's getting confused."

When Shana's son, Jeremy, was born, Shana told me, "You know what Aunt Rose said? She said, 'Not at all like Yankel, thank goodness.' "

Shana's second was born in June, a year after Aunt Rose's death. Shana named her Rose. "It will be as if she had a real child now," Shana said. "Yankel won't be her only descendant."

"I'm glad you named your daughter after Aunt Rose," I said.

"Jeremy left his trike in the driveway and said Rose did it." Shana laughed. "She's Yankel's sister in true spirit."

Aunt Rose's child.

Sharon Pomerantz

Grinder

The grinder she used for gefilte fish was old and heavy. The metal color sometimes came off on your hands, especially if they were sweaty, and they were sweaty that day. The grinder didn't quite grip the way it was supposed to, was missing a piece at the base. I remember her shoving it to the edge with gentle force, the way she did everything back then.

"Hold on to it for me," she said, "you can be my holder."

I stood on tippy-toes and gripped the table with all the force of my five years, reaching over my head, straining just a little. "Ummm"—I made a noise to show I was working hard.

"Good," she said and smiled. "Now we can grind the fish."

I watched her feed the pale, pink-beige carp corpses into the mouth. They slid through and came out in a stream of tiny pieces, spitting bits onto the waxed paper on the table. It smelled stronger after it had been ground; the fish smell blended with that other smell, the Grammy's-kitchen-sugar-and-strudel-dough smell. She had just baked. Before I came she always baked, even that day, even on the hottest day of summer with nothing but a fan in the window, the air barely moving the thin, spotless white lace kitchen curtains.

"Hold on," she said, "hold on." The grinder rocked back and forth. My hands gripped tighter around the base.

"You know where it's from, this grinder?" Tiny droplets of sweat gathered on her forehead.

I relaxed for a moment. Don't move, I told the grinder, stay put.

"It's from Poland," she announced, squeezing more fish into the wide mouth. Her fingers and hands were shiny wet. "I brought it with me. See this fish, the way it's eaten and spit out the other side. That's what happened to our people in Poland. That's what happened. Want to taste a piece?"

She held it, raw and pale, in my face. I shook my head.

"EN-O," I sang. "EN-O."

She laughed, bending down to kiss me wetly on my cheek. She was small, not so much taller than I was. The corner of her heavy bosom under the soft apron momentarily grazed my bare shoulder. She smelled of talcum and salty, peppery fish seasoning.

"Such a speller," she said. "You're my speller." She laughed and made a little snorting sound, then fed more fish into the mouth, and it came out in a stream on the other side. The base of the grinder tilted back and forth, harder this time. I could feel it wobbling under the weakness of my grip. I strained my shoulders harder, reaching farther over my head. Something tickled and irritated the back of my neck. A fly landed on my sweaty neck, attracted by the fish's decay. It paused there, waiting for a piece of the action. I shook my head back and forth, swatting it with my ponytail.

"Hot," she said, wiping the sweat from her eyes with the back of her long-sleeved cotton blouse.

"Hot," I repeated, feeling the apparatus begin to slip. "Help . . ." I looked up at her, "it's going to . . ."

"Hold on," she said, her mouth setting suddenly back to a serious expression as she caught the grinder by the neck, its lead weight about to cave in my direction. Holding the last piece of beheaded fish in her right hand, she shoved the thing with her left, once, twice, until it was temporarily back in place. "You just hold on, baby," she said. "Don't let anybody tell you it's any different."

Grace Paley

In This Country, But in Another Language, My Aunt Refuses to Marry the Men Everyone Wants Her To

My grandmother sat in her chair. She said, When I lie down at night I can't rest, my bones push each other. When I wake up in the morning I say to myself, What? Did I sleep? My God, I'm still here. I'll be in this world forever.

My aunt was making the bed. Look, your grandmother, she doesn't sweat. Nothing has to be washed—her stockings, her underwear, the sheets. From this you wouldn't believe what a life she had. It wasn't life. It was torture.

Doesn't she love us? I asked.

Love you? my aunt said. What else is worth it? You children. Your cousin in Connecticut. So. Doesn't that make her happy?

My aunt said, Ach, what she saw!

What? I asked. What did she see?

Someday I'll tell you. One thing I'll tell you right now. Don't carry the main flag. When you're bigger, you'll be in a demonstration or a strike or something. It doesn't have to be you, let someone else.

Because Russya carried the flag, that's why? I asked.

Because he was a wonderful boy, only seventeen. All by herself, your grandmother picked him up from the street— he was dead—she took him home in the wagon.

What else? I asked.

My father walked into the room. He said, At least *she* lived.
Didn't you live too? I asked my aunt.

Then my grandmother took her hand. Sonia. One reason I
don't close my eyes at night is I think about you. You know
it. What will be? You have no life.

Grandmother, I asked, what about us?

My aunt sighed. Little girl. Darling, let's take a nice walk.

At the supper table nobody spoke. So I asked her once
more: Sonia, tell me no or yes. Do you have a life?

Ha! she said. If you really want to know, read Dostoyevsky.
Then they all laughed and laughed.

My mother brought tea and preserves.

My grandmother said to all our faces, Why do you laugh?
But my aunt said, Laugh!

Jennifer Futernick

Comfort

I wore new white socks to my father's funeral. My navy blue corduroy jumper felt soft and close against my chest. The socks and the softness of the corduroy and holding my mother's hand were the only comforts I could find. I was nine years old. It was the day after my brother Elliot's birthday.

My family sat in the front row of the funeral parlor. I looked at my father's face, lying in the open casket, his face handsome and serene. His eyes were closed. Just two nights before I had watched him and my brother Elliot stretched out lazily on the white chenille bedspread, watching Ward Bond on *Wagon Train* in my parents' bedroom. Their heads were resting against the headboard and a bunch of pillows. My father had his arm around Elliot's shoulder. I sensed an instant similarity between Ward Bond's huge comforting face, the symbol of American patriarchy, and my father's—though they looked nothing alike. My father had fine chiseled features and soft hazel eyes, thinning brown hair. I went in and kissed them both good night.

When I got home from school the next day, Irene and Janice, my mother's friends, were there. They told me my father had had a heart attack that morning and was in the hospital. He must have collapsed at work while I was studying the oceans in geography. "I want to see him now!" I begged them. They told me I would have to wait until we heard from my mother at the hospital. They offered me cookies and milk. I wondered where my brothers and sister were.

I went to my bedroom and crouched behind the door. I read a prayer from the siddur I received from Hebrew school and then made up some prayers of my own. I whispered that even if I wasn't sure that there was a God, I would believe fervently, if only my father would come home healthy, soon.

About an hour later my mother came home, feverish, floating. Her words were gibberish. She couldn't stand unless someone supported her. She looked strange but very beautiful, backlit against the window, with her light pink shirtwaist dress looking a bit like gauze and her hair wavy and full, almost like an angel.

At the funeral home, we sat together, my mother, thirty-six, and Elliot, turned fifteen just the day before, my brother Larry, eighteen, and Nancy, my younger sister, four years old. I got a lot of kisses. Everyone I liked was in that one overflowing room.

The year before, when I was eight, we belonged to Sons of Israel synagogue. It was Purim and I won the costume contest, dressed as Queen Vashti in four lacy bedroom curtains, my mother's slinky silver belt and no shoes. I was so amazed I won, and so cold wearing nothing but those thin curtains in the chilly social hall, that I began shaking. I was asked to lead the oneg shabbat, singing the blessings over the wine. My synagogue sang the extended version of the kiddush prayer and I was afraid I would forget the words, though I'd learned them in Hebrew school just the month before. But as soon as I began to sing, I saw my father, who was sitting next to me, silently mouthing the kiddush, coaching me all the way through to the end of the prayer. When I sat down, he put his jacket around my shivering shoulders.

The next August my father took me shopping at the most expensive children's store in Newburgh, New York. He was a factory worker with four kids and a pink-and-gray Chevrolet in need of repair. But that month my best friend, Lois Shapiro, the daughter of a doctor, had gotten a new brown-and-white T-shirt with matching pedal pushers, and I wanted an outfit just like hers. I was thrilled to be shopping with my father and I loved that he spent more than he should have, just so I could look like Lois.

I wore that outfit the next week on my ninth birthday, when we visited the Catskill Game Farm. I fed the baby goats dried corn right out of my hands and they nibbled my palm, too. The odor from the zoo was ripe, but I mostly remember the freshly ironed smell of my father's white cotton shirt as I stood next to him and he encouraged me to feed the animals.

"Don't worry, they won't hurt you," he nudged.

At the funeral home the rabbi praised my father, Baruch Moshe ben Leib, his Hebrew name. He could calm an argument with the clasp of a hand, a few well-placed words or even a joke. He was always trying to coax a son or nephew to recite his bar mitzvah torah portion in front of a family gathering. Once, at our Cousin's Club, he convinced my cousin Brucie to chant his entire haftorah, too.

At the graveside, each of us threw a handful of dirt onto the lowered coffin. The dirt felt dry in my palm, though it had been an unusually wet spring. Everyone was crying, even my cousin Barbara's fiancé, Sandy. My grandfather Louis knelt at the grave calling "Benny! Benny!" Even at nine I knew that it was against the law of nature for children to die before their parents. I couldn't take my eyes off my grandfather and wondered if he would ever get up off his knees again.

Standing there I realized I had given my father a gift. I had spared him a parent's worst grief by outliving him. At least I had that.

Amy Bloom

Light Breaks
Where No Sun Shines

I didn't expect to find myself in the back of Mr. Klein's store, wearing only my undershirt and panties, surrounded by sable.

"Sable is right for you, Suseleh," Mr. Klein said, draping a shawl-collared jacket over me. "Perfect for your skin and your eyes. A million times a day the boys must tell you. Such skin."

No one except Mr. Klein had ever suggested that my appearance was pleasing. My mother, who was small and English and had decorated half the houses on Long Island with small English cachepots and porcelain dogs, bought me clothes at Lord & Taylor's Pretty Plus and looked the other way when the saleswomen dragged me out in navy blue A-line dresses and plaid jumpers. My eyes, which are almond-shaped and dark, were concealed by grimy pink-framed glasses, and my creamy, rolling flesh was too much a reminder of dead Romanian relatives and attic photographs to be appealing.

I stood on a little velvet footstool and modeled fur coats for Mr. Klein. He had suggested I take off my perpetual green corduroys and hooded sweatshirt so we could see how the coats really looked. I agreed, only pretending to hesitate for a minute so I could watch his thin gray face expand and pinken. I felt the warm rushing in my chest that being with him gave me. He also gave me Belgian chocolate, because he felt Hershey's wasn't good enough for me, and he told me that if only God had blessed him and Mrs. Klein with a wonderful daughter like me, he would be truly happy, *kayn ahora*. My mother never said I was wonderful. My father, who greatly admired my mother for her size and her accent, was not heard to thank God for giving him the gift of me.

"This one next, Suseleh." Mr. Klein handed me a small mink coat and set a mink beret on my unwashed hair.

"This is my size. Do kids wear mink coats?"

If you had to dress up, mink was the way to go. Much better than my scratchy navy wool, designed to turn chubby Jewish girls into pale Victorian wards. The fur brushed my chin, and without my glasses (Mr. Klein and I agreed that it was a shame to hide my lovely eyes and so we put my glasses in his coat pocket during our modeling sessions), I felt glamorously Russian. I couldn't see a thing. He put the beret at a slight angle and stepped back, admiring me in my bare feet and my mink.

"Perfect. This is how a fur coat should look on a girl. Not some little stick girl in rabbit. This is an ensemble."

I turned around to see what I could of myself from the back: a brown triangle topped by a white blur and another smudge of brown.

I modeled two more coats, a ranch mink, which displeased Mr. Klein with its careless stitching, and a fox cape, which made us both smile. Even Mr. Klein thought floor-length silver fox was a little much.

As always, he turned his back as I pulled on my jeans and sweatshirt. I sat down on one of the spindly pink velvet chairs, putting my sneakers on as he put away the coats.

We said nothing on the drive home. I ate my chocolate and Mr. Klein turned on WQXR, the only time I have ever listened to classical music with pleasure. Mr. Klein rounded my driveway, trying to look unconcerned. I think we both always expected that one Monday my parents would come rushing out of the house, appalled and avenging.

I went inside, my shoelaces flapping against the hallway's glazed, uneven brick. Could anything be less inviting than a brick foyer? It pressed into the soles of my feet, and every dropped and delicate object shattered irretrievably.

I don't remember which cleaning lady greeted me. We seemed to alternate between elderly Irish women who looked as though they'd been born to rid the world of lazy people's private filth, and middle-aged Bolivian women quietly stalking dust and fingerprints. I cannot remember the face that came out of the laundry room to acknowledge my existence, but I know someone let me in. I didn't have a house key until I was nineteen.

Every dinner was a short horror; my eating habits were remarked upon, and then my mother would talk about politics and decorating. My father's repertoire was more limited. He talked about his clients, their divorces, and their bank accounts. I would go to my room, pretend to do my homework, and read my novels. In my room, I was the Scarlet Pimpernel. Sometimes I was Sydney Carton, and once in a while I was Tarzan. I went to sleep dreaming of the nineteenth century, my oldest, largest teddy bear held tightly between my legs.

Mr. Klein lived two houses down and usually drove up beside me as I was walking to the bus stop. Every time I saw the hood of his huge, unfashionable blue Cadillac slide slowly by me and pause, I would skip ahead and throw my books into the front seat, spared another day of riding the school bus. If you have been an outcast, you understand what the bus ride was like. If you have not been, you will think that I'm exaggerating, even now, and that I should have spent less time being sorry for myself and more time being friendly.

He dropped me off in front of Longview Elementary School as the buses discharged all the kids I had managed to avoid thus far. The mornings Mr. Klein failed to appear, I kept a low profile and worried about him until the routine of school settled upon me, vulnerable again only during recess. The first two days of kindergarten had taught me always to carry a book, and as soon as I found a place on the hardtop, I had only to set my eyes upon the clean black letters and the soft ivory page and I would be gone, spirited right out of what passed for my real life.

Our first trip to Furs by Klein was incidental, barely a foreshadowing of our afternoons together. Mr. Klein had passed me on the way home from school. Having lost two notebooks since school began, I'd missed the bus while searching the halls frantically for my third, bright red canvas designed to be easily seen. I walked home, a couple of miles through the sticky, smoky leaf piles and across endless emerald lawns. No one knew I liked to walk. Mr. Klein pulled up ahead of me and signaled shyly. I ran to the car, gratified to tears by a smile that I could see from the road.

"I'll give you a ride home, but I need to stop back at my shop, something I forgot. All right?"

I nodded. It was better than all right; maybe I'd never have to go home. He could have driven me to Mexico, night after night over the Great Plains, and I wouldn't have minded.

Furs by Klein stood on the corner of Shore Drive, its curved, pink-tinted windows and black lacquered French doors the height of suburban elegance. Inside stood headless bodies, six rose velvet torsos, each wearing a fur coat. There were mirrors everywhere I looked, and a few thin-legged, armless chairs. The walls were lined with coats and jackets and capes. Above them, floating on transparent necks, were the hats.

Mr. Klein watched me. "Go ahead," he said. "All ladies like hats." He pulled a few down and walked discreetly into the workroom at the rear. I tried on a black cloche with a dotted veil and then a kelly green fedora with a band of arching brown feathers. Mr. Klein emerged from the back, his hands in the pockets of his baggy gray trousers.

"Come, Susie, your mother will be worried about you. Leave the hats, it's all right. Mondays are the day off, the girls will put them back tomorrow." He turned out the lights and opened the door for me.

"My mother's not home." I'm really an orphan, adopt me.

"Tcha, I am so absentminded. Mrs. Klein tells me your mother is a famous decorator. Of course, she is out—decorating."

He smiled, just slightly, and I laughed out loud. He was on my side.

Almost every morning now, he gave me a ride to school. And without any negotiating that I could recall, I knew that on Monday afternoons I would miss my bus and he would pick me up as I walked down Baker Hill Road. I would keep him company while he did whatever he did in the back room, and I would try on hats. After a few Mondays, I eyed the coats.

"Of course," he said. "When you're grown up, you'll tell your husband, 'Get me a sable from Klein's. It's Klein's or nothing.' " He waggled a finger sternly, showing me who I would be: a pretty young woman with a rich, indulgent husband. "Let me help you."

Mr. Klein slipped an ash blond mink jacket over my sweatshirt and admired me aloud. Soon after, he stopped going into the workroom, and soon after that, I began taking off my clothes. The pleasure on Mr. Klein's face made me forget everything I had heard in the low tones of my parents' conversation and all that I had seen in my own mirror. I chose to believe Mr. Klein.

At home, to conjure up the feeling of Mr. Klein's cool, round fingertips on my shoulders, touching me lightly before the satin lining descended, I listened to classical music. My father made vaguely approving noises from behind the *Wall Street Journal.*

I lay on the floor of the living room, behind the biggest couch, and saw myself playing the piano, adult and beautifully formed. I am wearing a dress I saw on Marilyn Monroe, the sheerest clinging net, with sparkling stones coming up over the tips of my breasts and down between my legs. I am moving slowly across the stage, the wide hem of my sable cape shaping a series of round, dark waves. I hand the cape to an adoring Mr. Klein, slightly improved and handsomely turned out in a tuxedo cut just like my father's.

My mother stepped over me and then stopped. I was eye to toe with her tiny pink suede loafers and happy to stay that way. Her round blue eyes and her dread of wrinkles made her stare as harsh and haunting as the eyeless Greek heads she put in my father's study.

"How are you keeping busy, Susan?"

I couldn't imagine what had prompted this interest. My mother always acted as though I had been raised by a responsible and affectionate governess, and guilt and love were as foreign in my house as butter and sugar.

"School, books." I studied the little gold bars across the tongues of her loafers.

"And that's all going well?"

"Fine. Everything's fine."

"You wouldn't like to study an instrument, would you? Piano? We could do a piano in the library. That could be attractive. An older piece, deep browns, a maroon paisley shawl, silver picture frames. Quite attractive."

"I don't know. Can I think about it?" I didn't mind being part of my mother's endless redecorating; in the past, her domestic fantasies had produced a queen-size brass bed, which I loved and kept into adulthood, and a giant dollhouse, complete with working lights and a chiming doorbell.

"Of course, think it over. Let's make a decision next week, shall we?" She started to touch my dirty hair and patted me on the shoulder instead. I have no idea what she thought of me.

I didn't see Mr. Klein until the following Monday. I had endured four mornings at the bus stop: leaves stuffed down my shirt, my books knocked into the trash can, my lunch bag tossed from boy to boy. Fortunately, the bus driver was a madman, and his rageful mutterings and obscene limericks captured whatever attention might have come my way once we were on the bus.

It was raining that Monday, and I wondered if I should take

the bus. I had never thought about the fact that Mr. Klein and I had no way to contact each other. I could only wait, in silence. I pulled up my hood and started walking down Baker Hill, waiting for a blue streak to come past my left side, waiting for the slight skid of wet leaves as Mr. Klein braked to a stop. Finally, much closer to home than usual, the car came.

"You're almost home," he said. "Maybe I should just take you home? We can go to the store another time." He looked rushed and unhappy.

"Sure, if you don't have time, that's okay."

"I have the time, Susie. I have the time." He turned the car around and drove us back to Furs by Klein.

I got out and waited in the rain while he unlocked the big black doors.

"You're soaking wet," he said harshly. "You should have taken the bus."

"I missed it," I lied. If he wasn't going to admit that he wanted me to miss the bus, I wasn't going to admit that I had missed it for him.

"Yes, you miss the bus, I pick you up. Suseleh, you are a very special girl, and standing around an old man's shop in wet clothes is not what you should be doing."

Usually what I did was stand around with no clothes on at all, but I could tell that Mr. Klein, like most adults, was now working only from his version of the script.

I sat down uneasily at the little table with the swiveling gilt-framed mirror, ready to try on hats. Without Mr. Klein's encouragement, I wouldn't even look at the coats. He didn't hand me any hats.

He pressed his thin sharp face deep into the side of my neck, pushing my sweatshirt aside with one hand. I looked in the mirror and saw my own round wet face, comic in its surprise and pink glasses. I saw Mr. Klein's curly gray hair and a bald spot I would never have discovered otherwise.

"Get your coat." He rubbed his face with both hands and went to the door.

"I don't have a coat."

"They let you go in the rain, with no coat? *Gottenyu.* Let's go, please." He held the door open for me, and I had to walk through it.

The chocolate wasn't my usual Belgian slab. It was a deep gold foil box, tied with pink and gold wisps and crowned with a cluster of sparkling gold berries. He dropped it in my lap like it was something diseased.

I held the box in my lap, stroking the fairy ribbons, until he told me to open it.

Each of the six chocolates had a figure on top. Three milk, three bittersweet, each one carved with angel wings or a heart or a white-rimmed rose. In my parents' fat-free home, my eating habits were regarded as criminal. They would no more have bought me beautiful chocolates than gift-wrapped a gun for a killer.

"Suseleh . . ."

He looked out the window at the rain and I looked up at him quickly. I had obviously done something wrong, and although my parents' anger and chagrin never bothered me a bit, his unhappiness pulled me apart. I crushed one of the chocolates with my fingers, and Mr. Klein saw me.

"Nah, nah, nah," he said softly, wiping my fingers with his handkerchief. He cleared his throat. "My schedule's changing, I won't be able to give you rides after school. I'm going to open the shop on Mondays."

"How about in the morning?" I had not known that I could talk through this kind of pain.

"I don't think so. I need to get in a little earlier. It's not so bad, you should ride with other boys and girls. You'll see, you'll have a good time."

I sat there sullenly, ostentatiously mashing the chocolates.

"Too bad, they're very nice chocolates. Teuscher's. Remember, sable from Klein's, chocolates from Teuscher's. Only the best for you. I'm telling you, only the best."

"I'm not going to have a good time on the bus." I didn't mash the last chocolate, I just ran a fingertip over the tiny ridges of the rosebud.

"Maybe not. I shouldn't have said you'd have a good time. I'm sorry." He sighed and looked away.

I bit into the last chocolate. "Here, you have some too."

"No, they're for you. They were all for you."

"I'm not that hungry. Here." I held out the chocolate half and he lowered his head, startling me. I put my fingers up to his narrow lips and he took the chocolate neatly between his teeth. I could feel the very edge of his teeth against my fingers.

We pulled up in front of my house, and he put his hand over mine, for just one moment.

"I'll say it again, only the best is good enough for you. So, we'll say au revoir, Susan. Not good-bye."

"Au revoir. Thank you for the chocolates." My mother's instructions surfaced at odd times.

I left my dripping sneakers on the brick floor and dropped my wet clothes into the lilac straw hamper in my bathroom. I took my very first voluntary shower and dried off slowly, watching myself in the steamy mirror. When I didn't come down for dinner, my mother found me, naked and quiet, deep in my covers.

"Let's get the piano," I said.

I took lessons from Mr. Canetti for three years, and he served me wine-flavored cookies instead of chocolate. One day, he bent forward to push my sleeves back over my aching wrists, and I saw my beautiful self take shape in his eyes. I loved him, too.

Ilana Girard Singer

The Secret

I loved going to my neighbor Patti's house. She had a TV and we didn't. Sometimes, we'd sit with her mother on their turquoise couch beneath a picture of pink flamingos and sing along with *Your Hit Parade.* Her mother looked just like Doris Day and wore red nail polish. Sometimes she played jacks with Patti and me.

One morning I knocked on Patti's door, but this time her mother didn't greet me with a smile. Patti wasn't home, she said. Her voice was cold. "Aren't your parents foreign-born?" she asked. "What nationality are you?"

"I'm American," I said warily. My parents had warned me about hidden loyalty questions. Patti's mother asked me outright, "Is your father a Communist?" I felt as though I'd been stabbed. I stammered, "No. He's a Progressive," and ran back home, confused and afraid I'd given away "The Secret."

"The Secret" made me feel different and scared. Each morning at my elementary school in the San Francisco suburbs, I said the Pledge of Allegiance, just like other kids. But in 1954, when I was in the fifth grade, the Pledge changed. Now when I placed my hand over my heart, I recited the Pledge but, as my parents had instructed me, I refused to say, "under God," which had been inserted in the phrase, "one nation indivisible." Father explained that in America, unlike the Tsar's Russia where he was born, our constitution separates church and state.

I tried to fit in, but the bullies pointed at my pink glasses and called me "egghead" and "four eyes." They snickered at my mismatched skirts and blouses, which my mother had bought at the rummage sale for the *People's World*, a Communist newspaper. Sometimes they pulled my braids until I cried.

They laughed and made fun of me because I didn't know who Buffalo Bob and Clarabelle the Clown were. They couldn't believe I'd never seen the *Howdy Doody Show*. How could I have? Father called TV a propaganda machine.

Then there were the bomb drills. Our teacher told us the windows were reinforced with chicken wire to protect us from flying glass when the Russian bombs exploded. One day, the sirens whined and Miss Meadows barked: "Drop! . . . Cover up and shut your eyes!" I scrunched underneath my desk, my legs cramping, my back to the windows, just like the other kids.

"Who drops these bombs?" one boy called out.

"The Jews. The Reds. The Commies!" another answered. I looked around. Who were they accusing? Did they know about my father the Russian, the Communist, the Jew?

Father was headmaster at San Francisco's Die Kindershule (The Children's School). Each Sunday I studied there with my true friends—children like me from secular, labor, and Communist families. I attended Father's Jewish history class. His dark eyes were intent behind his wire-rimmed spectacles as he told stories about how Jews were an oppressed people— enslaved by the Pharaohs, burned at the stake during the Spanish Inquisition and exterminated by the Nazis. At Die Kindershule, no religion was taught, no Hebrew prayers and no Torah. We did not celebrate Yom Kippur or Rosh Hashanah, or ever hear the ram's horn. Instead, we celebrated holidays of political freedom and emancipation such as Purim, Chanukah, Passover. I loved seder. I loved decorating the long tables with white bedsheets and spring blossoms for our seventy Kindershule families who celebrated together. In 1954 my father wrote a special Haggadah emphasizing dignity and emancipation. On each student's mimeographed copy he wrote a little note. I still have mine, his inscription hand-printed in the corner: "Sweet Ilana, many happy Pesachs to you, daddy Al."

The story of *Pesach*—escaping oppression—was my father's story. He'd fled persecution in Siberia to Harbin, China, where he grew up along with hundreds of Russian Jews. When he was a teen, he immigrated to Seattle, Washington, to study at the university. Later he became a political activist in California, organizing migrant workers and leading protests against unsafe working conditions and high food prices. Father was charismatic. He stood on soap boxes and spoke to street-corner crowds, demanding unemployment insurance and Social Security for all Americans.

Father was also a charismatic teacher. The Die Kindershule children loved the stories he told about struggling peoples— Jews, Irish, Mexican. He made American Negro heroes come alive for us: Harriet Tubman, Nat Turner and the Scottsboro Boys. Like us, they were former slaves.

Paul Robeson was the son of a former slave, a black activist, actor and opera singer. He was barred from concert halls all over the country because he was a Communist. So my parents and their friends organized Robeson's concert in an Oakland ghetto church. That evening, as he sang to an overflowing crowd of Jews, Christians, Negroes, whites, Latinos, Asians, longshoremen, teachers, lawyers, I handed him roses. I wore my hair in my Russian-style braids. I was so proud.

Pete Seeger, another blacklisted singer, brought his banjo to Die Kindershule, where we sang folk songs at a hootenanny. I loved the one about striking miners fighting the capitalist owners. I bellowed its refrain: "Which side are you on? Which side are you on?" I was always choosing sides, always trying to fit in.

Father must have understood my conflict because he encouraged me to think for myself. My schoolbooks were boring, so he gave me books about real people, about suffering and injustice: stories of the children in the Warsaw Ghetto, Howard Fast's *Sacco and Vanzetti*, about the Italian anarchists who were executed, Herbert Gold's *Jews Without Money*, about poor immigrant Jews in New York.

It was not safe to keep certain books at home during the McCarthy era. Many Americans were suspicious of anyone who read "too much." That's why my parents told me never to let neighbors into our house. They'd see our house was crammed full of "subversive" magazines, newspapers and books that had been banned and removed from library shelves in many states. They might snitch to the FBI that we had many of these banned volumes, books by Thomas Paine, Emile Zola, Upton Sinclair and Dante. Even my beloved book *Robin Hood* had been called "Communist doctrine." I had to be careful.

Father taught me how to spot the FBI men in snap-brimmed fedoras and gray flannel suits. They looked like "Fuller Brush" salesmen, but without the sample cases. One day Mother was in the backyard hanging out the wash and Father, an electrical engineer, was at work. I answered the doorbell and saw two stiff-looking men who asked to see my mother. I knew who they were and just as my parents had taught me, I tried to shut the door, but one of them stuck out his foot and blocked my attempt.

Mother came in and saw me struggling. She nudged me aside, but I hid behind our bookcases, listening, as they interrogated her. "Give us names of your friends and we'll help you," said one of the men. "We know you're not a citizen."

Her voice trembled as she told them to go away. Although Mother, a Canadian citizen, was a permanent resident and a legal alien, she was afraid of deportation. After the FBI men

drove away, she left me alone in the house and rushed out
to a pay phone to call her attorney. We didn't use our own
telephone because it was tapped.

One night after a hootenany at Die Kindershule, my father
was driving us home and telling my little brother and me the
story of Robin Hood. Suddenly, he stopped the story.

"I'll pull over and park," he said abruptly. "I'll tell them I
know they're FBI." But Mother urged him to keep driving, to
lose them in the hills. Father zigzagged through the dark,
narrow roads, trying to shake free from those headlights behind us that kept piercing the veil of fog. "The FBI wants us
to know they're following us," my father explained. The FBI
was trying to intimidate us and I was scared.

Even when my family listened to the radio, I was afraid.
On June 19, 1953, we were listening to Berkeley's KPFA,
America's first member-sponsored, public broadcasting radio
station. It was accused of being run by "subversives."

We heard the announcer say that Julius and Ethel Rosenberg, the Jewish couple convicted of selling atomic secrets to
the Soviet Union, had just been executed. I imagined I was
one of the two Rosenberg sons, Robby and Michael, in the
death chamber of Sing-Sing Prison trying to unstrap my
parents from the electric chair. But it was too late . . . too
late . . .

I was very sad for their sons, and lived in fear that if I gave
away our secret, my parents could get taken away.

My father was taken away—one year later. He was killed
in a car crash when I was ten. He left me a forceful Jewish
legacy that has shaped my life: Contribute to society and think
independently, for myself.

Susan Terris

Baba

1. Baba

In the cellar, on a rusted lawn chair
beside the water heater, I find
our Baba. Wearing black lace-ups
with cubed heels, a dress with
handsewn buttonholes—identical except
where her waist makes one grin,
she stares at me until hectic spots stain
cheeks. Light penetrates high,
fly-specked windows and illuminates
hairnet spider-webbing
her forehead below folds of

pale sheitel. Around her: detritus
of decades. Our cellar is for things
which have no use. First we stockpile
them at the stairs. Then by the door.
At last, below, they molder on shelves
or atop the child-sized workbench:
flower pots, old Lincoln Logs, last year's
cancelled checks. Eyes passing over

all, aware of heat and drip of
water heater, I stare again at Baba.
What are you doing in the cellar? I ask.

Rolling socks, she tells me. *Like most
bubbes I stay at home and roll socks.*
Now her cheeks deepen. *Or sometimes,
at night, I roll in sweet-scented hay . . .*

                   Baba, it's dark and damp,
I tell her. *You don't belong down here.*
She smiles, layers one thick-fingered
hand over the other. *But I do, my Dumpling,*
she replies slowly, *because upstairs
in your fine house, I forget to
roll and can't ever remember my name.*

2. Mother

Poised before her scale, Mother—arbiter
of family myths—weighs truth against
fabrication. *But it never happened,*
she insists, balancing her perceptions,
discarding mine. *Baba
was Grampa Jack's mother's mother,
dead before you were born.*

                   Still, I insist, *she was
there, sitting in the dark dressed in
worsted. With hands shaped like mine,
and a long face. She spoke to me.*

Mother, unwilling to pardon unreality,
adjusts her blindfold, recalibrates,
scoffs at me. *Then it's
her photograph you remember.*

Just a picture. We used to store it in
the cellar wedged between
our old furnace and the hot water heater.

3. Self

Shuffle, step, shuffle, step. Down in
the cellar I am tapping out all the bright
things that Mother and everyone tell me
are not true. *Shuffle, scuff, turn.*
Look at me. Then look again.
My cane, my hat—both are props,
for I am not yet Baba, not yet my mother.
Still, upstairs, I can't practice on
satin-finish floors, because I'll scar them.
So, between furnace and water heater,
using the workbench as barre,
I dance.

I dance against time, against rage. Days
are short now.

                    Baba danced in Szumsk,
I'm sure, but never here. Looking on,
she finds me as disconcerting as my house:
strong-hipped, grown woman in black
skivvies, socks, and TeleTones tapping
into gathering darkness. *Why?* she asks.
Because, I answer, eyeing squared hands.
Shuffle, flap. Shuffle-hop, toe.
Because as winter comes, I, too, need
time—*shuffle, roll*—to contemplate
sweet-scented hay.

Jane Bernstein

Baby-Sitting

Pop was delighted when Rickie suddenly wanted to work. He never questioned her motivation and instead offered her some pointers before she set out on her job hunt. First: She couldn't go out like she usually did, in holey jeans and sneakers, or people would laugh in her face. She had to wear a skirt and a blouse and stockings without runs and well-shined shoes. Whining would get her nowhere, and if she didn't scrub all the dirt out from under her nails and get her hair out of her face, people would slam the door when they saw her coming.

Anything to get away. Rickie, looking like a graduate of Miss Pritchard's, set off down Broadway in a white blouse and navy skirt, her hair held back with a fake tortoiseshell hair band. She applied in every store, but none of the merchants would consider her. Discouraged, she forgot to come home for dinner. The hysteria level rose that night, and when she finally slipped into the apartment, her brother Michael punched her, called her some juicy names, then suggested she slide notices under the neighbors' doors, saying she was available to do odd jobs.

Rickie designed a note, offering to wash cars or walk dogs or water plants or—her deepest wish—to be taken away to someone's summer home where she could do manual labor at peace. "Have work? Will travel," she wrote. "I am (almost) sixteen, strong! able! willing to do anything (preferably outdoors)! Contact Rickie Bokser, 9G."

At last her name delighted her. The thought that people would assume she was a guy was great, since girls were only hired for baby-sitting jobs. They never got to do any of the really cool stuff like washing windows or laying bricks.

Despite her attempts at hiding her sex, when in July she did land a job, it was as a mother's helper for Renee Rubin, 4D, wife of Charlie Rubin, the new president of I. Rubin and Sons, an outfit that manufactured hand-painted glassware. Rickie's new charge, Cliffy, was sixteen months old and weighed thirty pounds. He was a placid baby, content to sit in his stroller all day, providing he had nourishment in both hand and mouth. Cliffy could walk, though he wasn't much interested, and he knew two words, *ma* and *gee*, both of which meant cookie.

Rickie had never done any baby-sitting for a kid who was awake. She knew, because of her friends, that the proper thing was to coo at strange babies and on occasion even kiss them, but Rickie found something mushy about babies that frightened and disturbed her. Their heads lolled, they drooled and cheesed. They cried if you did the least little thing to them or if they did not like your looks. Still, her best friend was at camp, her parents were crazy, and all that remained of her brother was a shell inhabited by an alien creature who spoke with an English accent. That left Cliffy as the best thing in her whole miserable life, and as such she felt obligated to make his day as much fun as possible.

Every morning she wheeled him to the basketball court in Riverside Park, stashed his diaper bag under the stroller, and gave him a cookie for each hand. Then she rounded up the best available athletes so that Cliffy would get to see a really great game from the best seat in the house. He got a cookie at the beginning of the game, one at halftime, and one when it was over. He got a bonus cookie for each of her free shots, too.

"Okay, now don't forget to applaud when I get a basket," Rickie told him.

"Ma," he said.

"Like this!" She clapped her hands and ran onto the blacktop. "Gee!" Cliffy screamed.

It was weird and wonderful to have everything go so well.

One day a nimble and tricky giant named Earl showed up at the park and Rickie had to guard him. First there was all this noise—hecklers, people chanting "De-fense!" Cliffy cheering "Ma," gulls squawking at her. And then nothing. It was the nothing that distracted her, made her look at the familiar playground, the grass, the bare dusty patches, the highway, the fast-flowing river. Why did the nothing make her feel so uneasy? It took a while for Rickie to realize that Cliffy was gone. So was the stroller.

What would she tell the Rubins? What could she possibly say? Why did all the bad things happen to her? Rickie tried to calm down by reminding herself that she was good in the clutch, that she had always been able to block out the jeers and the mockery from her opponents. Think good thoughts, right? Cliffy would get hungry, and she was the one who had the cookies. Of course he would come back . . . assuming that he had left of his own volition and not been . . . No, think positive. No one would want to kidnap Cliffy. He looked so waterlogged and shapeless. He wasn't the least bit cute.

Rickie headed north through Riverside Park. She knelt in front of every stroller, expecting to see Cliffy's round face and gap-toothed grin, but each time it was someone else's strange, soft baby looking up at her. "How adorable, excuse me," she said, hurrying on, intoning with each step: He's okay, he's okay. He had probably just wiggled out of his safety belt and walked off. Where? Home? The jeering got loud as she thought about Cliffy crossing 96th Street, pausing to sit between parked cars, stumbling on a pothole as the light changed. Rickie started to run.

By the time she reached Harlem, she was shaking her head to clear away the bad images, and praying aloud to silence the razz.

"Please, God, please." Everything terrified her—a man with a shopping bag, a tiny lady wheeling a cart. Pop was right to say that her brain was polluted from all the horror movies she watched—axe murderers, body snatchers, corpses with twirling eyeballs. "If I find him, I promise . . ." She would take better care of him, be nice to her parents, go to temple every Friday night, and really pray if only Cliffy would come back.

Behold the Boksers in their natural habitat. The mother sets the table, the father adjusts the waist of his trousers and growls. Coins jangle. "She's not in the bathroom."

"So? She'll be here in a second. Sit down, forget her. Tell me what you want, rye bread or melba toast."

Michael puts his head under the kitchen faucet. As the water drips from his ears and nose, he transforms himself into Sir Michael, shrewd analyst of Bokser behavior, a naturalist among this wild tribe. "The Boksers are a nomadic people, believed to have migrated by foot to the New World," he notes.

"Rye, is it six yet?"

"Stop, you're driving me crazy. She'll be here!"

The father closes the faucet, the hot tap first. Icy water pours down Sir Michael's ears and scalp. "Some day because of people like you, the water will be all gone. Do you know how many gallons go down the drain while you stand there playing?"

Sir Michael tries to be serene but thinks that he will kill his sister. "How many gallons go down the drain while I stand here playing?"

"Thousands, Essie, is it six yet?"

She could just say he ran away, which was almost the truth, she hoped.

"I stopped to tie my shoe and while my eyes were down
. . ." Renee had cautioned her never to take her eyes off Cliffy.
Even to tie her shoes?

"Not for the slightest second."

The bridge was up ahead. Traffic was so thick the cars
looked as if they were connected, like the cars on a subway.
Rickie ran on the promenade beside the highway, wondering
whether to continue uptown or backtrack through the park.
It seemed as if she had looked everywhere on her way up
here, that she couldn't possibly have missed Cliffy, who, she
remembered quite clearly, had been dressed in his bright
blue Snoopy shirt. Was it possible that he had crossed the
bridge? What if he was still sitting in the stroller, if she had
panicked and started running through the streets, while all
along he was strapped tight, crying, "Ma, gee," his cookie
long gone?

She reversed direction and ran back to the courts. If she
found him, she would keep every promise she made plus
miss the game against the Blue Hawks that night without a
word of protest. But if she didn't find him her only job would
be to write up the guest list to her funeral.

Rickie had made her parents mad before by getting caught
missing school, stealing a key chain from Woolworth's, playing doctor in the closet with Barry Gluck, but this was the
worst, this was major league. Her parents were probably
screaming and being insane. Their voices made her ears
throb. Cliffy couldn't have crossed the bridge—even she
didn't know how to get on the walkway. They never gave
her a moment's peace. She said, "One second please," so she
could finish working on a blackhead deep in her ear, and
they went on pounding on the bathroom door, hollering,
"Rickie, Rickie," like deranged birds. They were too dumb to
understand that all that noise made her nervous, that the mirror she had carefully angled against the mirror in the medicine
cabinet got out of whack and the whole operation took her
much longer. She had to find Cliffy no matter if it meant the
worst punishment imaginable, like having to stay inside for-

ever. Please, God, yes, let them do it, as long as I find Cliffy, I swear I won't complain. .

Her hopes did not rise even once as she ran. There were no children outside anymore, no almost-Cliffys, no moment when with relief she saw a small boy, and thinking he had returned, thanked God. Rickie's stomach growled, but she was determined never to go home until she found Cliffy. She would wander through the park forever, if necessary. This proclamation, "I will never go home until I find him!" made her hope that maybe now, because she was showing God how serious she was by searching like this on an empty stomach, she would be forgiven and Cliffy would come back.

"Out!" says the father, clutching the edge of the table, as if he means to upend their meal.

"Michael, give me her plate, I'll put it in the refrigerator."

"Throw it out."

As the mother picks up the plate, the Boksers enact another ritual. The father, who considers waste the worst sin, has made the mother heap food on the daughter's plate just so he can throw it out. This enables him to get furious with Rickie not merely for being late, but for forcing him to do what hurts him most.

The dinner slides in the trash. The mother implores the father to sit down, but he hovers in the doorway, checking his watch, calling out the time minute by minute.

"Call," says the mother.

She could not afford to break her promise, not while she was appealing fervently to God, but she made a modification she did not think He'd mind. She would never go home—that still held. Maybe she would go to Claudia's apartment and get Claudia to—she admitted it—give her something to eat and then call up Renee and ask where Cliffy was. . . .

Rickie left the park and headed toward Claudia's building. In order to reach it, she first had to pass her own. Someone was waiting under the awning, and even with the sky as dusky as it had grown, she could tell it wasn't her father. She had a moment of feeling safe before she recognized the man as Charlie Rubin. Her first impulse was to run as fast as possible, and she turned away, ready to do that. Then she heard her name, and the next thing she knew, she had startled both Charlie and herself by flying into his arms and sobbing, "I've lost him, Mr. Rubin."

Charlie was by nature a mild, peaceable guy. He had been furious with Rickie, but now the sight of her sobbing just did him in. He put his arm around her and walked her into the building. A woman, a Good Samaritan, had found Cliffy pinned under his stroller, screaming his poor head off. She had picked him up and then the diaper bag, which had a tag on it with Renee's name and address. Charlie could not understand how that happened when Rickie seemed like such a nice, responsible girl.

Rickie was going to tell him she had just leaned over to tie her shoelaces, but she never got beyond a staccato "I-I-I-I."

"I know you're sorry," Charlie said, punching the elevator button.

"I-I-I-I," she tried as the elevator door closed behind them.

"I know," Charlie said. "I was a kid, too."

The doors opened at the fourth floor and Charlie said, "What a thing it is to love so much," and started down the hall. Rickie, weak from gratitude, followed Charlie down to his apartment. When Renee spied them, she pushed past her husband, and with a stupendous leap, one which Rickie admired for a moment before the sting, she raked her nails across the babysitter's face, nicking her eye with a sharp talon.

In the time between Papa's call to the Rubins and Rickie's return an hour later, only one thing was discussed: What would they do when she came home? How could they make her see that her carelessness could have caused a tragedy— the baby lying helpless on the ground. Where had she been then? And now? Pop had never touched either of his children in anger, but he could not see beyond his wish that Rickie was smaller so he could take her over his knee. . . .

"What happened?" Mama asked, following her into the foyer. Rickie was crying and sniffling; all her words sounded foreign except "My eye—"

Rickie did not mean to cry when she came home, but it felt as if a dagger had lodged in her eye. Every blink was punishment.

Her parents came toward her. Rickie covered her face.

"What happened?" Mama asked, following her into the kitchen.

"My eye!" she wept. Her words were garbled in her palms.

Pop moved Rickie's hands off her face. Her eye was blinking spasmodically and tearing by itself, as if it was sad before she, herself, could figure things out.

Papa rifled through the phone book, and a second later was on the phone. A second after that, or so it seemed, they were riding downtown in a bouncing Checker, Rickie between her parents, hiding her face like a criminal besieged by the press, sniffling continuously. In the darkness her hands made, the awful possibilities took shape. Cliffy on the ground. Cliffy dead.

The doctor lived nine floors above his office and was not yet there when they arrived. They clustered in the hallway until his wife turned on the lights in the waiting room. There they sat on a molded foam couch until the ophthalmologist showed up, in khaki shorts and a T-shirt that said "Virginia is for Lovers."

Rickie sat in the odd, high chair, and the doctor perched on a low stool and looked into her eye with an ophthalmoscope. He breathed heavily in her face. "Some fight," was all he said. He put an antibiotic in her eye and covered it with a thick white patch held in place with broad strips of adhesive.

Rickie walked back to the waiting room. She was ready for anything. She was hoping her parents would hate her. Pop looked up when he saw her in the doorway. "You weren't there, so you don't remember the day I carried you home from the hospital. Five days old, Mama had wrapped you in blankets and put you in my arms."

"I was there, Papa," Rickie said, daring a little smile.

"I was so frightened, I didn't think I'd be able to make a single step. Such an awesome thing to be trusted with a human life. Essie, do you remember what you said? How you have to know that danger is everywhere but live as if you've forgotten it? But first you have to *know*, Rickie."

Pop took Rickie's arm. Rickie remembered what Charlie had said earlier. "What a thing it was to love so much."

To love so much they could love even her. Rickie walked in silence between her parents, awed and disturbed by the depths of parental love.

Jane Yolen

Names

Her mother's number had been D248960. It was still imprinted on her arm, burned into the flesh, a permanent journal entry. Rachel had heard the stories, recited over and over in the deadly monotone her mother took on to tell of the camp. Usually her mother had a beautiful voice, low, musical. Men admired it. Yet not a month went by that something was not said or read or heard that reminded her, and she began reciting the names, last names, in order, in a sepulchral accent:

ABRAHMS
BERLINER
BRODSKY
DANNENBERG
FISCHER
FRANK
GLASSHEIM
GOLDBLATT

It was her one party trick, that recitation. But Rachel always knew that when the roll call was done, her mother would start the death-camp stories. Whether the audience wanted to

hear them or not, she would surround them with their own
guilt and besiege them with the tales:

HEGELMAN
ISAACS
KAPLAN
KOHN

Her mother had been a child in the camp, had gone
through puberty there, had left with her life. Had been lucky.
The roll call was of the dead ones, the unlucky ones. The
children in the camp had each been imprinted with a portion
of the names, a living yahrzeit, little speaking candles; their
eyes burning, their flesh burning, wax in the hands of the
adults who had told them: "You must remember. If you do
not remember, we never lived. If you do not remember, we
never died." And so they remembered.

Rachel wondered if, all over the world, there were survivors, men and women who, like her mother, could recite
those names:

LEVITZ
MAMOROWITZ
MORGENSTERN
NORENBERG
ORENSTEIN
REESE

Some nights she dreamed of them: hundreds of old children, wizened toddlers, marching toward her, their arms over
their heads to show the glowing numbers, reciting names.

ROSENBLUM
ROSENWASSER
SOLOMON
STEIN

It was an epic poem, those names, a ballad of alphabetics. Rachel could have recited them along with her mother, but her mouth never moved. It was an incantation. Hear, O Israel, Germany, America. The names had an awful power over her, and even in her dreams she could not speak them aloud. The stories of the camps, of the choosing of victims—left line to the ovens, right to another day of deadening life—did not frighten her. She could move away from the group that listened to her mother's tales. There was no magic in the words that told of mutilations, of children's brains against Nazi walls. She could choose to listen or not listen; such recitations did not paralyze her. But the names:

TANNENBAUM
TEITLEMAN
VANNENBERG
WASSERMAN
WECHTENSTEIN
ZEISS

Rachel knew that the names had been spoken at the moment of her birth: that her mother, legs spread, the waves of Rachel's passage rolling down her stomach, had breathed the names between spasms long before Rachel's own name had been pronounced. Rachel Rebecca Zuckerman. That final *Zeiss* had burst from her mother's lips as Rachel had slipped out, greasy with birth blood. Rachel knew she had heard the names in the womb. They had opened the uterine neck, they had lured her out and beached her as easily as a fish. How often had her mother commented that Rachel had never cried as a child. Not once. Not even at birth when the doctor had slapped her. She knew, even if her mother did not, that she had been silenced by the incantation, the *Zeiss* a stopper in her mouth.

When Rachel was a child, she had learned the names as another child would a nursery rhyme. The rhythm of the passing syllables was as water in her mouth, no more than nonsense words. But at five, beginning to understand the power

of the names, she could say them no more. For the saying
was not enough. It did not satisfy her mother's needs. Rachel
knew that there was something more she needed to do to
make her mother smile.

At thirteen, on her birthday, she began menstruating, and
her mother watched her get dressed. "So plump. So zaftik."
It was an observation, less personal than a weather report.
But she knew it meant that her mother had finally seen her
as more than an extension, more than a child red and white
from its passage into the light.

It seemed that, all at once, she knew what to do. Her mother's duty had been the Word. Rachel's was to be the Word
Made Flesh.

She stopped eating.

The first month, fifteen pounds poured off her. Melted. Ran
as easily as candle wax. She thought only of food. Bouillon.
Lettuce. Carrots. Eggs. Her own private poem. What she
missed most was chewing. In the camp they chewed on gris-
tle and wood. It was one of her mother's best tales.

The second month her cheekbones emerged, sharp reminders of the skull. She watched the mirror and prayed.
Baruch atah adonai eloheynu melech ha-olam. She would
not say the words for bread or wine. Too many calories. Too
many pounds. She cut a star out of yellow posterboard and
held it to her breast. The face in the mirror smiled back. She
rushed to the bathroom and vomited away another few
pounds. When she flushed the toilet, the sound was a hiss,
as if gas were escaping into the room.

The third month she discovered laxatives, and the names
of the containers became an addition to her litany: Metamucil,
Agoral, Senokot. She could feel the chair impress itself on her
bones. Bone on wood. If it hurt to sit, she would lie down.

She opened her eyes and saw the ceiling, spread above her
like a sanitized sky. A voice pronounced her name. "Rachel,
Rachel Zuckerman. Answer me."

But no words came out. She raised her right hand, a signal;
she was weaker than she thought. Her mother's face, smiling,

appeared. The room was full of cries. There was a chill in the air, damp, crowded. The smell of decay was sweet and beckoning. She closed her eyes and the familiar chant began, and Rachel added her voice to the rest. It grew stronger near the end:

ABRAHMS
BERLINER
BRODSKY
DANNENBERG
FISCHER
FRANK
GLASSHEIM
GOLDBLATT
HEGELMAN
ISAACS
KAPLAN
KOHN
LEVITZ
MAMOROWITZ
MORGENSTERN
NORENBERG
ORENSTEIN
REESE
ROSENBLUM
ROSENWASSER
SOLOMON
STEIN
TANNENBAUM
TEITLEMAN
VANNENBERG
WASSERMAN
WECHTENSTEIN
ZEISS
ZUCKERMAN

They said the final name together and then, with a little sputter, like a yahrzeit candle at the end, she went out.

Carolyn A. Rogers

The Get

In the thirties we lived in a little flat on New York's Lower East Side. It was depression times and we were all poor. My father was sick in bed. He coughed a lot. He worked, when he could, at odd jobs. My mother mostly stayed home to take care of him and took in ironing and sewing. Late at night I could hear her at the old treadle machine mending sheets or sewing a dress she'd promised a customer.

"It's a good thing there aren't any more of us, Becky, or we'd all starve," my mother would say when I begged her for a brother or sister to play with. "There are lots of kids in the building. You can play with them."

It was true. We played games in the street, stick ball and Keep Away and jump rope. We used stones to play hopscotch. In the winter when our flat was cold, I walked to the library where it was warm and quiet and I could read until it closed.

Josh was a boy in our building. He was a few years older than me, maybe fifteen. There was something strange about him. I guess he was sick because he didn't go to school like the rest of us. He wasn't stupid and he looked all right, he wasn't crippled or anything like that, but he acted kind of funny. I never knew what to expect. Sometimes he would get real mad.

"Those kids are teasing me," he'd yell. "They've stolen my books again." He would sit on the stoop staring straight ahead, not talking to anyone. Other times, he was nice and we would sit on the stoop together and make up stories to tell each other.

I had just started having my period. When I asked my mother about it, she scowled and handed me some cloths and a box of stuff and a pamphlet. "Here, Becky. This will tell you all you need to know."

That summer I turned thirteen. It was real hot in New York and I slept on the roof and spent a lot of time sitting under the fire hydrants when the kids turned the water on. When there was nothing else to do I sat talking with Josh on the stoop. It was more fun talking to him than to the girls. He didn't giggle and make fun of me, and from his being home all the time and reading he had lots of good stories to tell. It almost made me forget the heat that steamed out of the old brick building even at night.

Mother didn't like kids to play in our flat and mess things up. My father was getting grayer and thinner and he wanted the apartment dark and quiet. I didn't much want to go to Josh's flat. It was small and crowded and smelled of meat cooking and garlic and turnips. Kind of a stale, sour, oily smell.

So we sat outside, where it was cooler. From time to time my mother looked out her window at us sitting there. "Keep your legs together, Becky. Make sure you come in before it gets dark." It stays light real late in the summer so we had lots of time to talk.

Josh's parents were Orthodox and I felt awkward around them. They used words I couldn't understand. I used to think they were talking about me, though I couldn't imagine why.

One day Josh and I were sitting on our favorite spot, playing our make-believe games, when he held out a little ring to me.

"What's that for?" I asked him.

"That's for you," he said. "Will you wear it for me?"

It had a little pink stone and the band was gold colored. I suppose it came from the five-and-dime store. He didn't have much more money than we did.

"All right," I said. Solemnly he slipped it on my finger.

"Thank you, kind sir." I laughed and my face grew warm. It was just pretend, but it made me feel grown-up, like a woman, like a beautiful fairy-tale princess.

When I went in for dinner, my mother immediately noticed the ring.

"Where did you get that, Becky?"

"Josh gave it to me."

"Vey is mir. They're Orthodox. That means you are as good as married to him!"

"I'm too young to get married," I said. "You're spoiling all my fun! And besides, I don't love him or anyone else for that matter."

"Wait. You'll see. This will be trouble with them." She chopped the cabbage harder and faster than ever.

It was a couple more days before I saw Josh sitting on the stoop. I didn't know what to say. I didn't want to hurt his feelings.

"Here," I said, taking off the ring. "My mother said I'm too young to take such presents from a boy."

He put the ring in his pocket. I thought I saw a tear run down his cheek. I was crying, too.

But my mother was right. There was trouble. His parents cried and howled and carried on for days. They insisted that we were engaged, as good as married by their rules. Josh himself looked pleased when they said that. Never mind that I had returned his ring. It didn't matter, I guess.

But I wasn't pleased and I wasn't about to be married. So finally to satisfy them and placate me, my mother went to the

council of rabbis to get me a divorce, what they call a "get."
I don't know how often she went or what it took because it
was fall and I was back in school by that time. But one day
when I came home she handed me a piece of paper.

"Now you are a divorced woman," she said. "You'll be free
to marry when you are of age. Don't bother me again about
this."

I was thirteen and still a virgin. But I was divorced. As for
my "husband," he sent me a book one year for my birthday.
In it he wrote, "To my best friend, Becky."

Laura Cunningham

Grandma

When I hear that she's coming to stay with us, I'm pleased. I think of "grandmother" as a generic brand. My friends have grandmothers who seem permanently bent over cookie racks. They are Nanas and Bubbas, sources of constant treats, huggers and kissers, pinchers of cheeks.

I have no memory of my own grandmother, who has lived in a distant state, and whom I haven't seen since I was a baby. But, with the example of the neighborhood grandmothers before me, I can hardly wait to have a grandmother of my own—and the cookies will be nice, too. For, while my uncles provide a cuisine that ranges from tuna croquettes to Swedish meatballs, they show no signs of baking anything more elegant than a potato.

My main concern on the day of my grandmother's arrival is, how soon will she start the cookies?

She arrives, flanked by Len and Gabe. Although her sons tower over her, she appears in no way diminished: she holds herself absolutely straight, and cuts a trim figure in a navy-blue hat, tailored suit, an ermine stole. She holds, tucked under her arm, a purple leather portfolio, which contains her work-in-progress, a manuscript entitled *Philosophy for Women*. She is followed by her custom-made white trunk, packed with purses, earrings, dresses, and more purple-inked pages that stress "the spiritual above the material."

At five feet one inch, she is not much taller than I am—thin and straight, with a pug nose, one brown eye (the good eye), and one blue eye (the bad eye, frosted by a cataract). Her name is "Esther in Hebrew, Edna in English, and Etka in Russian." She prefers the Russian, referring to herself as "Etka from Minsk."

It's not immediately apparent, but she is also deaf in her left ear (the bad ear) but can hear with the right (her good ear). As the good ear is on the opposite side from the good eye, anyone speaking to her must run around her in circles or sway to and fro, if eye contact and audibility are to be achieved simultaneously.

Etka from Minsk has arrived not directly from Minsk, as the black-eyed ermine stole seems to suggest, but after many moves. She enters with the draft of family scandal at her back, blown out of another relative's home after assaults upon her dignity. She holds the evidence: an empty-socketed peacock pin. My cousin, an eleven-year-old boy, has surgically plucked out the rhinestone eyes. She cannot be expected to stay where such acts occur. She has to be among "human beings," among "real people" who can understand. We seem to understand. Uncle Len, Gabe, and I encircle her, study her vandalized peacock pin, and vow that such affronts will never happen with us.

She pats my head—a good sign—and asks me to sing the Israeli national anthem. I have the impression that I am auditioning for her, and I am. I sing "Hatikvah" (off key, but she can't quite hear me), and she gives me a dollar: a wonderful start.

Uncles Len and Gabe go off to their respective jobs, leaving me alone with Etka from Minsk for the first time. I look at her, expecting her to toss off her tailored jacket, tuck up her cuffs, and roll out the cookie dough. Instead, she purses her lips in an expression she learned as a child, and tilts her head in a practiced way: "Now, perhaps, you could fix me a little lunch?"

"It isn't supposed to be this way," I think as I take her order: "toasted cheese sandwich and a sliced orange."

Together we unpack the massive white trunk. She instructs me to stack her belongings—dozens of silk blouses, custom-made suits, spectator pumps, and a queen's ransom in costume jewelry—on my bed. I'm dazzled—and dazed. It had not occurred to me that she would sleep in my room: I am eight and she is nearly eighty. But my uncles don't see the incongruity, only the affinity of sex. Now, my old room is dubbed "The Girls' Room" by Uncle Gabe.

What goes on in The Girls' Room proves the name is apt: I've acquired not the doting Nana of my dreams, but an aged kid sister. Within hours, the theft and rivalry begin.

The first night, Etka from Minsk makes an official presentation—performed as if in an operetta. She walks to the dinette in full evening dress, holding in her outstretched hands three ornate beaded evening bags. "These are the three evening bags I have saved for my three daughters-in-law."

Even I hear one false note: why does she still have three gift purses when she has only two unmarried sons? *Ah ha . . .*

"I lost one son, a war victim" is how she describes Norm's marriage to Barb. The result is now she need save only two beaded bags; it is out of the question to reward Barb with a beaded bag. Therefore, one bag is available, to be given to someone worthy of owning it. Etka's good eye seeks me out at my place at the table. She holds out the most beautiful of the evening bags: a violet flapper-style purse, with long, sparkling fringes. I am beside myself: I would rather have this shimmering accessory than a lifetime of cookies or rolled strudels.

And yes, "I am giving this beautiful beaded bag, which I had saved for my third daughter-in-law, to my only grand-daughter, Lily." She pronounces my name "Leeli," adding to the foreign feel of this presentation. I love every second of the ceremony, which reminds me of tableaux depicting Indians trading for the Island of Manhattan.

I rise, bow, accept the beaded bag. I thank her, and, for free, throw in a few verses of the Hebrew national anthem.

On impulse, I rush to my room and open my treasure chest (a lavender metal candy box), and run back with an offering of my own: my most prized piece, the ivory heart-shaped pin I had planned to give to my mother. I present this pin, with a set of matching earrings, and Etka nods. This seems appropriate. Uncle Len and Uncle Gabe exchange a glance. Gabe cannot resist saying, out of Etka's "good" earshot (the first of our many mouthed asides), "See, they're getting along beautifully." Uncle Len, in response, raises his eyebrow, Marx brothers style.

That night Etka and I share the large bedroom. (Have there ever been two more disparate partners on twin beds?)

I spy on her, through not-quite-closed eyelids, as she prepares for sleep. She wears a matched peach set of European-style underwear. Her legs are slim and well-shaped. Her entire body is, in fact, surprisingly intact. Her small breasts droop, but not much (not as much as Ava's, anyway), and her white skin appears smooth, although she wears, here and there, tiny cysts—skin cells no longer incorporated—and, near her collarbone, a small garnet brooch of blood blisters. (Soon I know her body as well as I know mine, perhaps better, as I spend more time studying hers. And, because I often escort her by the elbow, I come to know the crushed flower-petal feel of her upper arm: cool and white, like the talcum powder that sifts from her skin.)

Etka takes to her bed with my kind of enthusiasm: a haven. She turns on her side, and nuzzles deep down into her pillowcase. I envy her swift snuggle into sleep. Within seconds, she is breathing evenly. Eventually, the sound must lull me, too, although throughout the night I seem to retain an awareness of something new, an unfamiliar form in the shadowed room. This is not unpleasant, only different, and tucked tight under my pink "Blanky," I pass a pretty fair night.

Which is why morning comes as such a blow. I wake and rush to my drawer to admire my new treasure, the violet beaded bag. I look through my scant possessions and there can be no doubt: the purse is missing.

Purloined. I look to my still-sleeping grandmother. Now she lies confident, on her back. On a hunch, I tiptoe to her file cabinet, and peek. Poorly concealed, under her manuscript, is a flash of violet fringe. I don't take the bag but run straight to Uncle Len, who is popping corn to accompany today's breakfast menu of tuna croquettes and baked beans. He wears his pith helmet and a professional chef's apron, over a tee-shirt and suit pants. I tell on Etka: she stole back the purse. . . .

Uncle Len doesn't look too surprised as he rattles his pressure cooker, and mini-explosions ricochet within. "Court will convene tonight" is all he says.

The decision goes against me. I can't believe it. They know she has that beaded bag. And, when confronted, she refuses to give it (or the ivory pin and earring set) back to me. They admit this is unfair, but they ask me to forbear: they don't want to upset Etka so early in her stay.

I burn at the injustice of it, and feel the heat of an uncomfortable truth: where once I had my uncles' undivided indulgence, they are now split as my grandmother and I vie for their attention. The household, formerly geared to my little-girl needs, is now rearranged to accommodate hers.

The crimes continue—I suffer serious affronts. Etka, in a fit of frugality, scissors all the household blankets, including "Blanky," in half. "Now," she says, her good eye gleaming, "we have twice as many."

I lie under my narrow slice of blanket and stare up at the ceiling. I think evilly of ways of getting Etka from Minsk out of the apartment.

Matters worsen, as more and more of my trinkets disappear. One afternoon, I come home to find Etka squeezed into
my unbuttoned favorite blouse. Rouged and beribboned, she
insists the size 3 blouse is hers.

Meanwhile, I am forced to adapt to her idiosyncrasies. She
covers everything black—from the telephone to the dog—
with white doilies. She leaves saucers balanced on top of
glasses. She tries to lock Bonny out of the apartment.

"Black, black, you never get back," she chants. In Russia,
her family had a white dog, which was kept in its own room,
a white room. The dog's name had been Belka, which means
"white" in Russian.

"We had a white dog," she says, as if that's that.

She also sings nonstop—Russian, Hebrew, and German
songs. Then, in a tuneless monotone, she chants her own
praises. She often takes both parts in a dialogue: "Who is the
most beautiful, intelligent woman in the world? I am. Who
has the most distinguished family? Who has the most perfect
legs?" She does, she does.

One afternoon, as we sit by the window (where she loves
to watch the neighbors in disapproval), she announces for
the hundredth time, "Once a beauty, always a beauty." Something in me snaps—she's wearing my pin, my earrings, my
blouse, and has been bragging for days. I say, with a child's
cruel honesty: "You have wrinkles."

To me her face appears creased, as if she has pressed herself against the mesh of a window screen. Etka doesn't see
herself that way. She purses her lip, exaggerating the "whistle
marks" and laughs as if what I've said is absurd. "Once a
beauty, always a beauty," she insists.

This stream of egotism would be intolerable—if she
sounded sure. But even an eight-year-old can hear a tinny
ring.

The word that Uncle Len uses to explain Etka from Minsk's
behavior is "arteriosclerosis." He tells me that sometimes not
enough blood reaches Etka's brain, and she "forgets."

She forgets so much that sometimes she locks me out of

the apartment. Other times she greets me by saying, "You look familiar." Sitting in our room, she asks, "What hotel is this?"

My answer, shouted into her good ear, is "This isn't a hotel. This is our apartment." Her response is another hoot of laughter: "Then why are we in the ballroom?"

In "the ballroom," one afternoon, I dance my old harem dance, wearing what little jewelry I can still find and a bath towel. "Very nice," she says.

But sex is on her mind, too. She tumbles out of bed one night, thrown by a nightmare that her sons are marrying "tramps." Uncle Len and Gabe must help me lift Etka into her bed. All the while they reassure her: "We aren't marrying tramps." She points to a red night light that glows near her bed: "Then what's that for?"

They buy a bed with crib bars—a hospital model that adjusts to full and semi recline, the better to secure Etka from her increasingly frequent apparitions. On most afternoons, an elderly woman, Mrs. Mark, is hired to mind my grandmother until I can return from school. This woman soon enters Etka's nightmares as a new persona: "I saw a blonde in a fur coat in here," she cries in the middle of the night.

I try to explain. That wasn't a blonde in a fur coat, that was another eighty-year-old woman, with yellowing white hair, wearing a fake mouton jacket. She'll have none of that: "I saw her, I saw that tramp, that bum in her fur coat."

When Mrs. Mark returns for the next grandmother-sitting session, we all hold our breath. Apparently Etka holds her tongue. In fact, when being cared for, she has all her senses. "Oh, you're so wonderful," she coos to "the tramp."

More of my clothes disappear. She has almost everything now. I have no necklaces—she's wearing them—and everything pink is also appropriated. My uncles keep replacing items only to see them disappear the next night.

Finally, we fight: arm-to-arm combat. I'm shocked at her grip, steely as the bars that lock her into bed at night. Her good eye burns into mine and she says, "I'll tell."

And she does. For the first time I'm scolded. She turns their love to disapproval, and, oh, how it chafes.

I throw a tantrum—the first under the uncle regime—and they stand by, helpless, as I pound the abraded floor with my fists.

That night, Etka from Minsk has a new nightmare. She screams, and I wake up . . . to hear her crying: "Where is my baby? Where is my baby?"

An eighty-year-old woman is dreaming that she has just given birth. Now she can't find the baby. She thrashes in bed, lifting her sheets: "Where is my baby? Where is my baby?"

I try to comfort her: there is no baby. "You were asleep," I tell her.

No, she insists: the baby was "just here" in the bed. Etka from Minsk starts to cry. I run to the other rooms and alert my uncles. Uncle Gabe, in striped pajamas, and Uncle Len, in tee-shirt and shorts, rush into The Girls' Room.

To prove there is no baby, we lift her mattress. There we discover a new secret: Etka's life savings, bound in a knotted lisle stocking, a wad of single bills, that she calls her "*knippl.*" Also: my stolen necklaces, cultured pearls, and pink hair ribbons.

It takes hours to convince Etka that she has not given birth and somehow misplaced her newborn baby. We usher her into the present. Uncle Len whispers her life history: "You had five babies, but that was a long time ago. . . ."

My uncles also bring me up to date. At the time when my grandmother had her children, women gave birth at home. Although my uncles, as young boys, were locked out of her bedroom, they heard her scream when their youngest brother was born. They tell me that babies were often kept, for the first few months, in the mother's bed. They believe that Etka's nightmare is a reprise of past maternal anxiety, suffered, most likely, after childbirth.

I say nothing, but I have my own theory. I believe Etka

cries for her lost daughter, my mother. By day, my grand-mother will not admit that Rosie has died. "My daughter was given a wonderful job. She's in Washington" is all my grand-mother will say. She incorporates this mythical promotion into her bragging monologues: "They don't promote just anyone's daughter, they promote *my* daughter. . . ."

There is much precedent in the family for pretending that the dead have not died but are living in other cities. Practicing a form of emotional etiquette, it is considered good form to spare elderly relatives sad news. Whenever we attend family reunions, the uncles give me a quick refresher course in who's officially dead and who's not. It would be helpful to maintain a cross-index, because some elderly aunts know while others don't know. Great Aunt Becky believes she has a nephew in Alaska, while her sister, Berta, knows that nephew died of heart failure three years ago. Entire sections of the family (the Kroll branch) have expired, but their sur-viving sister, my grandmother, has been told the whole group "moved to California." (When a cousin actually did move to California, no one believed it—the other cousins all believed this was a euphemism for the much-longer journey.)

My grandmother had been spared the news of Rosie's death for several months, but an aunt finally told. Etka did not ac-knowledge the death, however, and she maintained the Washington myth for another few months. I sensed she knew the truth but chose not to say so. When someone said the name Rosie, she would turn pale.

The way my grandmother mourns for my mother is some-thing I understand. I recognize her nightmare too. We both know the Night Witch may hide behind our closed closet door, filling all shadows by assuming new, awful shapes. When Etka insists her baby is stolen, I secretly agree.

Over the next several nights, I lull my own fear by com-forting Etka. If I can tuck her under the covers, and sing her to sleep, maybe everything will be all right.

Uncle Len tells me that my grandmother's distaste for the

color black has nothing to do with disliking the dog or being racist. She fears death so much she cannot cope with the color of mourning.

After that explanation, I keep the doily over the telephone, never wear black, and put a red collar on the dog (to minimize the effect). As time passes, my grandmother's night panics become less frequent, and I take a certain pleasure in offering her the reassurance she needs. "Who is the smartest, most beautiful woman in the world?" she asks.

I know the answer, and she knows enough to laugh.

"You are!"

As Told to her daughter, Ruth Weisberg

Theresa Weisberg's Wedding

(Daughter: You got married on July 17, 1932, a forty-four-year marriage that never ended in divorce in spite of the conversation you had before getting married . . .)

Yes, a friend predicted that as long as the two of us dance together we'll stay married, but once we stop dancing we'll get a divorce.

(And you never stopped dancing . . .)

And we never stopped dancing, so she was right. But the wedding was a real fiasco, the wedding to end all weddings . . .

First of all, you know Dad was an only child. I never met his father, who had died. His mother was not only Orthodox, she was ultra-Orthodox and superstitious and everything that goes with that. She didn't want him to marry me once she met me because to her I was like a shikse, I was a Jewish girl that was not religious. She said she would rather that he marry a non-Jewish girl and then she would help convert her, but she wasn't going to teach me anything. She was very unhappy.

My mother, on the other hand, thought Al was a great guy, which he was. She was happy.

For the wedding, we didn't have very much money, since it was the depression. But still my mother invited everybody, my brothers invited their friends, I invited my friends, and Al invited his fraternity brothers. The wedding was in my house on the hottest day of the year.

My father was in Birobidzhan, a part of the Soviet Union designated by Lenin as the Jewish homeland, and we were waiting all morning for a cable from him. My father, Isaac Herbst, had gone to Russia after the stock market crash in 1929 because he lost his job as a civil engineer in Chicago, where he was helping to build the first subway. Before that, we all lived for three years on a utopian Jewish commune in Clarion, Utah, with Zionists, socialists and anarchists until the farm failed. My dad was secretary-treasurer of the commune.

Jews in those days had no real hope of getting a homeland in what was then Palestine, so when he lost his job in Chicago my father thought he'd go to the new Jewish homeland and send for my mother in a few years. We hadn't seen him in three years by then and we were all waiting for a cable from him for my wedding. Telegrams were coming from all over. Still no cable from my dad.

I was eating a peach and ironing my wedding dress when the doorbell rang. I ran downstairs to get the wire, and I swallowed the peach pit. I couldn't bring it up again. It was stuck. Everybody kept giving me water and milk and bread, all the home remedies. Finally it went down.

Then my mother insisted on helping me pack, though I told her to leave my things alone. But she thought she should help me.

I worked then at the V.A. Hospital, so I would get my eye wash and other medicinals like alcohol from the hospital. The eye wash and the alcohol were both colorless and in bottles. So my mother packed away my eye wash. I went to put some of the colorless fluid in an eye cup, I put it in my eye, and it's alcohol. My eye blew up. So I had makeup on one eye, and no makeup on the other eye. The beautiful bride.

Then I'm ironing the wedding dress, and you know I used to get nose bleeds. And I get a nose bleed right on the wedding dress. We had to wash out the wedding dress, and we never got the blood spot out.

Then the guests start coming. Now my mother-in-law brings ten old men from her little shul as witnesses and mine is not a kosher home so they stand around not knowing what to do with themselves, and she clung to her son Al.

While I'm getting dressed upstairs at the neighbors, Al's mother asks the rabbi, Is there any way of stopping this wedding? It's the wrong thing for her son. She knows a rabbi who has a daughter, and that's who she'd like him to marry.

The rabbi says about me, She's a very nice, educated girl, you should be very proud. She said No, I want a religious girl, she doesn't have to be educated, I want a religious girl!

So the rabbi talked to her, finally quieting her down. We come downstairs and there's a *chuppah*, my brothers are holding it. Well, two of my brothers. My third brother, Dave, wasn't there. That morning, when I was cleaning up the house, I asked Dave if he's coming to the wedding. He says Who's getting married? I said I am. He said No, I'm not interested. And he left. So Dave, my older brother, was not at the wedding.

Anyway, my two other brothers and two of their friends are holding the *chuppah*, and the rabbi tells me in English that he's going to do the whole thing in Hebrew. But at one point he says he wants to have me walk around Al seven times. It was a religious ceremony. Do I have to do that? I ask. He says yes. I say Well, I don't think I want to do that. He says You have to do it for this kind of ceremony. So I say Well, I'll think about it. He says You have to do it. I say okay.

Meanwhile, Al is saving his travel shoes so he won't spoil them and he's wearing my brother Maury's shoes, which are a size smaller than his feet. And he's uncomfortable, and he can hardly stand, and he can't wait for this wedding to be over.

Just as the wedding starts, Al's mother gets hysterical. She starts screaming in Yiddish, "She's taking my only child from me! She's taking my only child from me!"

And my sister Maria, not to be outdone, starts to yell, "He's taking my only sister from me! He's taking my only sister from me!" And everybody is saying, "Quiet, quiet. We can't hear the rabbi." The room is full and it's hot, and finally the rabbi says what he has to say and he starts moving me around Dad seven times. After each time I stop; I don't want to go around another time, and he makes me finally go around a seventh time.

Finally Dad has to break the glass. But he wasn't so sure of himself because they weren't his shoes, and he klunked on the glass so hard that all the plaster from the ceiling below fell down on my brother's bed. This was a good omen.

Al couldn't wait to take those shoes off, and he went in the bedroom, and he got on his travel shoes. My sister was in there crying, and I said, "What in the hell are you crying about?"

"I don't know," she says. But she was crying, so I cried with her.

Well, meanwhile, the ten men who were so kosher decided to sit down and they practically ate up the entire wedding feast. My mother had made all the gefilte fish and the strudel, and everyone else brought dishes of food. That's what you did in the depression, you know, like for rent parties. They sat down and took up the whole table, and kosher as they were, it didn't bother them that they were eating in a very non-kosher home.

And then started the reading of the telegrams. This was left to my older brother's friend Lou, an attorney with a really lovely voice. And he's reading the wires and people are saying, "Read the cable!" meaning the cable from my dad in Russia. But he has no cable, so he decides to make one up.

But before that happened, some man got up and made a whole speech on behalf of Birobidzhan. My friends who weren't Jewish, from the hospital, thought that this was a request for money for the bride and groom as a wedding gift, which was done in those days.

The hat went around, people were putting money in, and my friends put the money they thought they were giving for the wedding couple into the hat for Birobidzhan. They never knew they helped a Russian communist colony. Oh, that was really funny.

But Al and I didn't ever get any of the guest money. We couldn't get it back from that man. And I was upset, I went and told my mother, Get him off the footstool, we can't let him make a speech now for Birobidzhan. But she said this is the only time we can make a speech for Birobidzhan, so she wouldn't stop him.

So they kept yelling at Lou to read the cable from Birobidzhan, as I've said, and he didn't have one, so he made one up. I mean, that's not hard to do, he made up a very nice long one, and then they wanted to see it, everyone wanted to touch it. A cable from Russia, you know, you don't get that very often. And, of course, he didn't have one. Well, they practically killed him. They were so mad at him. They had him down on the floor and Al and I and my brother had to separate them from Lou, before they'd kill him.

And then Al and I just decided we're hungry, there was nothing left to eat, so we're leaving. We were going straight to New York on the cheapest Red Star bus line you can go on, twenty-five dollars. It was the worst. We made every stop and the bus didn't have the inside toilet you usually have now on the big Greyhounds, so I wasn't in tune with their toilet schedule. When I had to go it didn't stop, and when it stopped, I never had to go. And I was getting crankier and more irritated, and Dad was getting irritated with me getting irritated.

By the time we got to Pittsburgh we weren't speaking to each other. And by the time we got to New York, to the Hotel Edison, I said to him You know, don't even register, I think I'll just turn around. I'll cash in some of our traveler's checks and go home. Al said, Listen, calm down, let's go upstairs and we'll work it out, as Daddy would say. We worked it out.

Part Two

"With all your soul . . ."

Marcia Falk

Home for Winter

Late Sabbath afternoon, remembering—
Father leaving through the snow for shul
to hear the final reading and the prayers,
mumbled cacophony in ten-part tune;
while here, Mama and I would sit and watch
the evening sky close down, unveil three stars
that marked the end to Shabbas. And between

the first three to appear and all the rest,
while Father, walking, bore the new week home
with spices in his pockets, light between
his fingers, sanctifying the mundane,
we knew a time suspended out of time,
not Shabbos, not yet week, and ours alone.

Then window turned to mirror by the night
would catch our eyes in accidental glance,
holding us there; and turning, she would ask
if I would spend the evening here at home.
Other things her eyes alone would ask:
Where would I be next winter? In whose home
and through what windows would I watch for stars?

Unspoken questions—how they echo through
the rooms of later weeks and later years,
for silence is a presence we still share,
and even under distant skies we trace
those same ascending paths of early stars.
Mama, if I knew—but you know better

where our stars gather, on what tangent curves
they bend their light, and where they congregate
in threes this Sabbath waiting, waiting for night.

Karen Golden

Big White Pushka

When I was in the first grade I had a Hebrew School teacher named Mrs. Rubenstein. She was a soft-spoken woman who taught us about Judaism through a long list of "do's" and "don'ts." At the top of the "do" list was giving to charity or tzedakah. This was more important than going to temple on Friday night, more important than lighting the Shabbat candles and even more important than knowing all the prayers in Hebrew. Each week she passed around a little blue box called a pushka for us to deposit our money in. It looked like a piggy bank with a wide slit on the top.

One Sunday, just before the pushka was passed around the room, I asked Mrs. Rubenstein for permission to go to the bathroom before recess. I ran down the long temple corridor, pushed open the heavy bathroom door and proceeded to find an empty stall, but then I stopped. There was a lady in the bathroom fumbling in her purse next to the row of sinks. I heard the unmistakable jingle of change that I heard each week as we took our money out of our pockets to put in the pushka. Then I saw it! I had never noticed it before. There on the wall of the ladies' bathroom was a big white pushka and the lady was making a donation. She put in some coins and the pushka spit out a prize in a white cardboard box.

The woman took the prize and went into a stall to unwrap it. This looked like a much better deal than what we got in our classroom. Here, you put in your tzedakah money and got rewarded instantly. You didn't have to wait to see if you made it into the Book of Life during Yom Kippur. I stared at another lady as she put in her money and got a prize. I noticed how both ladies wouldn't look me in the eye and they both went into a stall to secretly unwrap the boxes. I remembered how Mrs. Rubenstein told us that giving charity anonymously was the biggest mitzvah. I understood that these ladies probably didn't want me to see them giving. They wanted to give secretly to get more points with God.

With great anticipation and excitement I ran back to my classroom and whispered to my friend Diana that there was a better pushka in the ladies' bathroom. One where God gave credit immediately with a prize. I convinced her to save her money until recess. Mrs. Rubenstein stood in front of the room and jingled the blue box. "Now, children, let's see if we can double the sound of this box." She passed the pushka around the room and little fingers eagerly put in money and shook the box vigorously. When I received the box, I passed it on. I had nothing to be ashamed of, I was just going to give later.

Soon the recess bell rang and Diana and I were looking up at the great white pushka on the ladies' bathroom wall. We took out our money, climbed up on the sink, put it in and out came the little cardboard box. We were so excited we could hardly wait to open it. What could God be giving us? We looked inside and in unison said, "What is it?" We had never seen anything like this. It was long and white and looked like a flag or a fat headband.

We ran back to the classroom, waving our prize overhead, and we shouted, "Mrs. Rubenstein . . . What is this?" Her face turned white and then red, and she said in a very unusual tone, "Where did you get that?" We explained to her that there was a pushka in the bathroom and this was the prize we got for giving in there. "It just fell out of the big white box." She stuttered and turned red again. This was in the days before sex education. She said, "I can't tell you what that is, you'll have to ask Mrs. Epstein." Out the door we ran, waving our prize again, all the way to the office. Inside, Mrs. Epstein was sitting behind her large oak desk. When she saw us coming, she took off her half glasses and let them fall from the chain hanging around her neck.

"Hello, children," she said with an air of preoccupation. "What can I do for you?"

"Mrs. Epstein, what is this?" I waved our prize in front of her face.

"Where did you get that?" We explained about the big white pushka in the ladies' bathroom and that this was the prize for giving.

"I'm too busy, go ask your mothers," Mrs. Epstein said.

After class, I ran out to meet my mom in her shiny 1966 pink convertible. I sat next to her on the black vinyl seats, closed the door, and soon I felt the breeze blowing through my braids.

"How was Hebrew School?"

"Great! But Mommy, what's this?" I took out my prize and held it in the middle as the two tails blew in either direction.

"Where did you get that?" she asked. Once again I told about the pushka in the bathroom and how Diana and I got a prize for giving. I told her how we had asked Mrs. Rubenstein and Mrs. Epstein what it was and neither of them would tell us.

"So Mommy, what is it?" My mom looked at me in the way only a mom can look, caring and wise, and without missing a beat she said, "Honey, that is a Barbie Doll mattress!"

"You mean that wasn't a pushka in the bathroom?"

"No dear. That was a Barbie Doll mattress machine."

"But Mommy, why do they have a Barbie Doll mattress machine in the ladies' bathroom?"

In a gentle voice my mom continued, "For all the little girls who bring their Barbies to services. You know how sometimes the rabbi's sermons are long and boring, well, the little girls put their Barbies to sleep on those mattresses." Her look was so loving that any flaws in her logic passed by me.

"Can I get a new Barbie Doll mattress when we go to services next week?"

"Yes dear," said my mom.

My mom and I never did have a heart-to-heart women's talk about the Barbie Doll mattress machine. Girls find these things out, one way or the other. But how soon do they need to know? Both wisdom and innocence are invaluable tools for healthy adult life. As a child, when the rabbi's sermon became unbearable, I envied my Barbie Doll for the comfy mattress she had close by. And if the truth be known, sometimes I still do!

Jyl Lynn Felman

If Only I'd Been Born
a Kosher Chicken

My mother washed us both in the same kitchen sink. Only I don't know who came first, the baby or the bird. First I am on the counter watching, then I am in the sink splashing. My mother washes me the way she washes her kosher Shabbas chicken breasts. Slowly and methodically, as though praying, she lifts my small right arm; she lifts the wings of the chicken and scrubs all the way up to where she cannot scrub any more, to where the wing is attached to the body, the arm to the shoulder. Plucking feathers from the freshly slaughtered bird, she washes in between my fingers, toe by toe. Gently she returns my short stubby arms to the side of my plump body, which remains propped upright in the large kitchen sink. I am unusually silent throughout the duration of this ancient cleansing ritual. Automatically my arms extend outward, eternally and forever reaching for her.

The cold wet chicken, washed and scrubbed, sits next to us on the counter. I weigh more than the chicken, but as far as I'm concerned we're identical, the chicken and I. Except for our heads and the feathers. The chicken has no head and I have no feathers. But I will have hair. Lots of body hair on this nice Jewish girl that my mother will religiously teach me to pluck and to shave until my adolescent body resembles a perfectly plucked, pale young bird, waiting to be cooked to a hot, crisp, golden brown and served on the same sacred platter as my mother herself was before me.

At thirteen I stand on the bimah waiting to address the entire congregation. I am also upstairs in the bathroom, alone in the terrifying wilderness of my adolescent femaleness. But I stand on the bimah and prepare to chant. On my head is a white silk yarmulke, held in place by two invisible bobby pins. For the first time in my life, I prepare my female self the exact same way she taught me in her kosher kitchen sink. *Borachu et adonai hamivorach.* I look out at the congregation of Beit Avraham. My mother is crying. I look in the mirror; I inspect my face, my eyebrows are dark brown and very thick. *Baruch atah adonai hamivorach leolam voed.* I place the tweezers as close to the skin as possible to catch the root, so the hair won't ever grow back. *Baruch atah adonai eloheynu melech ha-olam . . .* My parents are holding hands as I recite the third blessing in honor of being called to the Torah. And then I begin. Although my haftorah portion is long and difficult, I want it to last forever because I love the sonorous sounds of the mystical Hebrew letters. But I am surprised at how much it hurts to pull out a single hair, one at a time, from under my pale young skin. When I reach the final closing blessings my voice is strong and full and I do not want to stop.

The rabbi asks my parents to stand. They are kissing me, their youngest baby girl. But I am surprised at how much it hurts to shape my thick Ashkenazi eyebrows into small, elegant, Anglo female arches. Then I remember the ice cubes that she soaks the chickens in to keep them fresh and cold before the plucking and how I used to watch her pluck out a long, hard, particularly difficult feather without a single break. She had special fleishech tweezers, for use in the kitchen only. The congregation sings, *Mi chamocha boalim adonai.* I return to the kitchen for ice cubes wrapped in terry cloth that I hold diligently up to my adolescent brow. *Mi chamocha adonai nedar bakodesh . . . Who is like unto thee,*

O most High, revered and praised, doing wonders? I have no feeling above my eyes, but the frozen skin is finally ready for plucking.

These first female rituals have no prayers as I stand before the rabbi utterly proud of what I have accomplished. He places his hands above my head, *Yivorech et adonai . . .* He blesses my youthful passage into the adult community of Jews. My eyes water as alone in the bathroom I watch the furrowed brow of my beloved ancestors disappear from my face forever. At the exact same moment that I become a bat mitzvah I begin the complex process of preparing myself for rebirth into gentility. I complete these first female rites in silence, without the comfort of my mother or a single Hebrew bracha. The congregation rises, together we say, *Yiskadal, Veyiskadash sh'ma rabah.* Today I am permitted to mourn publicly. I have become a beloved daughter of the covenant, only the covenant is confusing. *Shema Yisrael adonai echad,* I love my people Israel, but I loathe my female self. Is this what my mother wanted for me? On the occasion of my bat mitzvah, my body splits apart and my head becomes severed from the rest of my body, a chicken without a head, a head without a body.

I am balanced precariously between the sink, the toilet and the cold tile floor. I use my father's shaving cream to hide all traces of the hair growing up and down my legs. I stand in a wide V and smother my right leg in white foam. My left leg supports my young body while my right leg straddles the sink. Slowly and methodically I scrape the hair off each leg. I have to concentrate very hard so I don't cut myself. Every two minutes I stop to rinse out the thick tufts of hair stuck in the razor's edge. Then I inspect the quality of my work. The finished skin has to be completely smooth, as though there never was any thick brown hair covering my body. Convinced that the right leg is smooth enough, I lower it to the floor. When I am finished shaving the lower half of my body, I raise my right arm and stare into the mirror. The hair under my arms is soft and there isn't very much there. At thirteen,

I do not understand why I have to remove this hair too. As I glide the razor back and forth, I am aware of how tender my skin is and how raw it feels once all the hair is removed. Rinsing off the now clean space, I notice that the skin is turning red. And when I roll on the sticky, sweet-scented deodorant, it burns. But I lower my right arm, lift my left one and begin again until I am fully plucked and have become my mother's chicken.

She shows me how to remove all traces of blood from the body. After soaking there is salting. But the blood of the chicken accumulates under the wings and does not drain out into her spotless kosher sink. She roasts each chicken for hours, turning the thighs over and over, checking for unclean spots that do not disappear even in the stifling oven heat. With a single stroke of the hand and a silver spoon, she removes a spot of blood from the yolk of an imperfect egg. First she cracks each one separately into a glass bowl; if the yolk is clear, luminous, she adds it to another bowl. But whenever the blood spreads like tiny veins into the center of the bright yellow ball, she throws out the whole egg.

For my turn, I roll the egg slowly in between my palms; I learn to feel the blood pulsating right inside the center so I don't ever have to break it open. I learn that the sight of red blood on the food Jews eat is disgusting. Red juice from an undercooked chicken always makes me gag. I stop eating red meat. I eat all my food cooked well done. I do not tell her when I start to bleed. Instinctively I keep my femaleness to myself. I watch her throw out a dozen eggs, one at a time, crying at the waste. To spill a drop of blood is to waste an entire life.

When she finds out, she is furious. How long? I cannot remember. She is hurt. When was the first time? I do not remember. She is almost hysterical, but I cannot remember. I remember only that all signs of blood on the body must be removed. I do not tell my mother when I begin to bleed. Instead I wrap wads of cotton in toilet paper so thick that no one will ever guess what's inside. I clean myself the exact

same way she cleans blood from the chickens in her sink. I
soak and I salt. I soak and I salt. For hours at a time. For years
I will away my own femaleness. I do not spill for months in
a row and then, when I do, it's just a spot, a small speck,
easily removed like the red spot floating in my mother's yolk.

Before I am born I float in my mother's yolk and I am never
hungry. Soon after I am born the hunger begins.

L. Schimel

Kiddush Cup

There is an instinctive recognition of one's own possessions; luggage is visible the moment it is placed on the
conveyor belt; a mother peeking into a classroom immediately spots her son among the rows of backs of heads. Call
it a woman's intuition, call it what you will, as I stepped down
from the cable car I recognized the kiddush cup on the
sidewalk.

It was not exactly mine, belonging in truth to my mother.
But it had lived my life with me, sealing off each week of my
childhood with its dark liquid, as if all the week's joys and
traumas were locked into a Ziploc bag and placed in a freezer
that was my life, to be taken out and defrosted at a later date,
when I could digest the import of each item.

A week always ended on a Friday, and always in trauma.
We would sit down for Shabbat, the cup so full I feared it
would spill when Dad rested his elbows on the table after a
long week at work, when my mother's chair bumped the table as she sat after lighting the candles. Once, when I was six
or seven, I had climbed onto the table to get the cup. I no
longer remember why, just the wanting of it. It had knocked
over, Manischewitz spilling across me, dark as blood. The tiny

wine handprints I had made on the tablecloth never came
out, no matter how many washings they went through. They
stared at me each Friday, peeking out from under my plate
in silent recrimination.

After the kiddush was said, the cup would be passed
from oldest to youngest, crossing over the table as it made
its way toward me, the final destination. And every week,
just as it had almost reached its goal, Debbie, my older
sister and the penultimate stop, would drain the cup completely.

"You're only supposed to wet your lips," she told me by
way of an apology as she handed me the empty cup each
week.

She knew she was guilty, but she said it as if she had only
done what she was supposed to do. I always wanted to
scream back at her, "Then why did you drink it all?" But I
never did. She would have calmly answered me with something like "So you wouldn't drink too much," and sounding
as if it were for my own good that she had made such a
sacrifice. That's just the way Debbie was. She could get away
with anything.

To console myself, I was always thankful that she hadn't
added, "because you're too young." It didn't matter that I
never really had these conversations with my sister; I lived in
terror each Friday when it played itself out again that this
week she would say those hated words.

"Spare some change, Miss," the homeless man sitting behind the cup asked. I stared at him for a moment, trying to
bring his face into focus. He was old, and obviously a Jew,
with the black skullcap and long, dangling peyot of the Has-
sidim. A tallis peeked from under a yellow-and-purple ski
parka torn down the left side to reveal its synthetic innards.

You hardly ever saw a Jew like that begging. They're always too proud.

Lost in memories, I hadn't even noticed him. I looked down
at the cup. It was empty, dry as the days between Fridays

when it sat atop the breakfront, between the candlesticks.

"It can't be the same cup," I whispered to myself as I continued up the street toward work. Sometimes you grab the wrong luggage off the rack; a mother confuses another child for her own.

Miriyam Glazer

Watchman, What of the Night?

For Tillie Abramson Bidnick, of blessed memory

Sooner or later on one of my ever rarer visits to New York, my Aunt "T" (as we called her) would chuckle: "Remember," she'd say, "your little hat with the feather?"

Shrunken by old age and osteoporosis, half-blind, but with every silver-gray hair still as perfectly in place as it was when it was black; eternally, as she used to say, "young at heart," Aunt T would turn into a little girl before my eyes, placing an imaginary hat with a long feather on her head. I saw that "Toby Myra" (as she would call me) had had a dogged determination set in her lips, intensity in her eyes. "You remember?"

I'd laugh and nod, though in fact I didn't remember the Little Hat with the Feather that had become so vivid in our family lore. But the expression on her face would flood me with memories, with enveloping sensations of a different era, a still-palpable past. For I had been determined. Though our family was kosher and my mother lit candles on Friday night, on Saturdays my father would drive across the Marine Parkway Bridge to his Brownsville store; my mother would shop in Waldbaum's, and my older sisters would sleep late. But for me, for years of my childhood, Saturdays meant Shabbat. Even if I had to walk the near mile to Temple Beth El on

Beach 121st Street alone, I went off to Junior Congregation. Me, another girl or two, and a couple of dozen of the Hebrew School boys. Berle lived on Beach 132nd, so often we could walk most of the way home together.

I wore a little hat with a feather when I went off to shul? How many lives ago that was: before Junior High School 198, where in classes we debated whether this new rock 'n' roll caused juvenile delinquency; before Far Rockaway High School, where we studied Manifest Destiny, the "white man's burden," and Kwame Nkrumah; before the Marshall McLuhan sixties at Antioch; the years of graduate school, strobe lights, antidraft counseling and "Paint it Black"; before I left the States to live in the Negev of Israel; before marriage, the women's movement, motherhood, divorce. In the 1950s, before the Arkins built their red brick "ranch-style" house, ours—old-fashioned, brown-shingled, three-storied—was the first off the beach. Every summer on our backyard patio, we Beach 136th Street kids put on plays we wrote ourselves, and sold clam shells we had gathered along the shore and painted to raise money for polio or for muscular dystrophy. One year we earned as much as fifteen dollars. My mother's mother, Bubby, pressed away on the treadle of her Singer sewing machine, making aprons she had designed for us, and Purim costumes my mother had chosen for my sisters and me. Not glamorous Queen Esthers ("frivolous!") and certainly not the blacklisted Vashti: Ida Glazer imagined great destinies for her daughters; she dressed us for the Temple Beth El Purim Parade as Abraham, Isaac, and Jacob. But always, no matter what we were wearing, no matter what we were feeling, what we were doing, we could hear the waves of the Atlantic break against the jetties from our backyard, from our bedrooms, from the attic of the house. Always the ebb and flow of that ocean, as if in counterpoint to our lives.

Mary Adrienne lived across the street. Her mother would study the Catholic newspaper on Sunday afternoons to check whether Mary Adrienne was permitted to see that week's dou-

ble feature at the Park Theatre with me. Sometimes w
do homework together; I would check Mary Adrien
echism. Name the venial sins. Name the mortal
brother's name was John Edward Paul, Jr.; we didn't have
names like that, we didn't have "juniors" or "name our children after the still living." But they didn't have names in foreign tongues, exotic names, sacred names, and from 3:30 to
5:00 three afternoons a week, at Junior Congregation and on
Sunday mornings till noon, I was no longer "Myra," child of
America. I became "Miriyam," the loyal sister hiding in the
bullrushes of the Nile, guarding her baby brother, cleverly
asking Pharoah's daughter if perhaps she would like a nurse
from among the Hebrew women. Three afternoons and two
mornings a week I ceased being the chubby and mischievous
third sister growing up in the beach suburb of Belle Harbor,
jumping the ocean waves, baby-sitting neighbors' kids, riding
my bike to the candy store, playing "Ten A's" for hours with
my pink Spalding ball. I entered, instead, the drama of another time, another place, cast back into the ancient past by
the name "Miriyam," cast back by the Hebrew language of
our lessons, cast back by the Hebrew songs. Who is responsible if your ox falls into your neighbor's well? To this day, I
remember every song Gladys Gewirtz taught us at Temple
Beth El Hebrew School music class on Sunday mornings.

I felt, as if in my pores, that Belle Harbor, New York, America, might mean home for Mary Adrienne, but it could never
mean that for me. Not my real home. Interwoven in the fabric
of our lives was the lesson that, as Jewish children, our real
home was across the ocean that started on our street, across
the continent of Europe my grandparents had fled, across the
Mediterranean whose sunlit blue I could only imagine. Our
real home was the place where our pioneers were draining
the swamps and making the desert bloom. It was the place
whose folk songs we sang on Sunday mornings; the place
where our trees were planted; the place we sent the coins we
had collected in our blue-and-white Keren Kayemet boxes

painted with the map of Israel. Watchman, what of the night? Peace reigns, silent and bright. Sleep oh Emek, Valley of Beauty. Sleep while we stand on duty. . . .

Someday, I knew, I would be the one on watch. I would stand tall on the hillside overlooking the Emek, dressed in my shorts and kibbutz hat, gun bravely at my side. Down in the valley my comrades in the simple settlement where we all lived would sleep soundly, peacefully, trusting I was there. Above me, in the great silence of my watch, would be the bulging full moon of Tammuz glowing in the sky, its light glazing the breadth and length of the land.

Midway through my years at Hebrew School, we stopped saying "aw" and "s" and said "ah" and "t" instead: our principal, Dr. Tepper, announced that from now on we would speak Hebrew in the "Sephardic" accent of the State of Israel (or at least in that "Sephardic accent" the Ashkenazis thought they heard). We relearned the songs, the stories. We disinherited the tormented eastern European past. We inched ever closer to the sunlight, the kibbutzim, the orange trees, our promised land. Dr. Tepper retaught us the prayers.

The truth is that it was the magic of Dr. Tepper that drew me to Junior Congregation week after week. He encouraged each of us children to lead the services, choosing a new "rabbi" and new "cantor" each Shabbat. He taught us how to sing the whole service together. Though at home my sisters made fun of my "monotone," at Junior Congregation my voice could soar. But it was the magic way Dr. Tepper unrolled the Torah scroll, the magic way he knew just exactly where to begin each week, the magic way he chanted the words, the magic way he wove meanings for us children from the parshah of the week, that swept me out of that bare basement room into the vast wonder of the ancient desert where God spoke. The rabbi of our synagogue wore black robes, was a professor at The Seminary, was intimidating; Dr. Tepper seemed close to us, the most learned man to touch my life. *Lech l'cha mai'artsicha u'moladicha . . . get thee out of thy country, and from thy kindred, and from thy father's house, unto a land that I will show thee.* My mother teases me that long after I learned how to read, I still insisted that she read me stories from The Home University Bookshelf every night. The way her voice strung words like precious beads into stories delighted me, entranced me, gave me an invisible necklace as of coral that helped me drift off into dreaming sleep. But Dr. Tepper's stories were different. They made my spirit soar.

I can see him now, standing in the left corner of the room, his kippah slipping on his shiny bald head, on again, off again, on again. He would begin by explaining what he had just read, speaking in a soft accent that reminded me he was of there, he had come from Israel, born in the days when it was still Palestine! He spoke so intimately of the heroes of the Torah, that I felt as if he were talking of his own family, of his brothers and sisters and uncles, or of mine. As he unraveled the terror of the Akedah, the dreams of Jacob and Joseph, the tumultuous exodus from Egypt, the hitting of the rock that changed the life of Moses forever, he gave me the gift of ancestors who were missing from my life. My Bubby Soroka lived with us, but where was her mother? Before Bubby Glazer and Zayde, who was there? Where was our family's history? Where was mine? The Glazers and Sorokas, the Cranes and the Friedenbergs, the grandparents of my grandparents, their brothers and sisters, uncles and aunts, were long dead in wars and pogroms, people never spoken of, people no one knew. Like the rejection of the Ashkenazi accent, my family had tossed their samovars on the garbage heap when they fled the bitter poverty and persecutions for America. "Feh!" Bubby Soroka would say when she saw Khrushchev on TV. "Feh!"

But the dramas of the Torah filled in the past. Dr. Tepper taught us that the lives of our biblical ancestors, their joy and their anguish, their struggles and their achievements, were inscribed on that scroll without vowels, without punctuation, and their stories were told for all time. They were scoundrels and heroes, searchers, and dreamers; there were desires, intrigues, quarrels, hope. Hearing the voices of the Torah come alive was like hearing the ocean's waves, ebbing and flowing, but always there, their rhythms the barely heard constant undercurrents of our lives. Dr. Tepper did more than explain what had happened so long ago. He explained why it mattered for us kids of Belle Harbor, New York, America, growing up in the 1950s, learning a history that never was ours and would never be ours from Mrs. MacNamara and Miss Maloney at P.S. 114 in Queens.

Spinning in the tales Dr. Tepper told, I longed for a coat of many colors even if my sisters threw me in a pit. I hauled water from a well to feed a stranger's flock. I stole my sister's blessing and cried that my blessing was stolen from me. My slingshot slew Goliath, my hair got caught in a tree, I was trapped in a lion's den, I gave birth to twins who fought in my womb, I married a king, I was a king. And for all my adventures, my dramas, my trials, for all those words in that scroll, Dr. Tepper unfailingly unearthed hidden meanings, stuff we had to remember, lessons, he told us, for our lives. How did he do it? How did he find secret meanings? How did he figure it out? Week after week, he astounded me.

Because my sisters teased me about my "monotone," I never had the courage to raise my hand when Dr. Tepper asked who wanted to be "cantor." But every week Berle pushed and prodded me into volunteering as "rabbi." He would help me, he said. It's easy, he said. Turn to page 10. Turn to page 12. Please rise for the Amidah. You know the service, he said. I can't, only boys do it, I said. Don't be silly, Berle said.

No, dear Aunt T, I really don't remember the little hat with the feather. But I will never forget that single Shabbat morning at Junior Congregation when for the first and only time in my life, I raised my hand to be rabbi and Dr. Tepper, putting his slippery kippah back on his head, smiled, and chose me.

S. L. Wisenberg

Shema, the First Prayer
You Learn

It begins in bed. Before sleepiness. "Repeat after me," says your father. "It goes like this: *Shema Yisrael adonai eloheynu adonai echad.*" You learn the English alongside, without punctuation: "Hear O Israel the Lord are God the Lord is one." You don't think about what it means. Later you learn it's "Here, O Israel, the Lord our God." And later you learn the next lines, less familiar and therefore more special, serious: "*Baruch shem k'vod,*" after which you begin the list in English, as a kind of translation: "God bless Mommy/ Daddy/ Rosi/ Greg the dachshund/ Grandma Bessie/ Grandma Dallas and Pa." The sleek black dog is in between the older sister and the in-town grandmother, which is where he stands in your affections. Where he belongs. He belongs outside, says your mother. Greg is an outside dog. You pray for him to be let inside.

The Shema, the first prayer you learn. A sign that the day has ended. Giving over to it. Separation of light and dark. The noise and the quiet. The door is closed.

As you grow older, you learn that the Shema has been written down. You learn other prayers, but the Shema keeps its status as the first, fundamental. It is not frilly, like its companion prayer V'ahavta further down the page in the prayer

97

book. The V'ahavta is coquettish, with its rhyming, wending *"echa"* suffixes: *"elohecha, levavecha, me'odecha."* This is the fancy stuff, more dazzling, almost prissy, or at least that's the way the Bat Mitzvah girls sing it. When the cantor chants it at services, his strong, slow voice re-ennobles it. But the V'ahavta does not sound like a prayer for the end of the day. It is not yet familiar enough.

In Hebrew School, you learn a joke. A dark, adult joke, different from the plays on words that the boys in the back of the class make. They sing, for example, "Elvin Hayes" instead of "el b'nai" during the Passover song "Adir Hu." And they say "Minnie Horowitz" instead of "mein ha'aretz"—from the earth—during the prayer over the bread. Here is the joke told by the Hebrew teacher who speaks English with an accent—it goes something like this: In the ancient times, the time of domination, the Jew with no money takes a job as the lion in the Colosseum. There is a 50 percent chance he will die from it. On all fours, deep inside of his hot, close costume, he sees the real lion charge at him. The Jew begins the Shema, the prayer of faith you will die with on your lips. He reconciles himself to this dance with death, this chance of death, because otherwise he and his family will die. Because they will starve. He cannot provide. He takes a breath open to the jaws of death. He hears the other lion, who finishes his prayer.

Both are impostors, it turns out. Impoverished Jews. Mere men. The joke ends there. The teacher then turns to the serious stuff. Hebrew grammar. Biblical kings. Does not continue, does not explain what the crowd, deprived of its daily or weekly bloodlust, will do. Will the mob kill both of the men?

Or do the men engage in a to-the-death struggle, each to kill his own, amid the cheers of the crowd, which does or does not understand what it is watching?

This is not a before-bedtime joke. It is an off-center joke, the way everything the Hebrew teacher does is hopelessly foreign, like the way she draws beards and mustaches on the boys' faces for the Purim play, using permanent markers instead of eyebrow pencil. This is like a wayward April Fools' prank, like when you told your mother there was a bee in the bedroom, and then, five minutes later, saw a real bee fly in. It is like a frog put in a cigar box as a surprise and then forgotten as it suffocates in the tobacco-moist confines. The story of the lion brothers comes back to you at night.

Hero Israel. The Lord is one. Abraham smashed the idols in his father's idol shop (something like a sculpture gallery, you always imagined), and God said, "Good," and Abraham said, "Fine," and "We will worship just one," and shaped some prayers just for Him.

You are in bed alone with the Shema, the first prayer you learned, the one your mother and father say to each other at night. In good faith. When you're older you'll learn to lilt your voice for V'ahavta like the other bat mitzvah girls, orchids pinned to velvets and moirés. Later you'll read that, when praying alone, you should add, "God, faithful king!" You never do this. Later you'll understand the translation: "And these words, which I command thee this day, shall be upon thine heart: and thou shalt teach them diligently unto thy children. . . ." Later you'll be faced with lions, wander wanting/hoping they are Jews underneath—soulmates who know the ends to your prayers.

By then you will have absorbed some history and culture, enough to know that the lion story is the quintessential Jewish joke, which traditionally involves smart, weak people in impossible situations. They have only words to save themselves. In this case, the words of the joke, in future tellings.

The Jew speaks, so that the future will hear it.

The Jew prays, using words that ancestors knew that their ancestors knew.

By the time you get to graduate school, much of your life is spent with Quakers and other pacifists, planning rallies and protests. You're an atheist, you think, but a Jewish atheist, and know that there's even a tradition of nonbelievers. Still, on Friday nights you have dinner with three Jewish friends and you light candles and drink wine and break bread, reciting the blessings. You discuss poetry and heritage. How do you explain it? A tidal pull.

At formal services, which you attend erratically, you say the Shema along with everyone else. Sometimes you're provided with a Hebrew term for the female aspect of God. The prayer is as familiar to you as your pulse. You welcome it, an old friend: Oh, you, still around after all these years?

Each time you come home it's a surprise anew that your parents still recite the Shema, each to each, witnesses, pajamas and cold cream and hot pad, and they are surprised that you have stopped something as natural and necessary as brushing your teeth.

All this time, they've recited it, without question, a matter of faith combined with habit, decided long ago.

And you try but you can't remember when you stopped saying the Shema. And it's not their faith that you envy so much as their daily acceptance of the mystery of oneness—the oneness of unbroken repetition, the chain they are still a part of.

Karen E. Bender

V'ahavta

In Hebrew School on September 9, 1973, I read the V'ahavta in less than nineteen seconds. I read it while my Hebrew School teacher, Adina, a UCLA student who wore T-shirts that said Coca-Cola in Hebrew, tensed her thumb along her gray Seiko; my V'ahavta tumbled into the room at a graceful, albeit breakneck speed, its inchoate syllables sending my classmates into their prayer books to see how they, too, could massacre letotofot or bein anecha. "Hold your breath," said Adina, and I did, leaning hard into my prayer book while everyone waited to see how fast I could chant the second most sacred prayer in the Jewish religion. I finished, gasping, and watched Adina, my entire body yearning for a V'ahavta score that would burn rubber—a score that would establish me as miraculous, as the Hebrew School queen.

I stopped. Everyone seemed to be tilted. The boys were mostly slumped; the girls leaned to the left side of their desks. At first I thought my V'ahavta had done something terrible to them, but then I realized they were just depressed. Adina held up her arm to the light fixture with a sweeping gesture and clicked off the Seiko. "18.7847," she said.

The boys on the other side of the room couldn't stand it. They said I skipped a word, uchtavtam maybe, they swore they didn't hear it—but they were five seconds behind me so uchtavtam or not, I was still ahead of everyone.

"The best ever," said Adina, and the boys on the other side of the room groaned all at once and stamped their feet against the green tile. "Best ever" meant that my score went into the showcase in Beth-Em Temple's lobby, beside the third grade's papier-mâché kibbutz and the ninth grade's letters to their Jewish pen pals in the Soviet Union. I pressed my mouth together tightly, filled with a ridiculous elation. I imagined my score being discussed at temple luncheons, at youth groups, at Social Action Committee meetings. ("Yes, Emily Boxman. She read the V'ahavta in 18.7847 seconds! She's going for the Kaddish in 33.") Or more than that—I wanted a big, deep voice to declare, "It's a miracle!" and deliver a lightning bolt to B-11. Adina was writing 18.7847 on the blackboard with blue chalk, making a big jagged circle like a blue ribbon around it. She turned around and fluttered chalk dust into the air. "Keep at it," she said, "and soon you'll be able to say it faster than Mark Spitz can swim the hundred meters."

There was one reason why a phenomenal V'ahavta score was not just nice but imperative; it would save me from total oblivion in Hebrew School. For one, I was not very good at the other thing we did during Hebrew School, specifically recess, where rankings of worth were quickly established and never forgotten. During Beth-Em sockball games, I was afraid of the magenta ball hurtling through the air toward me; I would close my eyes and hold my arms out like a hoop, hoping that the ball would somehow fall into it. I wanted to catch that ball, to feel that smack against my hands and know the immediate acceptance. I wanted to be like the two favored members of our Hebrew School—two dark girls named, naturally, Tracy.

I envied the Tracys for their ability to throw themselves at a tetherball without worrying what it might do to them. The Tracys were fluent in the preferred language on earth—not one that involved alephs and gimels, but instead, an ability

to throw things, quick arms and legs. I may have been somewhat proficient in this other divine language, but in theirs, the
important one, I was unable to speak.

For me, coordinating my arms and that ball occasioned a
special entry in my diary. "Kicked a good one in kickball
today!" or "Caught sock by Dena!" were entries when I took
risks and actually tried to catch the ball; mostly I was afraid
of getting killed by it. All the V'ahavta required was a flexible
tongue, and to possess one that could trip through the prayer
in eighteen seconds seemed a great gift from this God who
supposedly listened to it. A speedy V'ahavta would, I hoped,
give me a legitimate place among the Yitzhak/Garys, Sarah/
Cynthias and Chayim/Jonathans who populated our class. It
might, I thought, make me a friend.

In addition to my inability to do anything physical was the
irritating fact that my Uncle Joshua was a popular drop-in
cantor at Beth-Em, chanting as a "special event" on certain
occasions. He would arrive on Friday nights after we had
been listening to Rabbi Sofstein remind us of the homeless,
starving Ethiopians, of Jews tortured in Russia, of missiles
around the globe poised to start our own destruction, of our
own latent evil. "You can never be reminded of it too often,"
he said. Perfumed, hose shimmering, we nodded. We were,
after all, "hip" Jews, living in the real world. We believed in
evolution, in individual responsibility, in the parting of the
Red Sea as a very strange tide. We wanted to be reminded of
the horrors in the world, to be prompted that we should do
something. But eventually an odd longing would sweep
through the pews. It was not for anything so archaic as "religion"; we were too smart for that. But when Uncle Joshua
lumbered in, chanting in his grand voice, it was as though
everyone softened. Uncle Joshua sounded like God.

It was not sheer decibel level, though Uncle Joshua's was
considerable. And it was not perfect intonation, as Uncle
Joshua destroyed an occasional note. Uncle Joshua's voice
rolled through the synagogue, enormous and reassuring; it
made us believe we were part of something good. I loved

listening to Uncle Joshua—his mighty lungs eliciting respect and piety from the congregation as reflexively as a hammer tapping a knee—but I also resented him. I would sit, nine and seething, and think that my uncle, by virtue of being born with vocal chords like railway cables, had become a legend at Beth-Em. I would roll the corners of my program and I hoped I, myself, was also special. My classmates' powerful arms and their kicks in kickball would mean nothing when I was placed in an upcoming book of the Torah and forced upon some future Hebrew class. It was crucial that I say the V'ahavta in a miraculous speed simply to save myself—to be known as something other than Cantor Bornstein's niece.

Normally, the V'ahavta, second only to the "Shema" in its sacredness in the Jewish religion, was not noted for its competitive value. Adina once mentioned that it was about the ways you were supposed to love God. "And these words I command you to this day," she read, trying to straighten an English-language version of the prayer on the overhead projector, "You shall love God with, um, all your heart, all your soul, and all your might." We stared, with great longing, at the silver chaparral-studded hills we would scramble across during break; we knew, thankfully, that she would not continue. In terms of raw holiness, Beth-Em was a joke among other temples in Los Angeles. We were getting off easy for our bat mitzvahs, with our dinky Torah portions and two half-page prayers; my friend Linda, who attended the Conservative Temple Sinai down the street, was preparing for a three-hour marathon in which she did everything but lead the Israelites out of Egypt. Adina, an education major at UCLA, liked timing us to practice techniques she was studying. Otherwise, our most memorable contact with the V'ahavta occurred the week after I said it in eighteen seconds; the day we went to visit Rabbi Sofstein in Beth-Em's synagogue.

All thirty of us zoomed across the temple grounds, the other girls clustering in small groups to trade Wacky Packs, and the boys turning their radios up so they could hear the

Dodger game. Everyone else was chattering about the Wacky Pack Cynthia had brought to class today—the rare and valuable Old Spit. I would have tried to negotiate for Old Spit with a fervor equal to any of theirs, but today I felt different from my classmates.

It was a glorious day to have performed a miracle. The sky was ribbed with silver clouds, thin and shining, and I felt a surge of belonging; the clouds, sky, and the whole arrangement seemed wonderfully, thoroughly holy. I felt I took to miracles like a hog to mud. I walked, my arms lifted a little, behind everyone else; I gazed expectantly, impatiently, into the dark September sky. Adina pushed open the heavy wooden doors of the synagogue and we rushed inside.

"AndPeteRose'sonsecondDonSuttonatbatit'sastrike" faded into a rush of static; the boys tucked their radios into their pockets and Adina hustled us into the sanctuary and up onto the bimah.

It was the first time I had seen the synagogue empty, and I felt as though I were backstage. Beth-Em, built during the 1960s, looked like a spaceship from the freeway that ran alongside it, but here, inside the synagogue, it seemed official in an exciting way. From the outside, the high, tilted ceiling looked like a strange conduit for alien (let alone divine) communication. Here we would learn important things.

Rabbi Sofstein said shalom to us. "Shalom," we answered back. I always felt fraudulent when he beamed back; it was so easy to make Rabbi Sofstein think we actually understood the few Hebrew words we had memorized during Hebrew school. He clasped his hands and walked slowly around us.

"In three years," said Rabbi Sofstein, "each of you will come up here and read from the Torah. You will chant your Torah portions and say two prayers—the V'ahavta and Baruch Avraham."

He raised his hands, slowly. "I want you to be able to say it like this." Facing us, he went into his rendition of the V'ahavta—an endless four minutes and thirty-six seconds of it. I waited for Rabbi Sofstein's V'ahavta to vibrate over the pews, to echo with the higher knowledge of the religious leader we (thought) he was. But his performance would not have made the top ten in my Hebrew School class; it would not even receive one of Adina's special awards for "enunciation." The prayer simply moved through the room like an old Buick. Everyone knew it, too; hazy purple bubbles of Grape Bubble Yum began emerging from certain mouths, popping quietly and then stuffed quickly back in.

"Oh, David," said a booming voice from the back of the synagogue. "Louder." It was easy to believe, when sitting in the big, empty synagogue, that any unexpected voice was *really* unexpected, that He had picked this moment to drop in, but I recognized it; it was my uncle.

"Joshua," said Rabbi Sofstein, stopping mid-V'ahavta.

"You might as well give them sleeping pills," said Uncle Joshua, and Rabbi Sofstein grimaced. Adina, not sure who to side with, proceeded to hiss a series of multitoned *Shhhhhs*, but she didn't need to; we were silent, curious as to how two Jewish role models would go at it if they were angry.

"Well," said Rabbi Sofstein, "why don't you try it?"

"Sure," said my uncle. "This is how you do it." I had heard my uncle chant many other prayers, but I had never heard him chant the V'ahavta; that prayer was mine, and now he was going to tackle it. He opened his mouth and the V'ahavta entered the room, big and solid, almost like another person, almost like Uncle Joshua. "*V'ahavta et adonai elohecha. B'chol levavcah uvchol nafshecha uvchol me'odecha,*" he sang, and I couldn't help myself—I practically laughed. Sounds like that didn't come out of other people. My uncle was strange—he was punching the air with fists, shaking his head, and bellowing the V'ahavta. He dug his heels into the carpet and closed his eyes, lifting the dark roses with his heels as he got louder and louder. "*Letotofot bein anecha,*" and I hated him for it, for his strength, for the way his voice contained these words. But I was also bubbly, silly with glee that I was related to this voice, that my mother's brother could roar a V'ahavta that shamed Rabbi Sofstein's, that his peculiar glow was also somehow mine.

We waited.

My uncle sat down.

The V'ahavta left the room and we were all by ourselves again. It seemed to me that the floor of the living room, the walls, had pressed out like lungs while my uncle chanted the prayer—now that he had stopped, the floor was moving back to its normal, boring position. I wanted Uncle Joshua's V'a-havta again.

The school bell sounded. "It's time to go," said Yitzhak/Gary.

"All right," said Rabbi Sofstein, looking relieved that there would be no time for a comparative discussion of V'ahavtas. "Walk, don't run." Everyone tore out, KNX's sports announcer's voice flicking on as soon as the boys were past the wooden doors: "Youwon'tbelievethiscatchfolks,nowit'sthree-totwo,Dodgers!"

I approached my uncle shyly. I saw him at Rosh Hashanah dinners, or Passover seders, but I was never really sure if he actually saw me.

"Hello," I said to his navy jacket.

"Emily!" he said, and I felt like I'd crumple with relief. "How's your mother?"

"Fine," I said, smiling.

"How's Hebrew School?" he asked.

"Um, fine," I said.

"Good," he said. He put his hand on my shoulder and turned to talk to Rabbi Sofstein. I stood there, mute. I looked up at Uncle Joshua, but he was ignoring me now, talking to Rabbi Sofstein about, of all things, golf. Finally Rabbi Sofstein left. I grabbed Uncle Joshua's jacket before he fled. I chortled, "I said the V'ahavta in eighteen seconds!"

He smiled at me, blankly. I held out my wrist and said, "Go!" then threw out a blizzard of words that, I hoped, approximated the V'ahavta.

He put his hand over my wrist. "What are you saying?" he asked.

"The V'ahavta," I said, patiently, bounding up and down on my feet.

"I don't understand," he said.

I was enraged. He was talking about the great miracle I had performed. "Watch," I said. I began again.

"Esther," he said to me, my Hebrew name; no one but Adina called me that. "Sweetheart. You're killing it. You think it's hard to understand here? Heaven's far away, and you have all those clouds to get through. They won't be able to make gobbledygook of it."

The air around Uncle Joshua's head seemed to shimmer! "Oh," I said. I drew back. I felt as though I had been beaten over the head. He patted me on the head. "Shalom, Esther," he said, and scurried off.

How had he not understood? How had I been left unrewarded for my miracle? I studied the watery, pinkish panes of stained glass on the sanctuary, the glass so thick it made the palm trees fuzzy, unrecognizable on the other side. I came to an explanation: perhaps no one had heard me. Perhaps there were too many clouds that day and my V'ahavta was too staticky. Maybe so many V'ahavtas simultaneously soaring toward heaven interfered with each other like competing radio waves. Maybe I needed someone to inform those in Heaven of my V'ahavta score: someone who was very loud.

I did not want to ask Uncle Joshua to remind God of my V'ahavta score, but he was the only person I knew who had the pure, raw lung power to get a message transmitted that high up. I ran to his office the next day after Hebrew School. He sat, silent, as I told him of my plan.

"Darling," he said. "I don't think . . ."

"Please," I said. "Please, please, please." It was not a series of words then, but a sorrowful incantation, a hopeful, confused, winding rhythm of sound.

If I had been older, I would have realized that he was tired;

burdened by his voice, his apparent strength, that caused in-
secure grade-schoolers, not to mention entire congregations,
to come to him for a word, a promise. I put my palms together in supplication, all the Hello Kitty faces on my fingernails lining up in a little row. "Please."

He looked at me with large, puzzled eyes. "All right. Let's
go."

I directed Uncle Joshua to drive us to the top of Parking
Structure B in Santa Monica; he steered his old Mustang
around the musty walls. He was silent, listening to KFWB,
voices I did not care about, nor want to hear. At the top,
Uncle Joshua slowly pressed down his emergency brake and
sighed. I hopped out of the car, staring into a cloudless blue
sky.

Uncle Joshua slammed his car door, a little too loudly. He
wandered to the edge of the parking structure, tucking in his
shirt. I stood looking over gleaming rooftops, toward the flat
silver that made up the Pacific Ocean.

"Is there anywhere you think I should aim this?" he asked.

I looked up anxiously. "No," I said.

He cleared his throat. "Hello," he called, uneasily.

"Try Hebrew," I said.

"Shalom!" boomed Uncle Joshua. "Emily said her V'ahavta
in eighteen seconds!"

"Emily BoxMAN," I said. "He probably knows more than
one Emily."

"Boxman!" boomed Uncle Joshua. "18.7847!"

A couple of seagulls landed, shuddered, poked at our feet.
Uncle Joshua leaned against his Mustang.

"Say it again!" I said.

"Why?" he asked.

"Because they didn't hear you!"

"You say it," he said.

"No."

He walked around the car, a big uncle, a black mountain
that everyone wanted to know. "You say it," he said.

"No."

"Say it so they understand you."

"They're supposed to understand me anyway!" I said furiously.

Uncle Joshua walked around his car, opened his side and shut the door.

"Where are you going?"

"Nowhere," said Uncle Joshua.

I tried to remember the words of the V'ahavta, all the syllables. They swirled inside my head, just sounds now. I couldn't remember any of it.

"*V'ahavta et . . . adonai elohecha*," said Uncle Joshua.

I could not remember the rest.

We stood there together a moment, waiting. He faced me. "*Uvchol levavcha, uvchol nafshecha, uvchol meodecha.*" His V'ahavta began tenderly in his throat and rumbled, big and sure, over the parking lot, as firm and logical as though he were pleading to somebody, as if he were trying to explain. His V'ahavta rose generously past the parked cars and I realized he was conversing with someone, trying to elicit an answer. I looked up at the sky and I wished I knew who he was talking to, who listened to Uncle Joshua; then I saw him looking right at me, two eyes bright as a cat's, and I knew he was saying it to me. I felt a sudden, desperate rush of love for my uncle, watching him pray to me respectfully, as though I were some sort of miracle or minor God, as though I were temporarily worthy. God was preoccupied and the sky shimmered a steady, indifferent blue, but Uncle Joshua was saying the V'ahavta to me and I was trying to listen.

tova

the mourner

(for mollie . . . always)

I.

gramma mollie
thought aunt bella would never die
but when uncle phillip called and said
      bella wasn't here
      bella wasn't here
      bella wasn't here any longer
mollie finally realized that aunt bella could.

aunt bella died.

II.

uncle phillip couldn't live without aunt bella
claimed he didn't know to make a cup of tea
without aunt bella phillip would cry i can't cut my meat
so gramma mollie would cut his meat
without bella phillip cried

and i shouted at mollie
how could one be so tied to another's life
how could one be so tied to another's death
how could one be so tied
                    to the lesson i became tied to
                    the deaths around my neck
                    the weight that pulls chin to chest
                    pose of mourning
                    life of death.

three months later
uncle phillip died.

III.

i sat outside the synagogue every yom kippur

        yiskor
        the mourners' *kaddish*
        death was for others
        older ones

i sat outside the synagogue every yom kippur

        wondering what exactly they did in there?
        death so overflowing
        there were no seats left in synagogue

        so they set up chairs in the basement
        where the mystery of death
        was below the floor they let me stand on.

i sat outside the synagogue every yom kippur

        jealous shut out
        a ritual i couldn't understand.

IV.

yisgadal v'yiskadash sh'ma rabbo
b'olmo deevra chiruseh v'yamlick malchuseh,
b'chayechon uvyonmechon,
uv'chayeh d'chol beys yisroel
baagolog uvizman koreeve
v'imrue omen.

     the mourners and readers recite.

V.

gramma mollie
said there's nothing worse than watching a child die
who would've thought cousin rhoda would go first
who would've thought cousin rhoda would ever die

rhoda died.

rhoda whose baby carriage mollie walked with
through that big cemetery on fort hamilton parkway
on sunny sunday afternoons
there were always family outings to the cemetery

     i was a child   they would bring me lunch
     mollie would talk to my grandfather's tomb
     tell him the news then say hello to her dead parents.

     i was a child   wandering through a cemetery
     putting rocks on tombstones
     wondering at mollie's tears her speaking to the dead.

       but i never really wondered that much
        at a life of
          rocks and cemeteries

talking with the dead
death overflowing
into white bread and
bologna sandwiches.

VI.

y'he sh'meh rabbo m'vorach l'olam ulomey olmayo,

responds the congregation.

VII.

uncle sam watched his daughter rhoda die
riddled with cancer he responded in like suit
in like suit
uncle sam died.

a year later gramma mollie went to uncle sam's *unveiling*
though she couldn't walk so well,
"respect the dead," she taught.
two weeks later mollie fell from the stairs.
three weeks later

mollie was dead.

VIII.

no one believed gramma mollie would ever die,
but really i knew
there were signs—
the dreams of her death
the frantic phone calls

uncomfortably assured
    by her life giving voice.

(mollie would never leave me)

    her homemade *blintzes*
    untouched in the freezer
      afraid i'd never eat them again

  it isn't hindsight
  despite what everyone says despite
  we all thought we all knew
  mollie would live forever.

(mollie would never leave me).

my grandmother who always lived with us
more my mother than my mother
feeding me hot milk with melted butter
in pink glass bowls.

my grandmother who was my security
giving me as no one else could ever give
no one else   could
      can   ever
          no one ever
will   again
mollie never stops dying

  the lesson of death she taught me
        the lesson i became tied to
        the deaths around my neck
        the weight that pulls chin to chest
        pose of mourning
        life of death.

IX.

*y'he sh'lomo rabah min sh'mayo v'chayim
olenu v'al col yisroel, y'imru amen,*

    the mourners recite.

X.

i saw cousin yeida at mollie's funeral
she was younger than my mother leah,
    and she looked to be in fine health
    and she looked to be in fine spirits
      who would've thought who
      would've believed
      just two weeks after mollie's death
      she would say to her husband:

        "joe, i don't feel well"

    and then die five minutes later.

XI.

a year later we took my sick and dying father
to gramma mollie's *unveiling*.
i walked him to the tombstone
he wept and sobbed no one knowing for sure
if he understood beyond strokes and leukemia,

    but he knew.

    for he wept for gramma mollie
    for he wept for aunt bella and uncle phillip
    rhoda and uncle sam and for yeida

for he wept for himself and he wept
for us   all.

XII.

i left my father's arm and wandered through the cemetery
like the child i was collecting rocks for the stones of the dead.

> i wait for all to leave and place my favorite
> purple crystal
> on mollie's tomb a rock not good enough anymore
> a crystal not understood by others

and death so overflowing

> and knowing somehow
> mollie would take the crystal through a child
> on a sunny sunday afternoon
> wandering through the cemetery
> eating white bread and bologna sandwiches
> collecting rocks for tombs.

XIII.

i never understood the years of my father's diseases.
there was parkinson's and clogged arteries and anemia
and they watched his blood
white blood cell counts red blood cell counts
            and i watched the life taken out of him
they talked about thinness and thickness
transfusions and aspirins
            and i watched the life taken out of him
and i said over and over this man will die soon
but i never believed he would die
            and i watched the life taken out of him

who would've believed in strokes
aphasia and leukemia and infections
gout and bouts in and out of hospitals
bad days and somewhat better days and worse
days
again

                    and i watched the life taken out of him.

and they said never until the next calendar year,
                              and he lived for that,
and they said never until his next birthday,
                              and he lived for that,
and they said not more than two months
                              and he lived for eight,
who would've believed he would live?

                                   my father died too.

XIV.

prayer books fill my life
in dresser drawers and desks
suitcases and backpacks
i compare funeral homes by their prayer books,
one year of mourning rituals into the next
death so overflowing into endless streams
of *ribbons black and severed*
shiva boxes molded to my body

yiskor

all the rituals denied in my childhood

                    i sat outside the synagogue every yom kippur

now known too well

                    the *kaddish*
                    the mourner's *kaddish,*

i am mourning
        in the synagogue in the basement
            death so overflowing

i am mourning
        in my home at my job on the street
            death so overflowing

        in the woods in the mountains
                i am mourning
                        in the bathroom in the kitchen in the
                        bedroom

i am mourning at the ocean
                i am mourning at the funeral homes
        i am mourning as the older one

                                i sat outside the synagogue every
                                yom kippur
                                too young for this age

i am mourning

                for
                        i am the mourner
            i am the *yiskor*

                        i am

                the *kaddish*

XV.

yisborach v'yishtabach v'yispo'ar b'yisromam
v'yisnasseaeh v'yis'hador v'yisal-ley v'yishal-ol
sh'me d'kud sho b'reech hu,
l'elo min col birchoso v'shiroso tushb'chosa
b'nechemoso daamiron b'olmo, v'imru amen.

oseh shalom bimromav,
hu y'asay shalom aleinu.
v'al col yisroael,
v'imru amen.

  the mourners and readers recite.

XVI.

the words of a poem finish, but the death in my life does
  not. there is no page to end on.

the day of my father's funeral was the day of my cousin
  yeida's unveiling. cousin melvin,
yeida's brother, had a heart attack that day. he died six
  weeks later.

how could everyone of this cycle be listed? family, friends,
  strangers. how would you
know them? sophie and may and jean; fifteen year old
  kisha; wally kills himself; ben's
face sprawled all over the newspapers. does a list of dead
  people constitute a poem?
does it constitute a life?

XVII.

it is passover. i am at a *seder* with about 200 people. one of
    the organizers, whom i have
seen at events, but do not know personally, asks me if i
    would read and lead a small part
of the 30+ page service. i agree to do this. he looks through
    the *hagadah* and asks if i
would lead the congregation in the mourner's *kaddish*. i
    dream of the letter "d" tattooed
on my forehead.

it is early winter. early morning. dark and thick fog. i roam
    the streets. i wander past an
unknown cemetery. i look up to see the spirits of my dead
    relatives dancing the
mazourka around the tombstones. i am with them and
    apart, like the child i was sitting
outside the synagogue during yom kippur *yiskor*, sneaking
    a look inside.

                  i watch these ghosts dance around
                       tombstones.
                  i watch this death overflowing

the lesson i became tied to
the deaths around my neck
the weight that pulls chin to chest
pose of mourning
life of death
                  joined by the heart and the hip
                  in the dance of the dead
                  joined by a single
                              breath
                of life
        in this dance
                of the living.

XVIII.

yea,
though i walk
through the valley
of the shadow
of death,
i will fear
no evil,
for thou art

                              with

         me.

Karen E. Bender

Inside the Ark

When I was almost thirteen and no longer wanted to be human, I watched carefully whenever my father, the rabbi, opened the Ark. Saturday mornings, he pushed open the wooden doors and parted the sheer white curtains that floated in the pale fluorescence of the Ark. Beth-Em's congregation squinted shyly at the bimah, as though trying to understand the shapes of huge, shining clouds. The soles of my feet got itchy, excited, for I did not want to be down on the maroon carpet with the rest of the congregation. For my bat mitzvah, I wanted my father to put me inside the Ark. That day, I hoped, the doors would swing open. My father would lift me onto his shoulder. He would carry me past the stunned rows and I would smile down, wondrous and benevolent, while everyone reached forward to touch me, with trembling, outstretched arms.

I imagined he had been saving this for me, his daughter, thinking about it during all the other bat mitzvahs of members he did not love as much as he loved me. I imagined him picking me up by the waist and placing me gently on the deep blue wrinkled velvet. Then he closed the heavy wood door, leaving me inside.

I imagined myself crouched, knees to my chin, shoulder to

shoulder with the three Torahs. Each one of them had a different personality. One was clad in worn, dark blue velvet, silver threads stiched in the word *Chai*; it was the most solemn Torah, prone to depression and thoughtful musings on life. Then there was a tough, gangster-ish, bulletproof Torah in an embossed silver metal case that in an alternative existence might have plotted international conspiracy or robbed banks. The third Torah, wearing a cover of fine, pearl-scattered white linen, had a snobby, exclusive aura. It always seemed to be evaluating what its reader was wearing, and whenever I saw it with its linen cover removed, it seemed naked and ashamed. All three were topped with jingling silver crowns that flashed, milky, in the white fluorescent light.

Inside the Ark, I first felt like nothing, like air.

It would be dark, a pure, complete darkness that poured into my eyes and throat. I touched the Torahs. I rubbed my fingertips against the side of the solemn blue-velvet Torah, which was as sleek and trimmed as the fur of a well-groomed cat. I put my lips to the dry, slightly bitter linen Torah cover, which had a faint saltiness left from hundreds of urgent hands. I flattened my palms against the bulletproof one, and it was surprisingly cold.

Then I felt myself: from the top of my scalp, the place where my hair began, my fingers traveling down the curves of my eyebrows and the wet swell of my gums. I rubbed the hard bone of my elbows and traced the new swell of my breasts, brushing the sparse hairs around my vagina, fingering down my legs. It was my body, but it had recently developed its own desires and dreams. I thought of the ways my family had made and tended the growth of this body since the day I was born. It had begun with my parents, linked completely one night thirteen years ago, with no knowledge of what I would be. Sometimes I wondered, as I toweled off after my bath, which parts of my body my mother loved most and which parts she wished had never been born. As my sister Janine and I lay in my bed at night, her breath Crest-sweet and sticky, we poked each other's belly buttons and ears, looking for the small ways we had missed being each other. We two were the only ones in the world who had lived inside our mother; I wondered what trace I had left, in that sound-lessness, for her. I hated the fact that a human body seemed a huge package of secrets, and one that was forever sealed off from everyone else.

I closed my eyes and tried to concentrate, for I had come here for a reason.

Slowly I began to change.

Finger by finger, I would turn to gold, my fingernails would glitter bright as rubies, my breath would become rose-sweet. My hands, new, incandescent, would squeeze open and shut, and I would breathe the Ark's tang of silver and velvet and dust. My tongue would become clear as glass. I would become unrecognizable to myself or anyone, and as there was a sudden swell of light from my fingertips, a pure, unreal happiness would pour through me, so overwhelming and perfect it would bring me to tears. I was not human anymore, but something far better, and no one would be able to criticize or advise me again. My fingers would lift the absolute darkness of the Ark to a faint, grayish color, and I would feel as though I were in the center of the world.

As I became gold, as I became magnificent, no one could hear me, but I could hear all the sounds of the world. I heard random sounds from the entire temple: the faint slosh of the dishwasher in the steel-countered kitchen, a toilet being flushed, the rapid rain of heels across tile, a single cough. Slowly, shaky on my new glimmering legs, I stood up. Pressing my ear to the thick wood door, I heard the bad, embarrassing sounds of human life—a fart, a whine, a sob. I heard Sheryl, the temple secretary, snap, "Don't yank the Xerox machine," and the slap as Linda Steinman hit Jessica Horwitz for leaving her out of the game of elephant tag. I heard Cantor Rossman say, clearly, "Shit," and Carl Shuberg mutter, "She's such a bitch." It was a ragged, rising cacophony, and I was thrilled by it, and I touched my glass tongue, tentatively, wondering at the new sort of sound I would be able to make.

The Torahs' silver crowns began to jingle. First one, and then all of them, in a raucous, ringing chorus, trying to either send out an SOS about my presence or, for their own purposes, speak to me. I held out my arms, all their fresh radiance, and the air took on the color of daylight. I was complete. Loneliness would not be able to live in me. The Torahs' strange music swelled, an almost tinny, childish sound; I waited for someone to come find me.

Judith Ungar

Prayers

Temples, churches, mosques, the heavens. Seekers find God everywhere, including the boy who asked, "Even in a banana peel?" As a young girl I knew where God was and that's where I talked to Him: the wooden bookcase in the corner of our living room.

The genesis of my prayers was personal and immediate. I hit my younger brother, ran down the hall, knelt with palms pressed together before the bookcase (like my school friends did beside their beds) and prayed.

"Please, dear God, don't let him cry."

Time was critical. This prayer was usable only if Larry had not started crying. If he had, I went directly to prayer number two.

"Please, dear God, don't let them hear him."

"Them," of course, were our parents. If minutes went by without Mama calling "Judith Sara, come here!" I was safe. If she did call me by my full first name and my middle name, I was caught. God was finished as far as being a help to me. I would have to manage on my own. Was Larry really hurt? Could he prove it? Was his crying real? Or just to get me in trouble? Who started it? Could I make a convincing case for having struck in self-defense?

My childhood prayers were freelance and self-serving.

"Please, make Lewis invite me," I petitioned God. Or, looking in the bathroom mirror, I beseeched God, "Please, let me fill this out," as I tried to be the most and the best that I could be, in my first double-A bra. God apparently was in the living room bookcase, where He couldn't hear me in the bathroom, because no matter how I maneuvered my meager chestly charms, the white cotton bra still had air pockets and wrinkles.

At Poe Elementary School we prayed every morning after the Salute to the Flag. Still standing, we bowed our heads and said in unison, "Our Father, whose hearts in heaven, Howard be Thy name," and so on. Then we said the Twenty-third Psalm by heart. I loved that psalm because of the exciting places named in it—places our family hadn't been to on vacation: "The Valley of the Shadow of Death," which was somewhere farther west of Texas and might be where The Shadow lived, the one we heard on the car radio on Sunday when we drove to Grandma Bell's for chicken dinner.

But when I recited The Lord's Prayer, with its hunger-inducing "daily bread," Mama said, "That's not our prayer." For a week after that she said Shema with me at bedtime.

LaVonne Northrup's family said grace with their heads down. LaVonne knew a better verse than Mr. Northrup did "Good food/Good meat/Good Lord/Let's eat." Her brother Paul knew one, too. "Over the teeth/Over the gums/Watch out stomach/Here it comes."

I did not learn prayers at Sunday School at Beth Yeshurun. We read Bible stories and watched Laurel and Hardy movies. The best year was when our teacher was absent a lot and my uncle Leon substituted. He told us all about mummies in Egypt. We brought charity from someone in Palestine named Karen-Ahmee. The year before confirmation we came to services on Saturday mornings. When Rabbi Malev finally read, "In solemn testimony to that unbroken faith which links the generations one to another, let those who mourn now rise to magnify and sanctify Thy holy name," a few grown-ups stood and said the Mourners' Kaddish with him. Then we all sang "Adon Olam" with a peppy tune, rose to be blessed, and left the sanctuary to eat refreshments in the hall. We knew to skip the sponge and honey cakes and get to iced brownies and the pastel petits fours before they disappeared.

On the High Holidays there were hours and days of prayers. The sanctuary wasn't big enough, so the synagogue rented the Houston Music Hall downtown. How different I felt dressed up, sitting on the crimson velvet chair (sit heavy in the center or it will fold up and swallow you), instead of wearing a tutu and dancing on the stage in Miss Emmamae Horn's annual ballet recital. I could read the English side of the prayer book, but the Hebrew prayers went on forever. I prayed faster than God listened and I was a lot younger. When could we go home and change out of our dark "transition cottons"?

When I was home sick from school, I listened to *Don McNeil and the Breakfast Club.* His radio program came from Chicago. He always said, "Now for a world united in peace, let us bow our heads and pray." Did God know that my prayer was coming from Houston, or did it get mixed in with the Chicago ones?

We had an Elaine May and Mike Nichols record that Mama laughed at. Elaine May was a mother who told her son who didn't call her enough, "I hope that someday you'll meet a girl and fall in love and get married and have children who will grow up and make you as miserable as you've made me—it's a mother's prayer."

Christians prayed to Jesus and God. Catholics prayed to Jesus and God and Mary. We had only God and were proud of it. Some people got dunked backward in water and some only got sprinkled like starched cotton. I took bubble baths and when I got older I was to shower. I heard about being washed in the blood of the lamb and wondered if the prayer-Mary was the same one who had the little lamb.

When I grew into my bra I decided that God heard me no matter what room I prayed in.

Kathryn Hellerstein

A Jewish Education

My parents sent me to a girls' prep school in the late 1960s because my mother had gone there thirty years before and it was still thought to be the best education available for a girl in Cleveland. They sent me, also, because my grades fell in the suburban junior high school, where I spent too much time combing my hair in the girls' bathroom or hanging out, trying to meet boys. Although at thirteen I was beginning to write poems, my moods and inspirations were pointing me more toward trouble than toward art.

When I got to prep school, though, I was lonely. Girls I had known when I was seven and who still lived across the street from me were now my classmates, but they walked past me in the halls without even saying "hi," as though we had never played kickball or spent the night telling secrets. Their parents had sent them to a dancing school to which I, a Jewish girl, was not admissible. Now they were preparing for their debuts. I was the only girl in the class not to be invited.

At school, I found myself marching in an alphabetical line from the tenth-grade homeroom into the chapel every morning, standing and sitting at command with 180 other girls in green skirts, white blouses, and saddle shoes. After the headmaster called us to order, we sang with our morning throats

the hymns from *The Book of Common Prayer*, strange to me
but as familiar as toothbrushes to the girls who went to an
Episcopalian or Presbyterian church every Sunday.

I soon felt uncomfortable. The daily opportunity to sing
words praising the Lord of Christendom seemed to most of
my classmates an innocuous school tradition; to me it was
coercion.

My strong response came as a surprise. I was not particularly observant or knowledgeable of Jewish traditions. My formal education as a Reform Jew had petered out after my
confirmation, the year before. During my Hebrew School
days, I had inklings of spirituality: I was sometimes moved to
tears during the Saturday morning service, while my Sabbath
school classmates fidgeted and passed notes. At temple, the
choir and the organ sent chords of holiness to the dome's
upper reaches. Light filtering through stained-glass windows,
set high between the pillars, seemed bejeweled with my spiritual longing. The rabbi, a hulking orator, intoned the Shema,
the Watchword of Our Faith, and the Kaddish, the Mourners'
Prayer, with an authority I was sure had been granted by God.
In such grandeur, I had only a whisper of a voice to answer
in the responsive readings.

Such devotions were not of my daily world. My parents,
both physicians and scientists, were essentially secular Jews,
as their parents, too, had been. All six of us children were
confirmed, but we soon stopped attending the Hebrew and
History classes on Saturday mornings. With cajoling from our
mother, we dressed up and piled into the old Rambler station
wagon every year for the Rosh Hashanah and Yom Kippur
services. We lit the candles for most of the eight nights of
Hanukkah; we recited the blessings haltingly. Our father led
the seder in English, mostly, throwing in a little Yiddish, and
using the Haggadah to test our oral reading skills. We didn't
keep kosher, although pork chops and shellfish never appeared on the supper table. It did not even occur to us to
observe the Sabbath, to light the candles or to bless the bread
and the wine, for such customs were not practiced by my

maternal grandparents, nor by their grandparents, who had
been Reform Jews since the mid-nineteenth century. My father's parents had passed down their immigrant rebellion
against religion, which did not keep my father from telling us
proudly about my grandfather's yeshiva education and my
grandmother's rabbinic lineage. At fifteen, I had forgotten my
earlier sense of holiness and knew little of the culture I would
later embrace.

Yet I was excruciatingly aware of history. I listened repeatedly to my father's stories of liberating Bergen Belsen
concentration camp, as a medical captain in the first American
armed division to witness the atrocities. With my brother, I
found in his attic room a shoe box filled with small, brown
photos of the piles of corpses, of the living dead reaching
toward my father's camera. I knew that only twenty-five years
before, six million of Europe's Jews had been murdered. Late
at night, hearing bombers and cattle cars in an airplane's rum-
ble or a train whistle, I felt like a younger, more fortunate
cousin.

As I slumped in the prep school chapel, the daily hymns
and prayers drummed a steady message: This education assumed Christianity as the universal truth behind everything
worth learning. I began to resist.

During sophomore year, I squirmed in my seat. As a junior,
I began to miss the 8:05 A.M. public bus that ferried me, a few
other students, and the Black women from the slums, headed
for their jobs as domestics, up along the grand boulevard,
arched by sycamores and giant maples and lined with stately
homes. I'd catch the next bus, tiptoe up those echoing granite
steps past the plaster cast of the headless, armless Winged
Victory, and slip into a chair in the last row. Chapel would
be more than half over. All I would have to hear were the
end of that week's Senior Speech and a few announcements
about intramural field hockey. The teachers at the back of the
chapel glared at me. In late October, my parents received a
stern note from the headmaster, threatening me with suspen-
sion if my tardiness continued.

By the time of the Christmas concert, my resistance blossomed into rebellion. The rehearsals were held every Thursday afternoon, and the whole Upper School would troop into the chapel to practice carols. The school's new choral director was Mr. Bard—one of the three men present in the school, besides the janitor and the headmaster. The history teacher and the sex-education instructor, George, were the others. Mr. Bard was teaching the girls a selection of lesser-known Christmas songs in medieval English and Latin. Although I liked the shape of those old words on my tongue, my throat tightened and I tasted gall when I remembered last year proceeding down the darkened aisle to the altar of St. Paul's Episcopal Church, carrying a candle.

After the first rehearsal, I walked up to Mr. Bard in the front of the room. He was a youngish man and dressed like an overgrown prep school boy. A lot of the girls had a crush on him. I asked him if he would possibly teach the school just one Hanukkah song or Jewish hymn to perform in the concert. He did a mock double take. "No. That would not be possible." How I longed at that moment to open my mouth, and out would come a Jewish melody as bold and pure as the Christmas songs! He turned away. I mumbled, "Well, I won't be in the concert."

I announced this decision to my parents. My mother worried aloud that I would draw too much attention to myself. In her day at the school, she told me, she sang the Christmas carols, whispering "Moses" for "Jesus." My father said heatedly that I had his support.

When I informed my homeroom teacher, she told me not to tell anyone else. I should simply go to the library during the all-school rehearsals. She would let the headmaster and Mr. Bard know.

The first week, while everyone else rushed to homeroom and then marched into the chapel, I clutched my notebooks and pulled open the library's glass door. I felt strange, happy, watching the leaves and clouds blow by from my carrel, a book of poems open before me.

The third Thursday, as I drifted between my book and the sky's small drama, a hand descended on my blouse collar. I was jerked to my feet. It was Miss Wicherly, my English teacher, beloved and much feared, who taught the Honors class Gerard Manley Hopkins and Chaucer, who supported Eugene McCarthy for president, who admonished us to wait to get married and to think for ourselves!

She pulled me around to her scowl, hissing, "What are you doing here?" She marched me down the silent hallway. She thrust me into a seat at the back of the chapel. The room was full and humming. As he beckoned the first sopranos through a difficult measure, Mr. Bard pointed at the second sopranos to hold their note and shushed the altos.

Miss Wicherly turned her face toward me. I could not see her eyes, only my reflection in her spectacles. "Do not think that you are exceptional," she told me. "You may be the only girl in the history of this school to refuse to sing in the Carol Service, but you are not exempt from what everyone else has to do. Whatever you think, you must sit here and listen. If I find you anywhere else on Thursday afternoon, I will have you expelled."

For the next three Thursday afternoons, I sat in the back of the chapel, swallowing tears of rage. I wanted to shout till my throat hurt. I wanted to sing out my own song, a Jewish song, but I didn't know any, and there was nobody in that dark hall who could teach me. I held my fingers in my ears. I did not want to hear the medieval lyrics or be tempted to hum with the first altos.

At eight o'clock on the night of the Christmas concert, all the other girls were standing in a tiered semicircle at the altar. They held candles that, flickering across their lips, illumined the gold cross in the shadows. And I was home, with my family, where I belonged.

Part Three

"With all your might . . ."

Sara Nuss-Galles

Schmutz

I was small, a seven-year-old shadow trailing my big sister. It was 1953 and we lived on the near North Side of Chicago. Our family had an apartment where we slept and changed clothes, but it was in the small grocery store that we actually lived. My brothers, Terry, called Avram, and Gerry, Gershon, six and twelve years older than me, were permitted their own lives. But Eve, Chava, a tall, thin, serious ten year old, was my friend, caretaker, playmate and occasionally my tormentor.

Our parents, who had survived Siberian labor camps during World War II, then five years of displaced persons' camps in postwar Germany, finally had come to share in the goldeneh medinah, the golden land of America. After years of working for others, they opened their own grocery store in the Polish working-class neighborhood. Their Polish was excellent.

But it seemed the store was cursed. No matter what they did, business was lousy. They worked from seven in the morning until eleven at night, charged fair prices and, in their way, tried to be pleasant. But they couldn't win people over. All day people walked by carrying bulging grocery bags from the nearby Grassi's supermarket or the distant A&P. The shoppers averted their heads to avoid the idle shopkeepers' ac-

137

cusing eyes. After the other stores were closed, they came for
an emergency item, like a sixty-nine-cent gallon of milk,
which we sold at a loss to attract customers.

In the store, Mother and Father were bound together seven
days a week, nurturing their misery. Day and night they bick-
ered; in the back room, at the front cash register counter,
while stocking the shelves, they blamed each other. The only
time they stopped was while waiting on customers or when
a delivery came. But let someone ask how business was, and
it started anew.

"I warned you. . . . You always. . . . We should never. . . ."
In their native tongue, Yiddish, their miserable lot in life was
their obsession.

Having lived among Poles all their lives, they now con-
cluded that the ones in America were no different than those
in Poland, willing to deal with Jews when they had no other
choice. But here they did.

We knew Grassi's. We'd been there to buy things for the
dinner soups our mother cooked on the backroom cooktop.
The spacious, brightly lit store was our local competition, run
by the two jolly olive-skinned Grassi brothers. One was short
and pudgy, the other, tall and thin. The store boasted a
butcher, fresh fruit and vegetables, and two checkout coun-
ters. Their flamboyant gum-cracking teenage daughters
worked the registers, and a radio played Top 40 music nonstop. It was a cheerful place to shop, in contrast with our
parents' store, hung thick with desperation.

"They have all the luck," our parents lamented. "They go
there because goyim stick together." While doing our homework on the backroom desk, which doubled as our kitchen
table, Eve and I once again overheard the familiar litany
against Grassi's. But one night a new ingredient was added.

"If only we had some of Grassi's luck," my mother was
saying, "our own luck would change. If we could get something, anything of theirs; even some of their dirt sprinkled
around the store would help us."

They spoke in Yiddish and the words that stuck in the mind

were mazeldich schmutz, lucky dirt. How could one person's schmutz be someone else's luck? This was an adult mystery.

Eve always tried hard to please our parents, even though she didn't understand them. But she wasn't too good at it. On weekends, when they went to the store and we dawdled at home, Eve had to dress me. One Saturday, I came to the store in a dirty shirt, the only one she could find. As we walked in, my mother spotted me and yelled at Eve right in front of customers. Eve knew better than to try to explain. That only made things worse.

But mazeldich schmutz stayed in Eve's mind. She talked about it to me. With lucky dirt, she'd be part of the outside world, able to play with friends, attend birthday parties, to live an "American life." How happy our parents would be. If business improved, the complaining and arguing would end.

Over the next days, Eve worked out a plan. An old photograph found in the store would serve as her dustpan. The receptacle was a paper napkin that Eve stuffed into her worn pants pocket. When finally she set off, I trotted behind her. It was nearly eight o'clock on a summer's night. People were out on the street. She walked purposefully to the next block, stopped in front of the store, and motioned for me to wait outside.

Eve entered Grassi's as it was about to close. Unlike our parents, who waited until the streets were deserted before they locked up, this store kept posted hours.

I peered anxiously through the plate glass window, my heart pounding fiercely. Eve prowled the aisles. From her desperate glances, I surmised that the store was spotlessly clean. At last, she bent down, disappearing behind a large baby food display. After an intolerable wait, she suddenly bobbed up. Discarding all pretense of ease, she hurried out of the store, balancing the laden photo in the palm of her hand.

On the sidewalk, she paused and pulled the napkin out of her pocket and transferred the precious schmutz into it. Her hands were trembling.

Now the door flew open, just a few feet from us. The short Grassi came out.

"Hey, you!" he called. "Hey, you girls!"

Eve crammed the photo and wadded napkin into her pocket, grabbed my arm, and pulled me down the street.

"They have plenty of luck," she insisted as we ran.

We didn't stop until we got home. We burst into the empty store, chests heaving. Our parents were leaning against the counter, arms crossed, waiting for customers.

"I've got it!" she yelled. Reaching into her pocket, she thrust out her hand to show them. They looked confused.

"The schmutz! I took it from Grassi's." Cautiously my mother opened the napkin. My parents looked at the contents in disgust.

Bewildered by their expressions, Eve repeated herself. "It's schmutz, from Grassi's. It will bring us luck, just like you said."

"You nahr, you fool," they said. "We were talking nahrish-keit, nonsense. It was a joke. Nothing can help us here."

Shaking her head, my mother walked over to the garbage can and tossed away the dirt and the napkin. My father picked up the Yiddish newspaper from the counter and was instantly absorbed.

My sister was silent, her slight body trembling. She walked out of the store and stood against a parking meter. She stayed there a long time, picking at the flecks of dust on her fingers. Eventually one of our "milk" customers came by, pulling a shopping cart full of groceries. Only I, standing in the silence of the store, was left to wonder, what would it have hurt if Grassi's dirt had been sprinkled on our parents' floor?

Enid Shomer

My Father's *Kichel*

Once or twice a year
he'd venture into the kitchen
to bake *kichel*—
cookies he made of sugar, flour
water and cinnamon. Rolled,
cut, then twisted into bows,
they puffed and hardened
like terra cotta pinch pots.

"He's making *kichel*,"
Mother whispered, as if the Messiah
might arrive on the cookie sheet,
mysterious as the first wild yeast.
She never suggested eggs or soda
to lighten the dough.
She filled the kettle
and lit the burner for tea.

Such an aroma I breathed then—
kichel browning in the oven
and steam swirling the air
like the grace that billowed
in Sunday school books,
foggy evidence of a God
who stayed behind the clouds.
My father, his dark arms white
to the elbows, wore a ruffled apron
and smiled faintly.

We ate and drank in silence,
dipping the stony *kichel*
into the tea my mother made,
biting down hard on his love.

Shirley Polinsky Fein　.

Down on the Farm

When people ask about Jewish life on our farm in northeastern Connecticut, I usually sugarcoat my memories with the picnics, hayrides and birthday parties of my childhood. I tell them how my father called the farm his own "Medina"; how Momma lit candles every Friday night and served a traditional meal. I tell them about the challah we baked and the gefilte fish chopped in the large wooden bowl, and the feeling of freedom for Mother and I, liberated from our usual kitchen duties and housework for that one day each week.

My happiness and contentment are only partly true. Grandpa Joseph, my father's father, lived with us on the farm, where he created a macabre museum of Old World attitudes and superstitions that he injected into our daily lives, causing me the unhappiness and misery that I remember to this day.

America must have been filled with men like Grandpa, eyes filled with pain, reliving a horror that for them could never cease. By the time he finally made his passage to America, Grandpa had witnessed more than twenty pogroms: the murder and terrorizing of the Jews. During attacks, he hid his three sons and two daughters in the dirt cellar of their meager cottage; until he died my father could not bear to be in a room without light. Grandpa was a leader of the local Chevra

Kadisha, the Jewish burial society, in Białystok. When a pogrom ended, my grandfather pulled the heavy wagon carrying
the bodies of his dead to the Jewish cemetery located miles
from town. By the time he left Białystok, his wife, Sara (I'm
named for her), was dead and he was a broken man.

Does this excuse the pain he caused us? It took me a while
to figure out that what the Tsar had done to the Jews, with
arbitrary rules and outbursts of anger, Grandpa did to us. He'd
march around the farm—a bizarre figure in high-top leather
boots, cap and a wool suit, appearing to be much less an
American farmer than a Polish nobleman on his estate. As
he'd walk about the land, he'd shake his walking stick, which
he fashioned out of a white birch tree. "Gay avek! Go away!"
he'd shriek at us, if we came too close. He scared the boys
and thought girls were worthless. That I was left-handed only
made matters worse, insuring I'd never get married. "A girl,
and not even all right," he'd say whenever I'd lift a pot. On
a rare occasion, we'd hear him playing the violin in his room,
the only indication that he carried memories of the life he led
long before.

Farming had been my father's dream, an escape from the
tenements of the Lower East Side. After World War I, Grandpa
followed Father to Connecticut, where the two of them lived
alone for three years until my parents married in 1925.

"You owe me a honeymoon," my mother used to tell him,
because he never left them alone, traveling in the back of the
wagon even when they first got married. He tolerated Mother
because she made him mushroom barley flanken soup and
did his laundry. When he was feeling generous, he would sit
in the kitchen near the wood stove, dressed in his starched
white shirt with the detachable high collar that took hours to
wash and iron. He would sit there, ever the gentleman, while
she cooked or scrubbed, and read to her the lovelorn column
and the letters to the editor from *Der Tog*, his Jewish newspaper, which came by mail once a week from New York City.

For a man whose ancestors had been bootmakers in Poland, he certainly had no trouble adapting to the life of landed gentry. Not for him a job in a shoe factory. In America he was a housepainter until my father's farm set him free. Grandpa never worked again. Mother's family called him "The Graf," the count. Once in a while he worked in the vegetable garden, but he didn't like to get dirty. Meanwhile, my three brothers, working alongside my father, did the heavy labor—milking cows, shoveling manure, cleaning out the barns, plowing and harvesting. I was my mother's helper, a scullery maid. I washed clothes in the old galvanized tub, fetching water and scrubbing by hand. I cleaned house, churned butter, cooked, baked, sewed and helped raise two baby brothers. In my spare time, I fed the chickens. Grandpa would stand on the sidelines and order us around.

Though there were no Cossacks in Connecticut, he lived in terror of others, and lived in isolation, refusing to speak to our visitors. He kept his hearing aid turned off. He spoke to few non-Jews other than the mailman. It was his way or no way. He taught us to play pinochle so he would have company on the lonely winter nights. But once I caught him cheating at cards, and that ended the games forever.

Because of Grandpa, Papa wouldn't let me drive the truck, not even around the farm. "Women shouldn't drive," he said. My mother was usually too tired to confront him, and she couldn't drive either, so what could she say?

Anyway, she had already won the only battle that really mattered, insisting that I finish high school. Grandpa thought education was wasted on a girl. But Mother wouldn't hear of it.

"I'm a high school graduate and all my children will be as well!" she said.

One day, Grandpa Joseph told me to get out of the dining room. It was evening and all the chores were done. My older brother Bernard was being prepared for Bar Mitzvah and Grandpa was going to teach him. Grandpa took out the siddur, the daily prayer book he kept in his room, and started

teaching Bernard the alphabet. They worked at it each evening, the sound of the ancient Hebrew filtering through the
house.

I wanted to learn. What was the mystery that Grandpa
wanted to keep hidden from me? One evening, I crept into
the room before the lesson started and hid under the large
round oak table. A floor-length tablecloth covered me from
view. Grandpa saw me and chased me from my hiding place.
He waved his walking stick and shouted at the top of his
voice, "A MADEL DOFF NISHT!" ("A GIRL doesn't need to
learn.")

But this girl did need to learn. It took me more than thirty
years to get the education I deserved and to put my bitter
memories to rest. I wanted the college education given to my
two younger brothers and for this I had to wait until my own
daughter was fifteen. I graduated cum laude!

Carol V. Davis

I dream of
railway stations

I dream of railway stations

and in these dreams
the ceilings are very high,
though the latticework varies:
a whole village
with small cottages and peasant
girls driving the cows home with
burnished sticks. The metals
too vary, iron dark with soot
or a filigree vine which glimmers
brass green in the afternoon sun.
Though I have children of my own,
I am always a child,
traveling with my father.
When my mother is present I am
grateful, for I know that she is dead
and here I can stroke her dress
and listen to her once again.
Sometimes we have to cross platforms
and I am afraid that a train will
turn the corner too suddenly and

there will be no escape.
We are lost and spend hours
wandering up and down stairs looking
for the right track. There are voices
around us, but the dialect is from
another region. It's a language I
might once have known. We must
hold onto our suitcases. They will
come for us if we don't board soon.

Dinah Berland

Sephirot

*According to the Kabbalah, creation began with the word of God in the
form of* sephirot, *letters of the alphabet that could be combined to gen-
erate everything in the universe. Traditionally, this knowledge was forbidden to girls.*

He was 81 years old when he drew the letters
in my tablet. I remember how he moved
the pencil slowly as he wrote my name
in letters that added up to numbers
the way he learned them in the village near Kiev
when he was a boy, before he was my grandpa.

I traced the pictures Grandpa
made: teapots, boxes, lamp-and-candelabra letters.
Girls, even at 13, were not taught Kabbalah in Kiev.
But *This is a free country*—so he showed me how he moved
the *aleph*, *mem*, and *shin* to make a riddle out of numbers
and I knew it was important as my name.

Sarah Bat Avram Yakov was my name.
When I was called to the Torah, Grandpa
closed his eyes. He was reciting Hebrew numbers,

turning them to songs with backward letters,
rocking back and forth as he moved.
He was so far from Jerusalem, so very far from Kiev.

Why did he and Grandma leave their village near Kiev?
When I asked him this, I could not name
the strange look on his face. Some said they moved
because Lake Michigan resembled the Black Sea. Grandpa
played cards in the park. Grandma wrote letters
and gazed across the water. How many did they number

when they climbed aboard the boats? They must
    have numbered
in the thousands—Jews who called Kiev
home for generations, fleeing the pogroms. Letters
clipped to our family tree told the story later, gave a name
to the horror, explained why Grandma and Grandpa
picked up their infant daughter and moved

with one small diamond sewn inside a coat. They moved
like skiffs on a wave, rising to join the numbers
of émigrés to Ellis Island. This is how it happened: Grandpa
heard his wife scream as she ran from the market in Kiev.
She had seen the Cossacks grab a woman and—in the name
of the czar—disembowel her, stuff her abdomen with straw.
    Some letters

have no sound. They moved like air, like fire, like water,
    with letters
that spelled the unspeakable name of God in numbers:
Grandpa Isaac, his wife Paula, and their daughter from Kiev.

Carolyn White

My Grandma
Had a Lover

My Grandma had a lover
I never knew 'til she was dead
my Grandma whom Mother said
lived before her time.
Why was that? I used to wonder.
Now I know she lived before the time
Grandmas had lovers.
I felt very proud.
My Grandma had a lover
15 years a lover/65 a wife
to Grandpa that tyrant
who couldn't walk and couldn't see
that Grandma had a lover.

And what was he like
this Cy I never saw
who died and left
my grandparents poor?
They paid the bills
and paid for thirty years
that's what happens
when you countersign a lover.

I think him very neat
a pious Jew
who gave it up in America
where piety won't do
always a little sad
and quite polite
he wore his hat and socks and garters
with Grandma in the single bed
in the daylight
of Brooklyn before the war.

It was the heyday of Schrafft's
Grandma and her lover on 2 stools
sipping coffee sodas
one hand on the straw
the other hand in Cy's
his hand upon her thigh.

I wish I'd been there.

I don't mean to stain Grandma's reputation
to bring a blush beneath her rouge
besides she's in her coffin
I want a past for her I love
I like the fact she held secrets
so dear she couldn't keep them
Grandma with her white white hair
and trim neat figure
who could send back the fish at Lundy's
"It's not done right, young man"
and I sixteen and blushing.
I inherited her clothes.

I hope all Grandmas had lovers.
For they each had homes
and they each had us and those
who came between, our parents,

but frankly I doubt
we were all that much
and they being special
deserve a lover saying:
       "Is there anything else
       I can bring you, darling?
       A cup of tea? Just ask,
       I'll order a trellis of
       yellow roses & 12 peacocks
       crowing in the sun"
and Grandma with her young young hand
draws back her golden hair.

Belinda Cooper

The Discovery

After my sophomore year of college, I took a summer job in Germany's Black Forest washing dishes in an isolated restaurant. It was a bit strange for the daughter of a Polish Jewish Holocaust survivor, but my father had lived in Bavaria for several years after the war as head of a Jewish refugee community, and had never imparted strong anti-German feelings to us.

True, he had been telling my brother and me of his Holocaust experiences since we were children—about the concentration camps and death marches and escapes, the murdered uncles and grandmother I never knew. But he was rational, almost too rational, about it all. He was often more admiring than critical of Germany, cheering for German sports teams at the Olympics and speaking highly of German politicians. I took German in high school and later college because it was rather like the Yiddish I had learned as a child, but also because he spoke it. After living in Berlin for years, I now realize some of his most basic traits are "Germanic"— the exaggerated need for order, the dogmatism, the inflexibility. But back then I knew only that his main hostilities were reserved for Poland, not Germany.

So Germany didn't frighten me. I wanted to spend time in

154

Europe, preferably in a country where I understood at least a little of the language. My father's main concern was that he'd never heard of the tiny village where the restaurant was located, and he made detailed inquiries at the German travel office. I don't remember what my expectations were, or if I even had any.

Right from the start, I found myself involuntarily wondering, whenever I saw an elderly German, what he or she had been doing forty years earlier. But the mostly young German apprentices who worked at the restaurant were friendly and fun, and everyone treated me well. One day the restaurant owner's father, a jolly white-haired old man who liked to hunt, proudly showed me the nautical mementos of his war years, when he served in the German navy. He didn't seem at all evil, but he also didn't seem particularly contrite.

That summer, I lived on a completely unaccustomed level, a level of physical rather than intellectual work, intensified by the fact that my undeveloped German reduced me to the vocabulary of a child. Reading German literature was hardly preparation for life in a Black Forest kitchen, where the most useful phrases were light-years removed from Goethe's *Faust*, and the accent so fractured many Germans didn't understand it. Yet I came to love the whole experience: the people, the food, the fairy-tale countryside, even the work.

At the end of the summer, my parents picked me up in a rented car; we were going to drive around Germany, which my father had last seen in 1949. It wasn't easy getting to know my parents again after the summer's experiences—after I'd come to know and like this very different world, these Germans. Their presence disturbed the summer idyll. My father met the friendly old former ship's captain, and they eyed each other, polite but wary. My reaction confused me; I resented the tension my father's presence created, and at the same time resented the old man for being proud of his wartime service, as though the Holocaust had never happened—torn between my new feelings for Germany and my Jewish loyalties.

Then we set off for southern Germany, snapping at each

other as we went. I was self-involved, trying to get used to my parents again after this first extended taste of independence; my father was dealing not only with an unfamiliar car and the unlimited speeds of the Autobahn, but with Germany, though he would never have admitted that this could be causing his emotional irritability. The country had changed enormously since his time, and he was constantly astonished at how modern it all was.

I wanted desperately to buy some jeans—they were cut differently in Germany. My father yelled at me; he couldn't understand why anyone would come to Germany to buy jeans. I hollered back, resentful that I was supposed to be sensitive to his feelings and guilty that all I felt was anger. We traveled through picturesque southern German towns, alternately bickering about jeans and reconciling long enough to admire the beautiful Alpine landscapes together. My father insisted we take the cable car up the side of the Zugspitze, Germany's highest point, with its beautiful view. He clambered cheerfully over a cliffside to retrieve something he dropped. In restaurants, we were seated at tables with other people, according to German custom; my father made a point of telling them he was a Holocaust survivor, making me feel defiantly protective of him, but also embarrassed and resentful. My American-born mother, who understood little German, marveled at how friendly and polite everyone seemed on the surface, and wondered what they were really thinking.

In a few days, we reached the area around the town of Straubing, in Bavaria, where my father wanted to trace his escape from the death march from Buchenwald to Dachau. He had always said that someday he would show us these sites, already familiar in the abstract from so many retellings. As the Allies closed in on Germany in 1945, concentration camp prisoners had been driven on foot into the country's interior, dropping by the dozens along the way from exhaustion or slaughter by their guards. My father watched friends and relatives die, and resolved to escape. One night the prisoners were herded into a barn to spend the night. Near the rafters, my father lifted down some tiles and slipped out onto the roof. He says he wouldn't have made any noise, but a fellow prisoner who tried to follow wasn't as careful. Prisoners and guards awoke, and chaos erupted as my father and the other man ran crouching between the barn's two peaked roofs, jumped down off the side and kept running. Later my father learned dozens of prisoners had been shot that night.

The two hid in the woods; when guards came after them with dogs, they miraculously failed to sniff them out. Not until the next day were they hunted down, taken to a German army camp and made to chop wood. My father tore off and buried the cloth numbers attached to his concentration camp uniform (after the war, he would return to dig them up). In the evening, an officer took them into the woods and said, "You tried to run once, now try again." The other man turned to thank him; my father, his instincts better honed, had seen the officer's hand reach for the gun in his pocket, and dove into the surrounding woods as the German shot at both prisoners.

My father ran. A storm broke, frustrating pursuit. He developed a fever. The American army was advancing, only days away. Wandering through the countryside, my father came upon a Polish slave laborer who hid him in a barn belonging to the German peasants he was working for. The peasants were called Bogner; they were decent, simple people, and in a day or two, after the Americans took over, they gave him a room and food. Later, an American officer brought him to a Catholic hospital; when he had recovered sufficiently, he was sent to a confiscated castle to recuperate.

We found the barn my father had escaped from; he spoke with the owner, who had heard the story before. We found the hospital, its old wing closed off, and an aged caretaker with a heavy Bavarian accent who found the room my father had recovered in. Outside the town of Geltolfing, we found the castle-convalescent home and the middle-aged German woman whose father, a minor Nazi, had once owned it. She'd been a young girl back then, and her obvious infatuation with my father, after all those years, was almost embarrassing to my mom and me. He barely noticed it. We found the cemetery, row upon row of white Stars of David, that my father had helped erect outside Straubing as a memorial to those shot the night he tried to escape.

And, following remembered landmarks, he even found the Bogners in their small Bavarian village. Quiet, dour peasants, they remembered my father and were pleased to see him. They opened a bottle of wine and fed us homemade ice cream, as grandchildren peeked from behind doors. I wish my German vocabulary had been good enough to ask them about their motives back then. Had they known my father was hiding in their barn before the Americans arrived? If so, why had they helped an escaped Jew? Because they knew the war was over? Because they were good people?

We also visited Straubing, where my father had headed the Jewish displaced persons community and worked in denazification. Some of the Jews were still there. He had helped a lot of people after the war; they were happy to see him, and everyone talked about the past. I couldn't understand everything. At one point, I was sure my father, glancing at me, said, "Shh—she doesn't know about that"—but I wasn't sure I'd heard right.

After that summer, my German was much better than before. One day soon after we returned, thinking about a subject for a college paper, I asked my father if I could look through some of his postwar documents. I shuffled through memorabilia—the concentration camp numbers dug up after the war, photographs, papers, some of which he had already shown me in the past, letters, documents, the business of Straubing's Jewish community. It all made more sense, now that I'd seen the places and met some of the people. In a pile of correspondence, I spotted a postwar identity card; my father's long, gaunt face stared up from it, dark eyes haunted. I examined the card more closely, deciphering the German. Under "marital status" was the abbreviation "*verw.*" As far as I knew, that could only stand for the German "*verwittwet*"— widower. A wife. A wife?

I told my mother I'd discovered a wife among the documents. She refused to tell me any more; instead, she told my father what I'd found. Then she sent me to talk to him, where he waited on the sofa in the basement to finally tell me the things I'd never known, never even suspected, though his age should have made it obvious.

This is what he told me: One day early in the war, he had come home from work in a distant town. A beautiful young woman walked in. It was, he found out to his astonishment, his sixteen-year-old cousin Sarah; he remembered her as a mere child. He was in his midtwenties. They fell in love. He showed me a photo from their wedding, a posed shot of the two of them, heads leaning against one another, looking young and beautiful. Later they had a child, a baby boy.

They lived in their shtetl, Strzemieszyce; when it was made into a ghetto, they starved. One day, tense and angry from the struggle to survive, he yelled at Sarah for something she did, for spilling some precious oil, and he's never forgiven himself. Recalling his frustration and impatience, he cried, the first time I'd ever seen him cry.

Then Sarah and the ten-month-old child were sent away— Auschwitz maybe, or perhaps a ditch outside the town that became a mass grave—and he went to the camps. It was almost a relief, he says, not to have to worry anymore, to wonder, to wait for the worst to happen—to know that it was happening.

I wrote my senior paper on Jewish Displaced Persons in Germany after the war. Then I went back to Germany, first for a year, then for longer; for many years, Berlin became my home. I learned more and more about the past, about the Nazis and about the relationship between Jews and Germans today. My father visited me a few times in Berlin, and we went to Poland together. In 1991 he lost a lung to cancer. Not long ago, he turned eighty, and my brother's wife had a baby—the first grandchild.

Except for that one time, and once on a survivor videotape, my father has never talked about his wife and child. He talks about everything else—about Poland before the war, about concentration camps and death marches, about his mother and his brothers, friends and relatives who died, horror and bravery in the camps. He talks about the boy whose life he saved in the camps, and about people he helped and ex-Nazis who caused him problems in Straubing after the war. He talks as though it were a mission, over and over and to any audience, and if you don't want to hear the same story for the millionth time, he looks at you as if you were personally responsible for it all, a look so furious that you stop arguing. He's talked in Poland, when we've been there together, to former classmates and professors and new friends; when he visited me in Berlin, he met my German friends and talked to them. He knows it's important to me, and I encourage him when he doesn't begin on his own.

The only things he doesn't talk about are Sarah and the baby. And I don't ask.

Part Four

"When you lie down,
when you rise up . . ."

Persis Knobbe

The Nose-Fixer

Before the acceptance of interesting noses, of wide hair and assertive behavior, before Barbra Streisand turned profile, it was not the best of times for a Jewish girl preoccupied with her identity and her nose. The curse of a funny nose and the fingers of a violinist were the result of being Jewish. I based that information on a visual survey. The equation at that time was: Jewish = different = almost but not quite equal.

"I hate my nose," I told Leah, my mother.

"Your nose is fine. It's in proportion to your face." What could I expect from Leah, straight-shooting and straight-nosed.

I had her gray eyes with a greener cast and my own good teeth, a bit larger than I would have ordered and what grown-ups told me was an Ingrid Bergman smile. On good days people asked me if I was related to Ingrid Bergman. Aunt Fay smirked when I told her that. Aunt Fay lived with us and thought that everything I did was a shanda to the Jewish people.

My nose was a problem I could do something about. I knew you could change noses because I watched my cousin

Mimi push up her baby's nose whenever she bathed her, an affectionate but deliberate push.

"I don't want her to have the Rabinowitz mountain," Mimi said to me with a certain lack of sensitivity.

"Bone?" I asked. "You can shape bone?"

"Babies are so flexible," Mimi said, letting her index finger slide across the baby's nose. I saw it happen. Now her little girl at age three had a darling button nose. Obviously it works, I told myself. It was too late for me to start from scratch with nose push-ups. That's OK for a pliable baby nose. By the onset of adolescence I needed a more drastic remedy.

Inspired by Amy in *Little Women*, who gave shape to her flat nose with a clothespin, I devised my own invention: a nose-fixer. It was composed of a Popsicle stick that I wrapped with a piece of mattress pad for softness. I attached it to myself with a thick rubber band that went around my head, forming a slingshot with my nose as the weapon. The stick went under my nostrils like a mustache. Every night before I went to bed I would put it on and adjust the rubber band for the proper slant of upness, something short of snooty that would still allow me to breathe.

Smiling at myself in the mirror, the nose-masked bandit, I knew I was smiling at my future. I quickly got into bed and turned out the light, afraid if someone caught me attached to my nose-fixer I would be teased for the rest of my life. But no matter how carefully I arranged myself the night before, I would wake up the next morning with my nose-fixer either on the pillow or twisted sharply to one side, my nose twisting along with it. Not discouraged, I promised myself as I slid the contraption into its hiding place behind the bed that one night I would figure it out.

Incredibly, such a night came to pass. I woke up in the morning, everything in place, as if I had not moved during the night. Flushed with the promise of an upturned future, I checked the mirror all morning, alert to signs of improvement.

I was investigating a small crease in the middle of my nose when I heard my mother's voice in the bedroom.

"What's this?" Leah asked in the midst of changing my bed. I didn't have to look; I knew what she would have in her hand. How angry would she be? The girl in the mirror looked guilty. Was admitting I had a funny nose a betrayal of our family? Of our heritage?

"What is this, a giant slingshot?" Leah wasn't angry; she was mystified. I shook my head. "Some kind of splint?" She put down the sheets she had been holding and looked closely at the apparatus, now a bit discolored from use.

"What is it?" she asked again, curious and a little worried. What did she think it was? I couldn't come up with a quick lie. A project for school was the only thought that came to me but that required an explanation. I had not prepared adequately for this moment.

"It's something for my nose."

"Your nose?" she said, turning the stick in her hand.

There was no other way; I would have to demonstrate. The ultimate humiliation. She'll laugh, she'll be hysterical, I knew.

"How do you use it?" she asked, holding it up. "Like this?"

I nodded. She got it right the first time. Very inventive, my mother. Good with jar lids, for which she once devised a special glove, demonstrating that nothing has to be stuck forever.

She looked at me the way my violin teacher did when we were in the middle of a difficult passage and he thought we should try it another way. "I don't think it's going to work," she said. I nodded, in spite of my recent success.

"You're so unhappy with your nose?"

"Yes."

"There's surgery," Leah said, sitting down on the bed. One hand on her lap, she ironed her housedress with the other. "Someday, if we have enough money and you're still crazy, we can talk about it. I'm sure it won't help if I tell you I like your nose."

She was right.

There was only one more thing. "Please don't tell Aunt Fay."

Leah shook her head as if the idea would never have occurred to her.

Vivian Gornick

That's Ridiculous

That's ridiculous. Sometimes I think I was born saying, "That's ridiculous." It shoots out of me as easily as good-morning-good-evening-have-a-nice-day-take-care. It is my most on-automatic response. The variety of observations that allows "That's ridiculous" to pass from my brain to my tongue is astonishing.

"Adultery makes modern marriage work," someone will say.

"That's ridiculous," I'll say.

"Edgar Allan Poe is the most underrated writer in American literature," someone will say.

"That's ridiculous," I'll say.

"Sports have an influence on people's values."

"That's ridiculous."

"Movies have an influence on people's fantasies."

"That's ridiculous."

"If I could take a year off from work my life would be changed."

"That's ridiculous."

"Did you know that most women refuse to leave the husbands who beat them?"

"That's ridiculous!"

Three years ago I ran into Dorothy Levinson on the street. We hugged and kissed many times. She stood there repeating my name. Then she smiled and said, "Do you still say, 'That's ridiculous'?" I stared at her. She hadn't seen me since I was thirteen years old. I felt the blood beating in my cheeks. Yes, I nodded, I do. She threw back her head and nearly had a heart attack laughing. On the spot she invited me to have dinner in a restaurant that night with her and her husband. What an evening it was.

Dorothy Levinson. So beautiful it twisted your heart. Now here she was, fifty, slim, lovely, full of shrewd Jewish wit and crinkle-eyed affection, her face looking remarkably as her mother's had at this same age: soft and kindly, slightly puzzled, slightly sad.

The Levinsons. I had loved them all—Dorothy, the four boys, the mad parents—but most of all I had loved Davey, the youngest boy, when we were both twelve, and how I had suffered because he hadn't loved me at all. There he'd been, thin and athletic, with a headful of glossy black curls and brilliant black eyes (every little girl had wanted him), and there I'd been, pudgy, sullen, superior. The whole thing had been quite hopeless.

The Levinsons were our summer people. Between my tenth and my thirteenth summers we were in residence at Ben's Bungalows in the Catskill Mountains. Two contingents dominated this bungalow colony: people like ourselves from the Bronx and people like the Levinsons from the Lower East Side. Or, as my mother put it, "the politically enlightened and the Jewish gangsters."

The Jewish gangsters had it all over the politically enlightened in the mountains. They learned quickly where good times in the country were to be had, and went after them as single-mindedly as they pursued their share of the action on Grand Street. They swam out farther in the lake than we did, roamed farther afield in search of wild fruit, trekked deeper into the forest. They danced in electric rainstorms, slept on the open mountainside on hot nights, persisted in losing their virginity whenever possible, and in making everyone else lose theirs as well.

The darkest and wildest of them all were the Levinsons—from Sonny the oldest son, to Dorothy the only daughter, down to my beloved Davey. They were so beautiful it was hard to look directly at them. Two summers in a row we shared a double bungalow with the Levinsons, and I was in a continual state as they slammed in and out of the screen door that hung on the same thin frame as ours. I remember those summers as flashes of black silky curls whirling by in the noonday sun, or quick darting glances in the bright shade from a pair of black eyes filled with scheming laughter. They were always going somewhere, planning something. Whatever they did it was the thing to do. Wherever they went it was the place to go. I longed to be asked to join them, but I never was. I stayed behind in the bungalow with my mother or read on the grass nearby, while they ran out into an intensity of sweet summer air to catch salamanders and frogs, explore abandoned houses, plunge repeatedly into the lake, feel sun burning into bare brown flesh, long after I had been called in to supper.

Dorothy and her husband and I went to a restaurant in the Village, and the talk plunged headlong into the past. Dorothy's husband, an accountant, knew he didn't have a chance and settled good-naturedly into playing audience for the evening. Dorothy and I, absorbed by every scrap of memory—Grand Street, the Bronx, Ben's Bungalows—talked over each other's voices, shrieking with laughter at everything, at nothing.

Dorothy kept asking if I remembered. Remember the abandoned house in the forest? Remember the berry-picking on the high hills far away? And the scratched asses from lying on the thorns to neck? Remember the warmth and vulgarity of the women on the porch on Sunday night? Dorothy's memories were richly detailed, my own sketchy. It wasn't just that she was eight years older. She was a Levinson. She had lived it more fully than I had.

Meanwhile, I kept asking, How's Sonny? How're Larry and Miltie? And your father. How is he? (I didn't ask for Mrs. Levinson, because she was dead, and I didn't ask for Davey, now a rabbi in Jerusalem, because I didn't want to know.)

Finally she said, "Davey! Don't you want to know how Davey is? Davey's wonderful! Who would have thought my baby brother would turn out spiritual? But he has. He's *spiritual.*"

I nearly said, "That's ridiculous." Stopped just in time. But I couldn't let it go, all the same. Silent throughout the recital on Sonny and Larry, now I felt I had to speak. "Oh, Dorothy," I said, very gently, I thought, "Davey's not spiritual."

Dorothy's eyes dropped to the table, her brows drew together. When she looked up again her eyes were very bright, her mouth shaped in an uncertain smile.

"What do you mean?" she asked.

"If Davey had left Essex Street at eighteen he wouldn't be spiritual today," I said. "He's looking for a way to put his life together, and he's got no equipment with which to do it. So he turned religious. It's a mark of how lost he is, not how found he is, that he's a rabbi in Jerusalem."

Dorothy nodded and nodded at me. Her voice when she spoke was unnaturally quiet. "I guess that's one way you could look at it," she said. I laughed and shrugged. We dropped it.

On we went, falling back repeatedly to stories of the bungalow colony. Dorothy did most of the talking. As the hours passed Dorothy did all the talking. She talked faster and faster, the sentences tumbling one after another. A mosaic of emotional memory began to emerge: how she had seen me, how she had seen my mother, how she had seen my mother in relation to her mother. I began to feel uncomfortable. She remembered it all so vividly. She had been so intent on us. Especially on my mother.

She laughed heartily as she spoke, a strong rocking laughter. Suddenly she turned full face to me and said, "You never really enjoyed it like we did. You were always so critical. For a little kid you were amazing. It's like you knew you were more intelligent than anyone else around, and you were always seeing how silly or pointless or ridiculous—your favorite word—everything was. Your mother, also, was so much better than anyone else around. And she was, she was. Your father adored her. She used to walk beside him, his arm around her and she holding on to him, God, did she hold on to him, holding on for dear life, clinging like to a life raft, and looking around to make sure everyone saw how happy she was with her lover-like husband. It was as though she wanted to make every woman there jealous. And *my* mother? My father came up once during the whole summer. She used to cry over your mother: 'Look how good he is to her, and look how Jake treats me. She's got everything, I've got nothing.' "

Dorothy laughed again, as though she were afraid to speak without laughing. "My mother was kind," she said, "she had a kind heart. Your mother? She was *organized*. My mother would sit up with her own kids when they were sick, and she'd sit up with you, too. Your mother would march into the kitchen like a top sergeant and say to my mother, 'Levinson, stop crying, put on a brassiere, fix yourself up.' "

More laughter, by now the taste of iron in it. Dorothy struggled with herself to stop, to get off my mother and her mother. Abruptly she took her memories back to a time before my time, and began to tell us of the Jewish mystics traveling around on the bungalow-colony circuit when she was eight or ten years old. "All the women would sit around in a circle in the dark," she said, "with a candle on the table. The medium would close her eyes, tremble and say, 'Habe sich, tischele.' Lift yourself, little table." ("And would it?" "Of course!") "Women would start to scream and faint. 'Is that you, Moishe? Oy gevalt! It's Moishe!' More screaming, more fainting."

Dorothy threw me a sharp look and said, "Your mother would have marched in, turned on the light and said, 'What is this nonsense?' " Dorothy's husband and I both stared open-mouthed at her. Before he could stop her she leaned toward me and hissed, "She never loved you. She never loved anybody."

The next morning I realized that although I had not said, "That's ridiculous" before I scored off Davey, Dorothy had nonetheless heard the words. The mother in her had heard the mother in me.

The New Girl

"Hey, Reuven! C'mere!"

I am standing at the corner of Albemarle and Alcott, talking to a girl named Esther. She lives on the other side of North Avenue, but she heard that a new kid her age had moved into the neighborhood and would be going to her school. She came over with a box of Barton's chocolates, the assortment called "TV Crunch." She is short and kind of funny-looking with curly hair that has been combed to look straight, glasses and stooped shoulders. Her clothes are too dark and serious for summer and she speaks in fast, assured sentences, sounding more like a teacher than a twelve-year-old kid.

Esther has just called to a lanky strawberry blond boy wearing a baseball cap, who was riding by on his bicycle. At the sound of his name the boy, Reuven, backpedals to stop his bike and gets off. He lets the bike fall softly on someone's front lawn, and then he walks over to where we are standing.

"This is Reuven Arnow," Esther tells me. "He lives about five blocks away on Dexter Street. Reuven, this is Joanie Jacobs, she just moved here. She's going to go to Westchester Hebrew Academy and she's also going into eighth grade."

"Jacobson," I correct Esther, instantly regretting my retraction. For a second I fear that Esther will stride off, offended, but instead my new neighbor shrugs her shoulders.

"Sorry."

"That's okay," I say quickly.

I look at Reuven. He is cute yet sort of dopey-looking, his ears stick out on the side, he has large splotchy freckles and his mouth is rubbery. It occurs to me that he bears a certain resemblance to Alfred E. Newman.

"Where'd you move from?" he asks.

"Pondview, New York."

"Where's that?"

"It's the end of Queens, just before Nassau County," I say, used to having to place Pondview geographically for other people.

"Oh," says Reuven, squinting at me.

"So, how many kids in your family?" Esther asks, looking around.

"Just me," I say.

"Really?" says Reuven, his eyes opening wide. "Wow, that's great. You probably have lots of things. Only kids are usually spoiled rotten."

"That's not always true," Esther says to Reuven, pointedly. "I have a cousin who's an only kid and she's not spoiled at all."

Reuven shrugs. "That's what my father says."

A sweet, late-summer breeze ripples down Alcott Road. I am beset by the sudden urge to run off, walk through the streets of my new neighborhood alone. Esther, with her authoritative voice and blue skirt, is creepy; she makes me feel like I am standing in front of a judge. And Reuven is just stupid and boring.

"Are you going on the September shabbaton?" Esther asks. "It's supposed to be great."

"Is that something from school?" I ask, fearful that my mother signed me up without asking my permission.

"No, it's from shul," says Esther. "The Young Israel has two shabbatons every year for kids seventh grade and up. You should ask your parents about it."

Relief courses through my veins. My mother told me that we were joining Emanu-El, the Conservative synagogue. The Young Israel must be the Orthodox one.

"Well," I say, swinging my arms, "we haven't joined the Young Israel. We're going to be going to Emanu-El."

There is a moment of palpable silence as Esther and Reuven exchange glances. I am keenly aware of being excluded from a crucial nonverbal communication.

Finally Esther speaks, her words slow and measured like a parent giving instructions to a slow child. "My mother told me that you were going to Westchester Hebrew Academy."

"That's right," I say. Again, Reuven and Esther's eyes meet. "So?"

"You're shomrei shabbas, right?" asks Esther, using a Hebrew term meaning Sabbath observant, peering at me intently from behind her glasses.

"Yes," I answer, feeling acutely uncomfortable, wondering why they are asking me these questions.

Esther's face relaxes and she gives Reuven a confident nod. "If you're shomrei shabbas and go to Westchester Hebrew Academy and live in Beechmont, you should join the Young Israel. The people at Emanu-El aren't religious, it's a Conservative shul." Esther speaks with an air of confidentiality, as if sharing a well-known but dirty little secret with me.

When I don't respond, Esther continues, getting to the heart of the matter. "My mother told me that they use a microphone on Shabbas at Emanu-El and they have an organ, just like in church. Men and women sit together and women can wear pants or shorts into shul. You don't even have to be Jewish to go into shul and most of the people there can't read Hebrew. And the rabbi hardly knows anything about the Torah. My mother told me she once heard him speak and he was worse than a goy."

I stand frozen in place, rooted on the corner of Alcott and

Albemarle, listening with incredulity to the words of my new neighbor. I am torn between a sickening anger and the desire to burst out laughing. I feel like Esther and Reuven are from another planet; I have never met kids who speak this way, who think this way. My father always told me that the first commandment of being Jewish was to love all Jews, even those who celebrate their Judaism in a different way. My mother taught me to respect people with different color skin and different religions. I shudder to think what Esther's mother told her about black people.

I am stunned beyond words. Esther, in her arrogance, takes my silence as compliance. "Your dad probably made a mistake," she says. "Tell him you should join the Young Israel."

Abruptly, I turn to Esther, lethal fury licking my skin, my face, locking my teeth into a grimace, narrowing my eyes, clenching my fists. I allow the murderous anger to overtake me for a moment as I imagine kicking her in the chest, tearing her hair out and beating her head against the pavement until she is dead. I envision jumping on her stomach up and down, up and down, until her guts spew out from the sides, her skin pops like an overextended balloon. I ride the crest of my anger until it washes over the shore of self and I am sensible once again, in control of my impulses. I allow myself to speak.

"I can't tell my father anything," I say calmly.

"Why not?" asks Reuven, face blank. Esther furrows her brow.

"Because he's dead," I say, dropping my words like a bomb, enjoying the way Esther's smug face reddens, the way Reuven's stupid mouth flops open. I feel suffused with power, watching the reaction of these sanctimonious schoolchildren. Esther, ever verbal, is the first to offer an apology.

"I'm sorry . . . I didn't know, my mother didn't tell me." She stumbles over her words. I want to strip her and make her run home to her mother, naked.

I cross my arms and take a step backward, regarding Reuven and Esther. I always thought that people who called themselves Orthodox were supposed to be better. I want to leave at this moment but there is a crucial piece of information I haven't yet imparted.

"By the way," I say, striving to keep my voice even, not betray the grief that is welling up inside me, following always on the heels of my anger. "You didn't ask me what my father did when he was alive. You know what he did? He was a rabbi. A Conservative rabbi. Do you hear me? MY FATHER WAS A CONSERVATIVE RABBI!"

Unable to control myself, my voice rises to a scream and I turn on my heels and run away. I sprint down Albemarle and up the steps of my new home, chest heaving, tears cascading down my face, snot running from my nose. I pull open the front door of my house, gallop upstairs to my bedroom and throw myself on my new bed. I cry and I cry, grabbing handfuls of my blanket and squeezing it just like I did when I was little. Is this the way everyone is in Beechmont? I lie face down on my new bed, sobbing vocally, my mouth open, until I hear the hurried footsteps of my mother, and feel her firm hand on my back. My sobbing ebbs, but the pain does not ease. My rage and grief gradually acquiesce to a numb understanding that I am alone.

Sheila Schwartz

Mutatis Mutandis

(LOVE)

There was evening and there was morning the sixth day, and for what? So that she, Miriam, could walk alone to her bunk every night while the others groped and rustled in the dark, so that her only friend, Renee, could ditch her just like that for a creep named Harvey Haas, so that Chaim Picker could torment her ceaselessly, interminably, with his obscure, a priori liking?

Everyone else that summer got smoke in his eyes, got satisfaction, got do-wa-diddy-diddy-dum-diddy-do. Not her. Not mutatis (though not yet mutandis) Miriam. All she got was, "Nu, Miriam?" All she got was the correct answer every time she raised her hand. All she got was taller and taller. (Five feet ten and who knew when it would stop? Tall like a *model*, her mother always said. An attractive girl. Only thirteen years old and so shapely. Wait!)

But there was no end in sight. Too big, too smart, and on top of all this—the teacher's pet (a real *drip* in other words). It was a simple concept with a simple proof: Chaim Picker was a real drip. Chaim Picker liked her. Ergo, *she* was a real drip.

And so the proofs of *his* drippiness, clear and manifold.

For one thing, he spoke way too many languages all of which were queer. According to the others, his Hebrew was queer, his Yiddish was queer, his English was *totally* queer. (What was all that "Omnipresence" stuff, anyway?) To make things even worse, he wore the exact same thing every single day—a creepy black suit, black shoes, black yarmulke, and tsitsit (the *epitome* of queerness). When he lectured the tsitsit swayed with him, back and forth, back and forth, Baruch HaShem amen v'amen! As far as anyone knew, these fringes were the only things he had ever kissed, in the morning when he put them on, and in the evening when he lay himself down to sleep.

Miriam saw him differently. He wasn't really a drip, just an "anachronism" (as she had discovered in one of her recent forays through the dictionary). For Chaim, it was clear, reminders of God and his commandments were everywhere, not only in the ceremonial fringes he wore, but in the whoosh of pine trees, in the birds flying overhead, even in his tea glass, spoon handle pointing upward like the metal finger of God, admonishing.

A bachelor, born circa 1930, he had a propensity for closed spaces and esoteric questions. Witness the inordinate amount of time spent in his tiny cabin. Witness the thick curtains on his windows, the hours spent in the library studying. Witness (they had no choice) his probing technique in class.

They groaned. Good Lord, more questions! He was going to kill them with all his questions. At every damned word he had to stop and wonder: who what where when and why, and sometimes why again. WHY does it say "in the beginning"? Hasn't everything always been here forever and eternally? So where did this "beginning" come from? And how could God precede it?

And furthermore. What is meant by "the face of the deep"? Wasn't this "face" covered by darkness? And wasn't it also empty and formless, but still visible in the "darkness"? (If it was *truly* darkness.) And how could this "darkness" *and* the spirit of God move upon the waters or whatever they were at the same time and in the same place and did this imply identity? And if so then what is meant by "in the beginning"? Miriam? Good, Miriam. *Correct.* For him, nothing in the stupid book was just simply what it was. Nothing in the whole damned world.

It was true, Miriam thought. Everything had its layers, its surfaces, its unexpected depths, even the riddle he asked them every day at the start of class: "Nu, children. What is the meaning of 'peel'?" Even the answer Barry Sternberg gave for the twenty-fifth straight day, "Miriam" instead of the true meaning "elephant." (Though it might seem otherwise, Chaim explained to her one day after class, Barry really was a good boy, he meant no harm by his remarks. "He's a sick boy," Chaim had said, "a boy with many problems. He needs people to pay attention, and not just *you*. Whom do you think has been scribbling on the walls all summer long? And other pranks I am not at liberty to mention. Just try to ignore him, Mireleh. The more any of us pays attention, the more he'll keep on doing it.")

Barry popped up and took a bow.

"Sternberg," Chaim said.

"What?"

Chaim pointed to the bench.

"Who *me*?" Barry pretended to be astonished. He spread his arms wide to capture his amazement. "What did I do? What in the 'H' did I do?" he asked the class.

"Please sit down."

"Why?"

"Sternberg. You may leave or you may sit down. *Choose.*" Chaim placed both palms flat on the table.

Barry pointed. "The right one," he said.

"Sternberg!"

"The left?"

"OK OK OK," Chaim told him. "That was an interesting

exercise. You have made for us a good variation on the state of innocence and on the meaning of will. But now, *we* will go on." He clasped his hands behind his back. "Nu, children?" He turned toward the class. "And vus is 'peel'?" His smile was hopeful. He waited.

"Oy!" Barry flopped back onto the bench. "Oy oy oy!" He shook his head. "These Jews. These Jews! They are *just never* SATISFIED." Then he went into his act. He made his eyes blink, made his jaws click-clack together. "Nu, Meereyum." His voice came out slow and underwater. "Why don't youuuu tell us vussss." As though drowning in precision, he sank to another octave. "Cumpute it for him, Meeeeeer-ee-yummmmmmmm."

They burst out laughing.

"Sternberg, *leave.*"

"Shtarenbeerg, *liv!*" Barry flapped his hands. Shoo! His grin implied a cheering crowd. He made no move to leave.

"OK OK. My accent is very funny; it's very funny indeed, I agree. There's truth in everything," Chaim said. "So, therefore, one more chance, Sternberg. This is Erev Shabbat and I'm giving you the benefit. Now what is 'peel-pool'?" He bent forward and nodded as if nudging him the correct answer.

Which gathered on Barry's face into a big, knowing grin. "An elephant pool—where Miriam swims." He sprang up from the table. "Shtarenbeerg—*LIV!*"

They laughed.

Miriam tried to ignore them, she tried to ignore Barry as Chaim had asked her to. After class he had repeated what he'd said before. "No matter how disturbing these events seem, we must pretend we don't notice. He's a child crying just to hear the sound of his own voice, a sad boy, a very very unhappy human being." And when she hadn't been convinced ("But why does he always pick on *me?*") he had added, "Listen, Mireleh. You are my best student. It's a shame that he spoils your concentration so I'll tell you a secret—for your ears alone, fashtays-tu?" When she'd nodded, he took hold of her hand, as if to prevent her from running in horror when she heard the truth. "Barry is an orphan," he whispered. "*Both* his parents at once—a terrible misfortune. He lives with his aunt. She's been very generous, but he has never gotten used to his fate. For this reason he sees a psychiatrist. A *psychiatrist*," he repeated. "You understand what this means? It's crucial for us to set a good example."

She tried, but it was difficult. Every day Barry sat down next to her. "Sha-loom, Meereyum." Winking to the class, he sprawled himself out until he was so close she could feel his tanned arms and legs glistening against her own pale ones, rubbing sweat. Every time she moved over, he moved over too until there was no place on the bench to sit. She tried to ignore him. She remembered what Chaim had said: "It is better to be persecuted than to persecute others." She tried to believe him. She stared at her hands, and at the trees, and at the big heart carved into the wooden table.

RANDY & JOSH IN '63.

That was the way the summer went; this was the pattern of love. Someone looked at you in services, in class, at dinner. Three times (a holy number). His friends noticed. They kidded him and giggled. *Your* friends heard about it and they told *you*. You blushed and shrugged your shoulders, not yes, not no. Sometime later (after a movie, or lunch, or Friday night dancing on the tennis courts) you heard footsteps on the path behind you, a voice which leapt to life in your ear, "Wanna take a walk?" Sometime later, the ID bracelet, a binding silver promise on your wrist. (Or was it the ID first and *then* the walk?)

That was the way it went and it happened to these people: David Stein and Leslie Gold. Yitzi Feinberg and Shira Oster. Josh Blum and Karen Bregman. Bennet Twersky and Susan Gould. The boys from Bunk 3 and the girls from Bunk 19. The kitchen help and Gladys Ticknor. Stacy Plisky and everyone. Once it almost happened to her, but it was only Norman Levine, the boy with the slide rule.

Still, even love with a slide rule was permissible in certain cases. According to the Talmud there were many faces to love—some smiling, some weeping. Love could be a wind, a deep well; it could be a tiger waiting to spring.

That was all well and good, but *this* was nothing of the kind. According to Leo Goelman, the camp director, love was one thing, *neetzool* was another. He gave them a long lecture about it the morning that this sign was discovered painted on the library wall:

SUZY CREAMCHEESE—WHAT'S GOT INTO YOU?

Whoever had done this, Leo Goelman shouted, had no idea what love meant, not a clue. Real love was sacred. It was not something to joke about. What *this* prankster had in mind was something else—"neetzool" he reiterated. "Neetzool" meant *exploitation*, a lack of respect, a lack of individuality. "Neetzool" was what you felt like doing with anyone at all.

His interpretation discouraged no one.

Every night there was the same rush for the woods, the same giggling in the bathrooms afterward. Every night Miriam listened to Shira and Renee whispering about what they had done (always just loud enough for her to hear, just soft enough to make her feel that she was eavesdropping).

"We went to second. What did you guys do?"

"Only first."

Everything was euphemism. First base. Second base. Making out. Popping flies. Once Shira looked at her and laughed. "You don't know what we're talking about, do you?"

When they got between the rough, white camp sheets, instead of saying their prayers, they thought of what they had done, of what they might do tomorrow. They dreamed of scratchy bark against their backs, and later, eventually, of their names carved into that bark.

Miriam saw things differently.

They would meet somewhere, in a park, in a cafe, in the

rain. He would be wearing a long coat, military style, black, but not as black as his hair which was blue-black, seething with midnight. He would smoke thin cigars and know everything there was to know about poetry and film. Whatever he stared at, he would stare at intently. "Ah! A reader," he would say. "That's good. A woman who thinks." His eyes would linger on her face.

She would hand him her copy of *Steppenwolf* and he would turn the pages slowly, his unnaturally delicate fingers slipping beneath the paper. He would pause to read some comment in the margin. "Coffee somewhere?" he would murmur.

Rain would fall. Time would pass slowly. They would go on and on.

Or it might happen like this:

They'd have something in common (a love of nature or justice). Both of them, hard workers, diligent believers in a cause. People with principles! (Civil rights, maybe? disarmament?) Whatever their protest, they would run from the tear gas together, find shelter in a burned-out basement, wrap their wounds, never come out.

Or it might be like this: Before she even spoke, he would love her.

Other girls got letters from their boyfriends back home: "Are you still stuck in that dopey Bible camp? When are you coming home? I have a great tan from hanging around the club. The women adore me. Ha. Ha."

And they wrote back, a big pink kiss on the outside flap: SWAK.

Miriam got letters from her mother every day. "My darling, Miriam," or "Dearest Miriam," or "My darling, little Miriam," they began. She hoped that Miriam was having a profitable summer, that the other girls were nice, that Miriam was wearing all her nice, new outfits.

And as if that weren't enough. "P.S." she said. "You're a wonderful girl. I miss you."

Another week passed and they were still crawling through Genesis. God had made light and plenty of it shining down on every corner of the field, making the air hum, making the horizon, through the waves of heat, seem to curl up into the sky. The grove where they had dragged their benches and table was no better. It was too hot to think. It was too hot to answer. Only Chaim, in his eternal, black wool suit, was moving.

They had been over and over the Garden of Eden. Chaim had delineated it for them in graphic detail, had made them sweat blood over it. The fragrance! The fruit trees! The making of each creature—how splendid! The perfection of the whole thing. Now they were stuck on Adam's rib (a difficult passage).

Why was it that Eve had been made from Adam's rib and not from dust, as Adam had been? God could do anything, correct? So why then from a rib?

Shelley Katz did not know.

Danny Goldfarb did not know.

Barry Sternberg did not give two hoots.

"*Think*, children."

"To make them fit?" As soon as she'd asked it she blushed. The heat of her mistake began to rise through her, to swell inside of her, to do something, at any rate, totally awful.

"Nothing would fit *you*," Barry said. "Not even *this*." He showed her with his hands.

"I didn't mean—!" But it was too late. They were too hot to answer, but not too hot to laugh. She wondered what the Talmud had to say on the subject of laughter. It could be a wind? A deep well? A tiger waiting to spring?

Chaim bent forward to block their amusement. "Don't be a clown, Sternberg. Do you never learn? Of course Miriam didn't mean this literally," he said. Then he frowned at them.

"You meant it *figuratively*, didn't you, Mireleh? A metaphor? Something for something else, wasn't that your intention?"

She nodded faintly. Something else—oh sure. The road was a ribbon of moonlight. My love is a red, red rose. That was what she had meant—some other perfect fit. "I guess so," she said.

"Correct, Mireleh. That's very good." Chaim patted the table in front of him as though it were her hand. "Very good indeed." He held up his Bible, print outward, and pointed to the passage. "You see, we have here, class, a metaphor—a lesson we can read between the lines—"

"Between the what?"

"Between the LINES, Sternberg." He tapped the page. "Beneath what is said literally, children, we have a second, more important—"

"Beneath *who*?"

Chaim sighed. "Beneath what is said *literally*, a second truth, as Miriam has pointed out—what is good is often hidden."

"You can say *that* again!"

Chaim set down the book. "Please, Mireleh. Please tell us simply and QUICKLY and in what manner, *figuratively*, these two fit."

"Yeah," Barry whispered. "Give us all the figures!"

The blush crept through her, literally, figuratively, fittingly and otherwise. However she had meant it she didn't know and didn't care. All around her they were grinning. Barry was grinning; he was coursing with possibilities (loose? tight? dry? deep?). Barry nudged her with his leg. "Nu, Mireleh—so tell us already."

She tried to slide away from him and when she did, her legs lifting from the bench made a slurping sound.

"Correct!" Barry exclaimed.

"That *is* correct," Chaim said as though she had answered. His eyes told her: "Bear with him. Ignore him. Be brave." As if to demonstrate how sufferance like this was achieved, he

ignored Barry and the sound and their laughter. He ignored
everything he could possibly ignore. He clasped his hands
together and squeezed. God made Eve from Adam's rib, he
told them as he started to sway, to insure a perfect match, to
make a coupling of the right and left halves so that no part
should be omitted, no part lacking. It was a union perfect
as the Garden, a union fragrant as a citron, alive with light.
"We're talking about the crown of creation—*you understand
me, class?*"

Sure. They understood.

On Friday nights it was standing room only in the woods.
She could hear them in there hugging and kissing, fondling
and caressing, zipping and unzipping, rubbing, pushing, their
desire shredding fabric. She could hear them giggling and
whispering and groaning, an ocean of sound that described
each touch, that rose like steam through the woods.

(THE LIBRARY)

No one knew as much about that library as she did, except
perhaps the librarian himself, and even *he* didn't know it in
the same way.

She knew that the wood smelled in the morning, and the
dust, of years of thought—resinous. She knew that the sun
lit the letters on the bindings, gold. She knew which books
had pictures, which ones had tiny, unreadable print. She
knew who came there, at what hour, and for what purpose.

Chaim was there every afternoon from lunchtime until dusk
poring over commentaries on the Bible. He didn't lean on
one elbow like the others, but held his arms stiffly at his sides
and swayed back and forth over the text as though he might
dive into it. Sometimes he closed his eyes. She could watch
him for hours and he never noticed her. Even when he lifted
his head for air, his eyes shone with a blank, unseeing light.

Often, after he'd gone, Miriam would slip into his chair. She would pick up the book which still lay open on the table awaiting his return, and she would try to read what *he* had read that afternoon. There were reams of words, some in Hebrew, some in Aramaic, all without vowels, mysterious, impossible. She could only read the very large print—the phrase, or word, that was the subject of all that commentary: IN THE BEGINNING. DARK AND UNFORMED. She sat with the dictionary and puzzled out words. She wrote down translations, verbatim, awkward, but no matter what she did, she found nothing. The words were just words. Chaim still remained a mystery.

Then, eventually, she discovered that the words didn't matter. Maybe she couldn't understand them, but she didn't have to because it was just as pleasant simply to sit in the dark and pretend, to slide her fingers over the page, (occasionally to sway a little), to skim the elusive grains of sense, silently, as though reading. She imagined that was what mystics did when they meditated. They chose some words, they shut their eyes, they rocked themselves to sleep. Every day she did this a little longer—a half hour, forty-five minutes, an hour—when she should have been playing basketball, or making lanyards, when she saw Barry coming toward her, over the hill.

As for Chaim—. One evening she hovered over the book he had left behind until it was almost dark. The librarian had gone home to his cabin. Dusk had thickened around her and she had let it, had liked it, the feeling of darkness melting into her, the way the words melted into her fingertips, and her fingertips melted into the pages, the way the pages melted back into the darkness, slowly, very slowly, and the darkness melted back into her. She was dreaming that the letters had become figures, tall and thin, in long dark cloaks, broad black hats. They had all joined hands and were dancing in a circle around her making the room quake with joy. Faster and faster they whirled until the walls fell away, the sky became a blur—stars, moon, night thrashed against the galaxy; she couldn't catch her breath.

Wood creaked.

She opened her eyes.

A dark figure was coming toward her. Tall. Twisting. A shadow that bent. Unfolded. Bent again as though searching for a path through the twilight.

"Who's there?" she whispered.

The figure stopped. "Vus?"

Not the spirit of a letter, but Chaim. She had conjured him, complete, in his long black coat, his round black hat. "Vus machst tu, Mireleh?" he inquired.

Still not seeing clearly, she blinked. The hat he wore cast shadows on his face making from his features, shapes—caves and crags. "Ah," he said softly. "You're reading. Please don't let me disturb you," as though this were the most natural thing in the world, to be sitting in the dark with a book. She glanced down. She must have fallen asleep right on top of it. The pages were all crinkled and there were spots of saliva. She thought she smelled the oil from her hair. Ashamed, she closed the cover. "I wasn't really reading," she sighed.

But he didn't answer. Instead, a white hand leapt to his beard and began stroking it, thoughtfully, gently, as though this were a demonstration of how to treat the world. Something about this puzzled her. Not the motion, but the whiteness of his hand. Her own hands were obscured by darkness, but his shone pale as though lit up from inside. She thought of miracles that she'd studied—the Hanukkah candle that burned for eight days; the bush in the desert exploding into flames. She thought it might be some strange effect from the Ner Tamid, the Eternal Light, that burned above the Ark against the wall. Or, she might have lapsed back into her dream, lulled by his silence.

"Mireleh?"

He was asking her something. One hand soared to his hat brim where it hovered as though waiting for an answer.

"What?"

"Pirkei Avot. The Ethics of the Fathers, you remember? It says there: 'On three things the world depends—on Torah, on work, and on the performance of good deeds.' Do you believe this?" He gestured. His hand swooped toward her like a dove, plummeting down.

Another magic trick? She pushed the book away. "I guess so." Why had he come back this late? Why hadn't he turned on the light? Did he come here to hide the way she did?

He did not help to make things clearer. Folding himself into the chair across from her, he said, "May I sit down for a minute?" Then the conversation began, a long conversation which made no sense, that seemed like words weaving through the darkness, occasionally surfacing, then dipping, then floating up again making strange ripples through all that had gone before.

"So how are you liking it thus far?"

"Liking what—the class?"

"The class. Anything."

"Not bad," she said.

"Ah, I see," he said sadly. His hat bobbed agreement. "At your age life is merely 'not bad.' I suppose God thinks you should be grateful for this. Well. Let's put Him aside for a moment." There was another long silence much more than just a moment, during which pause she wondered, was this really Chaim sitting across from her saying: *Let's put God aside?* She could feel him staring at her, his gaze like the hour after midnight, a mournful, naked look that made her lose her balance, made her fall slowly toward the center of the earth.

Finally, he sighed. "You know what is my favorite poem in the English language?" He recited it for her: "Sonnet number 73," he announced, as though it were a psalm. " 'Bare ruin'd choirs, where late the sweet birds sang'—that's Shakespeare. Isn't it sad?"

"I guess so." She didn't understand at all, really. Shakespeare. The Torah. Sweet birds and ruined choirs. What did he want from her?

He didn't explain. Instead, he wished her a good evening

as he stood up, then drifted from the room. "You'd better go too, Mireleh. Your counselor will be worried."

But he came back again the next night. Again, he settled himself into the chair across from hers and began speaking as though no time at all had intervened. Perhaps it hadn't. Whatever was on his mind was still there, pressing him, tugging at logic, winding good sense up into a ball—that came unraveled as soon as he opened his mouth to speak: "Do you know 'Ode to a Nightingale'?" he asked her. "Do you know this one by Hopkins?" Again he recited to her, his voice trembling as though *he* were the poet falling over the edge of the world into discovery. She knew this must be another secret he was telling her; something else he believed in besides God and good deeds and the Talmud Torah, a secret she must not divulge to anyone. The verses frightened her. In bed, after lights out, she chanted to herself all of the lines she could remember: "All is changed, changed utterly . . ." . . . "Though worlds of wanwood leafmeal lie . . ." . . . "I have been half in love with easeful Death . . ." —lines that went against what they prayed for each morning: "Blessed art Thou O Lord, King of the Universe, who removest sleep from mine eyes and slumber from mine eyelids, who restorest life to mortal creatures . . ." It was as though she'd seen Chaim wandering through a new landscape—a shadowy glen drenched with mist, moss-covered, hopeless.

By the third night, she was waiting for him, for the conversation that made such confusion, that made her grasp the arms of the chair she sat in, so solid, so wooden. He didn't greet her this time, just picked up the threads of their last talk and began braiding them, rocking back and forth as though praying, as though fevered. He spoke until the dark became as thick as a trance, until she leaned into this, waiting, bending toward him so that their knees brushed under the table, his—rough and woolen, hers—bare and tender, very warm. She wanted him to say something that would break the spell, something ordinary: "That's fine, Mireleh," as he would have done in class, "You're a good girl, my *best* student . . ." But he didn't say a word, and what he didn't say gathered between them.

She tried to think of a question to ask him, a polite question to engage his interest, but the only ones that occurred to her pertained, oddly enough, to his legs. What were they like beneath the fabric of his trousers? Pale? Calloused? Were they as white as his hands? As smooth?

Suddenly, he leaned forward as if he had been speaking to her all this time. "And you know what they say? They say that the Torah was written by men."

"What?" She was still thinking of his legs, white as paper, the black curling hairs.

"By *men*," Chaim repeated. His words rushed through her. He was looking at her earnestly. For a minute she imagined he had heard what she was thinking, that this was the way scholars made passes, by a reference, that he would reach across the table and draw her to him; they would kiss across the table, only the outstretched Talmud between them. Then she realized he wasn't looking at her at all. He was staring the way he did when he was unable to pry himself loose from his holy books and go back into the world. "That's what they think!" he exclaimed. "Can you believe it? By men and not by God. That there isn't any absolute and, therefore, no suffering. It's as simple as that." He laughed, incredulous. "There are no *real* laws. Only *human* laws. Is that ridiculous? We should think like the others, they say. The Chinese. The Hindus. They think it's better to meditate, that it's all right to leave the suffering of this world behind, while we Jews, we *real* Jews," he shook his head, "*we* stay and suffer, throwing our souls into the fire and groaning when we are burned. And then we think we know." He slapped the table. "And then we think we have done our part!" His fist came down.

She tried to make sense of it later. For several days, she added up the evidence, subtracted what didn't fit at all, and divided by what was obscure. On the one hand, there was the lateness of the hour each time they talked; there was his prolonged stay, the personal nature of his questions, his lingering over the poems, his knees brushing hers. On the other hand, there was his unexpected leap to the Hindus, his discussion of suffering, and after his fist struck the table, his apology: "Never mind," he had told her. "It's late and I've probably driven you crazy with all this nonsense. I keep forgetting you're only thirteen. Thirteen in America is an easier age."

Than what? she wondered.

She began to dream of him at night, a dream bathed in different lights. Gold. Dark green. Over and over.

In her dream it was a Sabbath afternoon, dry as ashes, like a day held under a magnifying glass to start a fire. Everyone was resting, tired, quiescent, in their cabins, reading newspapers, or poems or love letters: "My darling, my dearest, sweetheart . . ."

Except her.

She had been walking for hours looking for something, her eyes were fixed on the road. Whatever it was she had lost it. A bracelet? An earring? She was looking for a glimmer in the road as the sun beat down against her back pasting her yellow shirt to her skin with sweat. It was hot. It was so very hot. The road was a dusty glare—empty, forlorn, forever.

Suddenly, she looked up. There were woods! From nowhere, green rushed out to welcome her. On both sides of the road, deep green, the trickling of running water, branches waving. Leaves. Meadows of thriving grass—Queen Anne's Lace and Wild Timothy.

Someone touched her arm. A tall figure dissolving into shadows in the woods. She followed though she couldn't see, could only feel the deep cool breath of the forest soothing her. She walked for hours, until the setting sun came through the trees in threads—orange, green, yellow sprays of light that dazzled her.

Against this light, she saw Chaim. In black as always, long

coat, velvet yarmulke, clasping in one hand his Bible, the special one from Israel with its silver cover beaten to the shape of tablets, a turquoise stone inset for each commandment. In his other hand, a bunch of flowers, white, which he handed to her, then kissed her cheek. A warm, moist kiss. "I like big girls," he whispered.

They lay down together.

He began to kiss her. Lips to her mouth, lips to her hair, to the hollow of her neck, to her lips again until she shivered though his lips were warm like cinnamon or cloves, and smooth as the wood of a spice box. Then stinging. Then sweet. Over and over, his lips, until his hands moved over her too, touching her and stroking her, unbuttoning clothes, sliding them over her skin as swift as angels, (she was naked; he was naked), reading her body with his fingertips, skimming her arms, her legs, her breasts, with hands that were lighter than whispers, than blessings, until light poured over both of them, into them; they were inside it. He was rocking her back and forth; she was curling herself around him.

By day what remained of her dream? He was naked; she was naked. Nakedness in all its conjugations. I was naked, she thought. *We* were naked. Had been naked. Would be. Might.

She watched him in class as he bent over his text and she didn't see his black clothes, she saw his skin, white and smooth and glowing. When he said her name, she could hardly answer. When he moved his fingers over the pages, she flinched. And when he started to sway she felt her body swaying with him; she couldn't bear to look.

(HUNGER)

Precedents for such romances: David and Abishag, Abraham and Keturah, Isaac (he was over forty) and Rebecca, Esau and

Judith, Joseph and Potiphar's wife (sort of), Pablo Picasso and what was her name? his latest wife, someone slim, exquisite; at any rate—a woman to be proud of.

She imagined how it would feel to look like that, as thin and graceful as a lulav—the wand made of palm fronds and myrtle and willow that the men waved on Sukkot, the harvest festival. She pictured herself that way, and then Chaim, taking her by the hand, introducing her proudly: "This is Miriam. She's not only a great reader, she's also very lovely— don't you think?" He would bow to his own words, dazzled, faithful. In private he would touch her as he had in the dream. "I'll tell you a secret, Miriam—for your ears alone. I'll tell you all of my secrets . . ."

But it wasn't just for Chaim she had decided to do this; there were the others as well. How wonderful, she thought, to leap and twirl and float right past them, to rise above their laughter like a wisp of smoke. How wonderful never to hear Barry say again, "Here she comes—THUMP! THUMP!" She would be thin as a switch, that's what she'd be. She'd lash the world with her beauty, make them all run before her— awed, delighted.

If not, then she'd disappear.

She had already given up lunch and sometimes even dinner; it was nothing to give up the rest. The first day she didn't even feel hungry, and whenever she did she drank a cup of tea.

Strangely enough, she seemed to have more energy, not less. Instead of going to meals and activities, she took long walks around the countryside. She hiked through the woods and trekked across pastures so that she could climb to the tops of hills rough with brambles, boulders. She searched for waterfalls, a far-off rushing sound. She made her way through marshes where only algae grew or the stumps of trees pointing upward for no reason.

Each day she dared herself to go a little further. Once it

was a walk to the next camp five miles down the road. The following day she went into town, then another five miles past an abandoned church with a cemetery plot, untended, crooked crosses scattered everywhere as wayward as weeds. On Wednesday it rained and still she hiked all the way to the lake at Equinunk. Because it was pouring no one was there, so she took off her clothes and swam. That was beautiful, floating in the lake, rain washing down through the trees, rattling in the leaves, drenching her face. The sky was iron gray, a ceiling of clouds descending.

But then, everything was more beautiful, she found. No matter what she looked at it seemed clearer as though it lit up under her gaze and announced itself: I am water. A maple tree. The sky. I am stone.

When she grew tired of just walking she began another kind of journey. She watched Chaim. A man mysterious. A man apart.

His curtains were always drawn, but she found some holes in the planking that allowed her to see different parts of the room, though never very much at once. There was the floorboard view and the closet view. There was the view of the bookcase, the view between the bottles and jars in the medicine cabinet. There was a complete view of the ceiling from underneath the bunk, but this required hardships that made it not worthwhile.

She settled for glimpses.

From various angles at various times, she saw his feet in socks, in slippers. She saw a glass of water placed on a chair next to the bed. She saw a handkerchief dropped, a handkerchief plucked up again. A bag of laundry set down in a corner. Often, a broom swept balls of lint and hair into a pile. Pantslegs! Coatsleeves! All of a sudden—his face! as he leaned over to collect the dirt into a dustpan, as beatific as though he were gathering manna in the desert.

What she hoped to discover, she couldn't say precisely, but

every day she made her pilgrimage. Every day she knelt, hidden behind the walls of his cabin, trying her best to peer in.

Some days were more rewarding than others.

On Friday afternoons, for instance, he always polished his shoes so that they would be bright and new for the Sabbath. First he removed the laces, gingerly, as though they were made of silk. Then he took a whisk broom and brushed off all the loose dirt. With a nail file he scraped mud from the welt of the shoe, then poked a pin into all of the perforations. When the shoe was finally ready, he shook the bottle thoroughly, a lurching sound, heavy, like medicine being mixed, then removed the applicator and began painting—first the sides, then the tongues, then the heels. Last, he let them dry for half an hour, then rubbed them with a cloth until they shone.

Another ritual was the preparation of tea which he drank without fail, at 4:30 in the afternoon. He had a small electric kettle stationed above the bookcase, a silver spoon, a china cup.

At night, instead of turning on the overhead light, he burned candles. Miriam could barely see anything then, but the flicker of shadows was enough to intrigue her, the occasional hiss and snap of flame made her shiver.

She shivered, too, the time she spied his slender hand lift a bar of soap from the shelf in the bathroom. As he removed the wrapper her heart leapt up, for had he not closed the cabinet door just then, she would have seen his robe removed as well, would have seen him stepping into the shower.

She never actually discovered anything she hadn't already observed just by sitting on her bench in class with the others. He was meticulous. He was thoughtful. He worshipped the acts of ordinary life the same way he worshipped knowledge. Nothing new.

But here, alone and unguarded in his cabin, he was framed in mystery. From her vantage point, each hint of flesh loomed

statuesque. Each gesture swelled with meaning. The smallest
act became a revelation.

Her devotion turned boundless. From his morning ablu-
tions to his nighttime prayers, she scrutinized every motion.
She was his prophet. In a thick notebook she wrote down all
he did, printing the words in straight, careful lines as though
they were already gospel:

"At dawn, he wakes . . ."

"Late afternoon: he groans and stirs—too much study in
one position? . . ."

"Evening: Walks to the window and stares into the woods
. . . He sighs . . . Eventually, he lets the curtain fall . . ."

"Later: Night has come. He waits for sleep . . ."

She studied these notes daily, searching for patterns. She
asked herself questions: which had more significance—the
order of his actions or the spirit in which they were performed? Could she estimate that spirit? Could she guess the
exact nature of the intention that informed each action?

No more than she could understand Barry, who daily grew
more bold in his troublemaking. She wasn't his only victim
anymore. Perhaps because the end of summer was approach-
ing he began to expand his horizons. From simple pranks
like graffiti and pool dunkings, he leapfrogged to more elaborate crimes—putting paint in the windshield washer of the
camp bus, hiding all the canoe paddles the night before the
big trip down the Delaware, making streamers of the underwear he pirated from the girls' bunks and draping them in
the trees. He stole cake from the baker's closet—poppy seed
strudel and cream puffs and chocolate eclairs, the spoils of
the camp director and the rabbinical staff always kept locked
up against just this kind of invasion. During Saturday morning
services he let loose a collection of live crickets that rasped
and whirred like a demented congregation. He ordered sub-
scriptions to the library from Crusade for Christ, from the
American Nazi Party.

Everyone assumed it was Barry. It had to be him. Who else would have had the nerve? Miriam, herself, saw him one night at the camp junkyard breaking windows with one of the missing canoe paddles. The junkyard was a clearing in the woods at the end of a narrow, rutted road. It was the place where they piled all the ruined furniture—the mildewed mattresses and ravaged sofas, the crippled chairs and tables, as well as things like martyred pianos, mirrors that were cracked, embittered.

Over this ruined kingdom, Barry reigned, forcing homage with beatings, breaking spirits that were already broken. He pounded and whacked and hammered and when he'd shattered every window into a thousand frightened splinters, he began ranting aimlessly, "Take *that* you bastard! Take *that* you bitch!" flailing and thrashing and smiting all of the unfortunate subjects in his path.

If his behavior in class was any measure of his loss of self-control then this was to be expected. Late in the season, he and Chaim had learned a new kind of dance—contorted, ugly. It drove away all peace and quiet, all possibility of reconciliation. By that time, it was just the two of them. As though Miriam were a shade that had been lifted to reveal his true enemy, Barry no longer bothered to tease her. Chaim was the target now, a willing target who bent to receive the arrows.

Each morning Barry strolled in an hour late: "Did I miss anything? Are we still on chapter two? That dumb old stuff? Lord! Will this ever be over?"

Each morning he pushed Chaim a little bit further: "Excuse me, dear Teacher, Moreleh, Your Highness, I mean. That just doesn't make any sense to me. Is that really the translation? Are you certain this is the answer?"

"Why do we have to study this boring garbage anyway?"

"Well that's a silly law if I ever heard one!"

He would goad and bully and impugn and just as Chaim was about to lose his temper, as his face began to redden and his voice began to shake, he would pull back: "Hey. Don't get excited, man. Take it easy, will you? I'm just an ignoramus, a clown, a boy who likes to sow his nasty oats—what do you care? Look. Don't pay any attention to me. I don't mean anything, you know. Not really."

Chaim appeared determined to endure. It was as if by yielding to his anger he would prove himself a liar; he would have to admit that Barry was not a "good boy," someone to "bear with." Setting an example was all that seemed to matter. Ignoring the price, he continued to sidestep these challenges and affronts, to pretend that they were merely bursts of high spirits. Kindling.

She was walking in circles. That's all she knew. She was further than ever from understanding him, from understanding anything. Further still the night she saw this, something so strange she was not convinced afterward that she had seen anything at all.

She had been fasting for a week, for two weeks, more. She had been living on tea and water and water and tea. Many times she had seen things that weren't there. Flocks of birds when she bent over, swarms of ants, dark fountains spouting from the ground. She saw afterimages of what she had just seen on top of what she saw a second later—trees on top of buildings, rocks on top of heads.

At night she couldn't sleep. She closed her eyes and had visions (she couldn't think of another name for what she witnessed). Big dots. Masses of color. Parades of geometric shapes. All the parts of the body, in parts: huge eyes, knees, foreheads, ribs. She saw lines, flashes of lightning; as before —letters from all of the alphabets dancing together without shame.

Still. Even this made a certain kind of sense. What she saw in Chaim's cabin—no sense at all.

First his feet walked over to the bookcase. They walked back to the bed and paused. She heard the sound of sheets of paper being ripped from a book, from many books. This went on for several minutes during which time the feet returned to the bookcase, presumably, to remove more books. Then she saw knees, hands, a pile of paper.

A coat was thrown to the floor, then a shirt. One set of ceremonial fringes. And just when her heart began to pound, thinking she would see him at last, she saw, instead, a pair of hands strike a match, reach forward to the paper; and when it was on fire (blazing in fierce darts of color) he muttered something in Hebrew, the hands came down; she saw him lay himself down, back first, on top of the flames.

What would it have meant provided she had actually seen it? After she awoke from her faint she thought of several possibilities. He had a rare skin disease that was held in check, though not cured, by daily doses of charcoal and extreme heat. He had decided to become a Hindu mystic. He was a magician. A pyromaniac. She was crazy.

She knew she should stop fasting. She told herself that every day. She was becoming very light. Much lighter than anyone else. Invisible. A wraith. It was true. She had found the trick. She could pass right through other people and they didn't even notice her. In turn, the words they spoke passed back through her and on into the night as if through ether. What they meant no longer sank into her flesh and lay there trapped.

But it wasn't only that. It was the strength she had achieved, the concentration. It was feeling that once she gave in, once she gave up just a little bit, she gave it all up; she gave up forever, herself. It was feeling that she might see again the flames in Chaim's cabin, and, like a ledge or a bridge, some wide open space between heights where she might fall, it was daring to see those flames again, wanting to see them rise through his back.

(CHAOS)

But that was cool, wasn't it? Barry had asked the morning they finally finished reading chapter three. Wasn't screwing on the Sabbath a double mitzvah? a double good deed? Wasn't that the law—double your pleasure, double your fun? So why did Adam and Eve get the boot? What was wrong with one little screw?

Smoke hissed from the torches. Her insides hissed with hunger. It was the evening of Tisha B'Av, a fast to commemorate the destruction of the Temple, the precedent (as Chaim called it) for all the two thousand years of suffering that came after.

They were sitting on the floor reading "Lamentations." By the waters of Babylon, remembering Zion.

He was standing, a man apart, a man mysterious, in a corner by the door, swaying as though he had been swaying for days and days and couldn't stop. The torch light swayed with him, and the congregation, sitting in the long shadows on the floor chanted: "From above he hath sent fire into my bones, and it prevaileth against them. He hath spread a net for my feet, he hath turned me back: He hath made me desolate and faint all day . . ."

Barry had disappeared. Three days ago. "Who needs your stupid class?" he had said. "Who needs your fucking Torah?" He had stalked off into the woods and they hadn't seen him since.

At first they thought he was just going in there to sulk, to make a scene. "You were right," they told Chaim. "He was really being a jerk"; and Chaim, still furious, still clutching his Bible, had called after him only faintly: "Sternberg, wait."

He hadn't appeared on the baseball field later that afternoon when they were scheduled to practice, nor had he shown up for dinner; and by the time "lights out" had rolled around, they knew he wasn't fooling. They knew they had to look for him.

But, by then, it was too dark to find anyone. The woods had filled with fog.

They were swaying together and the room was hot. They were packed together on the floor, sitting cross-legged, swaying back and forth, voices rising with the smoke. "I am the man that hath seen affliction by the rod of his wrath. He hath led me and brought me into darkness, but not into light . . ."

"Fool!" At Barry's question, Chaim had banged his book down on the desk. "For *this* you suddenly come alive? For *this* you are suddenly familiar with the text? For *this* you open your foolish mouth?"

Whatever had gotten into Barry had gotten into him as well. He was more than just angry. He was a pillar of smoke, an avenging cloud. "How many times have I asked you, children, and nobody knows? How many times and no one has even bothered to ask me themselves or to look? What's wrong with you? Can't you think? All summer long I ask you questions. All summer long you sit there like death!"

But this was not the worst. He had slammed his Bible down on the desk—a vast sacrilege; in the old days, a sin almost equal to murder. When he saw what he had done, how he had crushed the pages and broken the binding he cried: "Ah, look! Look! Look what you made me do. This is what comes of 'peel-pool'!"

But he hadn't explained.

Instead he had picked up the broken book and cradled it in his hands, turning the pages gently, slowly. Then, sighing a cold, deep sigh, as though he had found an irreparable injury, he had hugged it to his chest and started swaying back and forth chanting in Hebrew, "Forgive me, forgive me, forgive me . . ."

It was the evening of Tisha B'Av, the start of the fast to commemorate the destruction, the suffering, the marching in of armies, the marching out of hope. The fast had begun at

*sundown, would continue until sundown, twenty-four hours.
They would pray tonight and all day tomorrow sitting on the
floor and fasting, praying, sighing.*

Barry had disappeared. Three days ago. "Who needs your
stupid class?" he had said. "Who needs your fucking Torah?"
He had stalked off into the woods and they hadn't seen him
since.

The next morning they had thought they'd find him
crouched behind the door of the bunk waiting for the right
moment to spring out at them. "Ha! Ha! Fooled you assholes.
You gave me up for dead, didn't you? Well, I'll tell you the
truth now. I had a superb night. On the town, of course."
(Though his clothing might be crumpled, though bits of
leaves might cling to his hair.) He had done this twice before,
they said. Each time, they had called his aunt. Each time, they
had called his psychiatrist. "It's just a manipulation," the psychiatrist said. "His version of suicide." And the aunt had said,
"It's true. He runs away all the time. He hides in some safe
place. He makes everyone suffer."

*"But Thou hast utterly rejected us; Thou art very much
wroth against us."*
*Now they were finished with "Lamentations." They were
beginning the long litany of suffering. Leo Goelman stepped
to the podium. "Two specialties we have," he said. "Suffering.
Memory. Of these we have made an art."*
*They were lighting candles—one for each phase of history,
one for each hallmark of the art. The First Temple and the
Second Temple. The exile in Babylon and the exile in Persia.
The Greek occupation and the Roman. The Inquisition and
the Dark Ages. The pogroms and the Cossacks. Treblinka and
Auschwitz and Dachau . . .*

Barry had disappeared, but he couldn't have gone very far.
The evidence was clear. There were signs of him everywhere.

Books pulled from their shelves. Benches overturned in the classrooms. Messages on the library wall.

And Chaim had not been in his cabin, had not been there for three days. There had been no shoes on the floor, no fringes, no pale white hand reaching toward her in the cabinet. She had waited for him and waited, had hoped he might be sitting there in the dark, within the curtains, clutching a pile of paper, maybe singing softly or muttering or clasping his hands together and curling himself up in prayer.

Barry had disappeared, but there were signs of him everywhere. In the prayer books that were stolen, in the candlesticks that had fallen down, in the pages torn from books and scattered in the grass, in the things that were missing— scarves, rings, bracelets, (handed back, lost somewhere). Some even said in the weeping at night in the cabins (from the upper bunks, from the lower).
Even here there were signs. The torches burned brightly. They swayed. She was hungry.

She had waited until after dark, herself, curled up amid the pine needles, the weeds and dry sticks, hungry and thirsty, until finally, when the first damp fog of evening began to seep into her skin, she felt she couldn't wait another minute longer. She had crept up the stairs, had nudged the door open, found a room completely empty. There had been no clothes in the closet, no books on the shelves, and, except for an old brown suitcase which stood by the door, there was only a dustpan propped against one wall, the faint smell of something burnt.

Smoke rose. Shadows rose. She could feel herself rising with them, lighter than air, so faint she felt like vapor.

Barry had disappeared. Chaim had gone after him. She had gone after Chaim.

All day long, on the hottest day of summer, she had walked. Through pine forests, through stands of maple, through shrubs matted with vines and creepers. There was no path, but she kept on going, drifting along in a cloud of hunger. Every time she moved, a trail of sound and light churned inside her, turning to heat and dust, a dry aching thirst that caked her throat, that made her lean against a tree and gasp.

But even this was not the worst, that she had walked until late afternoon, until her thirst was so great that it pushed her through the underbrush to a stream where she drank and drank and drank. Even this was not the worst, that when her thirst stopped, when the roaring stopped in her ears, she had heard weeping, had looked up and seen a man in black sprawled on the ground weeping and weeping and weeping. Nor even this. She hadn't gone to him and caressed him. She hadn't knelt and kissed him; nor had he, in his turn, kissed her, had not said "I like big girls," had not held her until the sun came through the trees in threads: orange, yellow, green sprays of light.

It was this—what he *did* say. "You know what is 'peel-pool,' Mireleh? I'll tell you what it really is. Not just the dictionary definition—*casuistry*, the athletic misinterpretation of words, in a quiet room filled with dusty old books . . ."

He had made her sit down beside him. He had held her hand.

"Listen. It was many years ago, not here, but in a village far away. There was a boy just about your age. It was going to be his Bar Mitzvah. He was coming of age. He was going to know what there was to know—about the world, about himself, and his family was very happy, very excited; or they would have been excited. But this was a bad time. A bad place. There was no Torah then. It was forbidden, strictly forbidden.

"The boy's father was a rabbi, the head of a yeshiva until they closed them down. After that, he was a rabbi in secret. He had hidden the Torahs, every single one of them. The penalty for this was death. For being a Jew. They were burning all the Torahs, burning the yeshivot; they were marching us all away.

"Every day whoever wanted to, whoever was brave enough, whoever was left, would slip out of their houses, go to this secret place to pray."

"And the Bar Mitzvah?" she had asked, though she already knew the answer. "Did he have it?"

He shook his head. "When they found the Torahs they would burn them. In a heap they would pile them in the street along with other holy books, law books, whatever they found that looked sacred. They would pour kerosene on top and set them on fire, let them burn into ashes. There were some Jews who tried to rescue them. There were some who believed in Kiddush HaShem, the commandment of martyrdom for God, for His word, a commandment outweighing all the others, but *never* to be invoked, some said. Others, like my father, threw themselves onto the flames."

"But did you—"

"I, Mireleh? Not I. Not then."

And that was not the worst. It was not only that, but this: Barry never knew when to stop. "Sure," he had said as Chaim rocked back and forth with the ruined book. "Sure, man!" He had raised his arms and held out both hands in benediction. "We forgive you—no problem. No fucking problem. Forgiveness, *free and complete*. Don't give it another thought."

Chaim had stopped swaying. He had set the book down on the table carefully, very accurately, had set it down in some precise diagram that only he could see of a Bible set down in anger. Then, as if it were also part of the same diagram, one which told him how to convert thought into motion, rage into sound, he had slapped Barry across the face, had shouted: "*You* forgive *me*? *You* forgive *me*? To whom do you think you're speaking? To some goniff? To the devil? Get out of here you little bastard!"

And this. Finally there was this: "Bergen Belsen, Madanek, Theresienstadt . . ." They were still listing, matching up the horrors with the lights. Barry still hadn't come back. She was still hungry. In his corner, Chaim was still swaying, back and forth, back and forth, Baruch HaShem, amen v'amen.

Behind him, the torches swayed, glowing. And for a moment, as he bent over his text, she didn't see clothes, but flesh, saw the pale skin of his back, on either side of his spine, saw letters (the ten commandments? the ten plagues?); she saw the torches burning behind all of them, saw all of them, like Barry, alone in the woods in the dark.

Alexandra J. Wall

The Way "We" Were

I was sitting at an off-campus bar with my friend Samantha. With my driver's license declaring that I was just a few months past twenty-one, even sitting on a barstool sipping a beer had a thrill. Though I was officially legal, I still had the uneasy feeling that any minute a bouncer might eject me.

"Howyadoin' this evening, ladieez?" a guy sitting a few stools down from us begged for attention. A dirty blond with a Marine-inspired flattop and a hot pink polo shirt, not like the usual hippie-type college students I was used to. When we ignored him, he got up and moved onto the stool right next to mine, brushing his leg up against me.

This is why my parents don't like me hanging out in bars. I crossed my right leg over my left to avoid him and began listening to the details of Samantha's last date, a guy that she met in typical Samantha fashion, at the grocery store. But in spite of the girl talk we were so involved in, Mr. Flattop was desperate to avoid drinking alone. He looked for a way in.

"Have you ladies seen this band before?" Mr. polo shirt slurred loudly over the guitar soloist.

"Yeah, they're okay," said Samantha without enthusiasm. We were trapped. Bob, he said his name was, flexed his Nautilus-trained biceps and moved in for the kill.

"You know I used to work in the music business down in L.A.," he said, name-dropping anyone we might know or be impressed by. He was boring and my mind wandered away. . . . Then my mind snapped clearly back into focus.

". . . And you know how Jews are," he was saying.

"Excuse me?" I said. Sam nervously shot me a quick sideways glance.

"You know, the Jews. They're everywhere in the music industry, in movies, television. They're everywhere."

My face flushed, from more than the beer.

"Hey . . . you're Jewish, aren't you? I knew you were! I could tell by your nose! You look just like Barbra Streisand!"

I should have seen it coming, but then again I never do. I've been hearing those words forever, and they always sting. Like a movie playing in my head, I faded out, back into the world of childhood . . .

"Mommy, do I look like Barbra Streisand?"

"No, don't be silly. Her nose is much bigger than yours."

But as often as I asked, my mother's soothing words never convinced me. Everyone always said I looked just like Barbra. After school I would go to my mother's record collection in the family room, always stopping at the gray greatest-hits collection. Barbra's tight, frizzy curls and infamous nose were in profile. Standing on a chair, I held it up to the bathroom mirror, studying my own face closely. Nope, no Streisand. I saw a blond-haired, green-eyed little girl, with a normal nose. Barbra's nose dominated her face, making the rest of her features insignificant. Surely I didn't look like that, a woman whose nose took over her face.

In fact, it was more that that. Barbra Streisand's looks were so obviously Jewish to me, when I wanted so desperately to look like everyone else. At my school there were only a few of us. During rehearsal for the third-grade Christmas show, set against a winter scene, two of the teachers sat in the auditorium. "Doesn't she look just like Barbra?" I heard one of them whisper. They meant it as a compliment, but I wanted to cry. I wanted to blend in with the other snowflakes, but instead I was doomed to look like Barbra, to *be* like Barbra. What could be worse than a Jewish snowflake?

I faded in, back to the bar to find Bob trying to excuse his bad manners.

"Don't be offended! I dated a Jewish girl for three years," he was saying. "You should go into business or something because I *know* . . . the Jews are really good in the business world. It's in your blood, you know. You should take advantage of it!"

"In my blood?" Quick repartee was beyond me now. Surely Barbra would have had a ready answer, a cutting jab. Surely she could dazzle this guy to speechlessness, just as she could wow those audiences in Vegas. I began to wonder: what would the Funny Girl do?

"Yeah, you know, just like the blacks are natural athletes, it's in the blood," he continued. "You should be proud of what you are."

I glanced up weakly at Sam, hoping she would come to my rescue. Sam had disappeared, but in her place was Barbra, fully decked out in a low-cut black evening gown, as if she were ready to perform on stage.

She nodded her head in greeting, but words escaped me. I studied her face, just like I used to when it was on the album cover. She had shiny straight hair, French-manicured nails and that same nose, but somehow it didn't look as bad as I'd remembered. She was a vision of glamour and poise and success. And I was a mess.

"Let's help this poor man rethink his position," Barbra said, with a flip of that shiny hair. "Tell him where he can go." I looked around me, at the couples flirting or playing pool. They were all too busy drinking to pay attention.

"I'm very proud of what I am, believe me," I said suddenly out loud. "And besides, I'd rather look like Barbra than look like you."

"Geez," Bob said, shot me a look and then got up and left.

"Where'd that come from?" asked Samantha, who suddenly reappeared.

"I got inspired. Was I too rude?"

"No way. Perfect."

As we left the bar, I could swear I heard the sounds of "Evergreen" in the air.

Hindi Brooks

The Wandering Jewess—20th-Century Style

The first time I made a stab at independence was when I was still in Detroit, and a student at Wayne University (now Wayne State University). My sociology professor would listen to my tales of woe about being a prisoner at home, and warn me that freedom can be a very lonely thing. But his was a different kind of freedom. His wife had recently left him. Mine was to be a freedom of beginnings, not endings.

By the middle of my sophomore year, I'd reached an impasse with my parents about my choice of friends and career, where I went and when I went there, and almost everything else I did or did not do. I had to get out on my own. So one day I packed a bag and my prize possession, a portable typewriter, and I moved into one of the old mansions across the street from campus that had been converted into rooming houses.

That night I opened my window to breathe in my freedom, feeling, I must admit, just the slightest bit apprehensive. There, facing me, not more than five feet away, was my sociology professor, looking out of the window in his rooming house . . . and well into the nightly drunk that his students all gossiped about.

"You see," he said across the night air. "It's a lonely thing, freedom."

I didn't really have a chance to find out for myself then because the next day my father marched into the rooming house with a military air quite foreign to him, and schlepped me home, suitcase, typewriter and all.

For a solid week I got "It's a shandeh for the neighbors!"

"It's ridiculous to spend money on a room, when you live a twenty-minute bus ride from school!"

"You can't live alone by the schvartzes!"

I knew there was no use debating those issues. I'd tried many times.

I also didn't have an adequate answer for "If you really wanted to leave home, why did you write your new address on the note?"

"I didn't want to worry you" came out rather limply, because I wasn't sure that it was the entire truth.

But, by the end of the semester, I really was ready to leave. And obviously, I could only do it by moving out of town. I just had to convince my folks that I wouldn't end up dead or in jail or worse. And I thought I knew how. They'd been right about one thing—that one day I'd be glad I went to Sunday School. This was that day. I was ready for them.

"Nice Jewish people don't go off by themselves who knows where."

"Abraham didn't go off who knows where? Lot didn't go?" And more important to this debate: "Lot's wife didn't go?"

A mistake. I knew the retort before Ma said it: "And she turned into a pillar of salt."

But I topped that: "Because she looked back!"

I thought I had them. Until the new round started.

"You're only twenty years old."

"You were sixteen."

"We were getting married."

Because they'd both been sixteen when they married, I was already over the hill. I sidestepped the new argument.

"You had to cross an ocean to get married?"

"We had to get away from the pogroms."

"Me, too, Pa."

"You have a pogrom here?"

"Well, Ma, a different kind of pogrom."

"What kind of pogrom? People spit on you in the street here? Gonuvim break your windows? Cossacks ride their horses over you?"

"Parents kidnap you."

I was challenging Pa's paternal rights. It led to a full-blown lecture—my parents finishing each other's sentences.

"For two thousand years we moved around looking for what you have now. A place. A home. Around the world, we went. A million miles we went. A million? A billion. For you. So you shouldn't have to do it. So you should stay put somewhere you should be safe, you should be free."

Ah, the magic word! "Me, too, Pa. I have to be free."

"You're not free here? You should never know what it means, not free."

"I know, Ma. It means not being able to live the way you want to live. Find the place, the home, that's right for you. Do the things you want to do."

"You're doing what you want to do. You're going to college." I could hear the familiar smirk in Pa's voice.

And Ma added her usual addendum, "Even though men don't like women to be so smart."

My folks, who had dragged my two brothers, kicking and screaming, into college, didn't believe women should have too much education.

"And now, right in the middle, you want to quit?"

"I want to learn how to be a radio writer. And a movie writer. And they don't teach that in Detroit."

I got the expected response from Ma. "Men don't marry women who write. Women who write live in attics and starve to death."

"Not in Los Angeles."

I'd been preparing for this. I pulled out my stash of *Writers Guild Journals* and pointed out the underlined women writers' names.

Pa was only mildly impressed. "Not very many of them."

"With me there'll be one more."

Ma was less impressed. "But how many are married?"

"With me there, at least one. I promise on Bubba Blima's, ole v'sholem, grave."

They weren't convinced, but the vow made it sound like a possibility. And since I was on the verge of becoming "an old maid," it was worth considering. While they considered, I packed.

All the way to the Greyhound Bus station in downtown Detroit, Ma waved clippings about crime from the Los Angeles papers at me. Pa kept trying to take my suitcase from my hand. But I had the typewriter, my bus ticket and sixty dollars wrapped in a hankie and stuck into my bra because Ma had done it that way when she left Poland, and it avoided another argument.

My friends were also there, with the farewell present they'd chipped in to buy me—a copy of Eric Bentley's *Writing for Radio.*

And me? And I was so terrified that if none of them had been there, I might have chickened out. But with Ma and Pa begging me to stay and my friends applauding me for going, I couldn't turn back.

The trip took three and a half very long days. In Chicago, my sixty dollars slipped into my cleavage, making me look as if I had three breasts until a three year old pointed it out to the whole bus and I shoved it back into place. In St. Louis, the straps that had held my suitcase shut all through Europe for my father twenty-five years earlier, broke open. In Texas, a cowboy in a hair shirt sat beside my sleeveless arm and rubbed it raw. And I was more certain with each passing mile that I'd made a dreadful mistake. But even more certain that I was not going to turn into a pillar of salt.

By the time we reached the Greyhound station in downtown Los Angeles, I was so exhausted that it took the driver and two porters to shlep me off the bus. At one o'clock in the morning, I staggered into a strange city, full of strange people, with a roped-up suitcase, a suddenly heavier typewriter and sixty dollars back in my cleavage.

But I was here. I was in Los Angeles. My career was just around the corner. And I was free!

And terribly, terribly lonely.

Jori Ranhand

Desert Song

Menstrual cramps prove it. G-d is a woman. Who else but a jealous Woman with G-d powers would even think of such a punishment? G-d is always just and jealous. I know all about G-d. She's a nice Jewish girl who lives in the north of Israel. I swear I met her there. I went to Israel to find G-d, and I did, on a kibbutz bounded by Akko, Haifa, and the sea.

G-d, who goes by the name of Yael, put me in the avocado fields my first morning, starting at four A.M.

"I am the field manager," she told me as we rode out on the tractor. "I decide all the work people do, planting, pulling weeds, picking. Or when a field needs rest, I decide. I am G-d in the fields."

"I always knew G-d was a woman," I told her. Ah, laughter.

She sent me out with two English guys to add white plastic sprinklers at intervals along all that black rubber tubing by the avocado plants. Our pipe in the desert, she called it. Israeli irrigation. My hands blistered from the work, my back blistered from the sun, my brain went soft, and blue whales spouted before my eyes. This is fun. I did it for a week.

The hard job was pulling weeds in the cotton fields. Jewish weeds in Israeli soil? It takes a Jew. They don't use hoes in Israel, too wimpy. They use their hands. I never failed to pull up a weed. Not one of them could resist a tyrant like me. I planted my feet on either side of the weed, a colossus of weeds, grabbed low, and hollered, "Jew. Yid. Semite." Yank. They came up fighting, landing me on my ass half the time, but I won. I was sent out to the cotton every morning, at four in the morning, until it was done. G-d, that is, Yael, worked with me, laughing at me the whole time. Once, she found a hoe rusting in the soil. She hoed and I heaved. We were the new comedy team, heave-ho. That joke is as old as Adam and Heave.

In August, after the cotton, I was given an easy job, washing glasses in the moadon, the kibbutz equivalent of a coffeehouse. They also served tea, lemonade, and as much gossip as we could handle. We, the volunteers, and they, the ulpanists, gossiped the most. We did it separately from them, and the kibbutzniks did it separately from all of us. They huddled in corners, far away from us, voraciously reading the Hebrew newspapers and not talking to us outsiders, suspicious even of those of us who could speak Hebrew. We weren't staying, not on this kibbutz, possibly not in Israel, better not to get too attached to us. Better not to think about or remember the possibilities of an easier life off the kibbutz, outside of Israel. I absorbed all this from Yael. We struggled along together with my bat mitzvah-lesson Hebrew and her high school English.

The true end of the harvest was marked for me by a week of assignments in the kitchen. During the height of the picking and weeding season, I had been a vital force. Now it was the kitchen and the factory for all my energy. Somehow, peeling onions and stacking cardboard boxes weren't quite the same as pulling feisty Jewish weeds out of Israeli soil, but Yael was G-d in the kitchen, after the harvest. Not even peeling onions on the back porch by the garbage heap kept me safe from her teasing. She would come out and watch me shedding onion tears.

"Don't cry, Yehudit," she told me all too often, "you don't hurt the onions."

"Yael, I pulled weeds with you for almost an entire summer. Are you really going to stand there and tease me now, with a knife in my hand?"

"You know all your onion peels are going to end up in that lovely green Dumpster you are so fond of sitting near. That garbage will go on the avocados, and grow killer weeds in the cotton, just for you, so you must stay."

"I know, all Jews should live in Israel."

"So you'll join the ulpan, it starts again soon. Go talk to Ahuvah. You'll have to learn when you go in the army anyway. If you live in Israel, you go in the army," she reminded me.

"What rank were you?"

"Sergeant."

So G-d created the Women's Army, too. What else could I do? G-d had spoken. I joined the ulpan, which meant giving over five and a half months of my life to the study of Hebrew. Classes began with Lily at six A.M. She then had until eleven o'clock to fill our sun-baked, sleep-glazed brains with new words and grammar. Actually, the second half of the class was devoted to conversation, an impossibility to the stupid sleepy, that is, me. I never believed, in class, that I got it.

It was only because I put into Akko regularly that I discovered I might actually be catching on. Cruising the aisles of the supermarket was a favorite pastime of us starved Americans, unused to the sparse, mostly vegetarian diet, and to the lack of readily available bottles of Coke. Going into town was a desperate need. When the labels started resolving themselves into words that made sense and had meaning together, well, my shock was great. Declining to conjugate in class was no longer feasible. My compatriot ulpan dwellers caught me understanding street signs. Too bad. I preferred the stupid look.

G-d was glad I was learning Hebrew. So were my Israeli cousins, who live on Beit Herut, a small moshav near Tel Aviv. They wanted me to live in Israel, as they had since 1947, as their three children and ever-increasing number of grand-

children do. Purely delightful was my own growing ability to
converse with my two-year-old cousin, Matan-el. I was ready
to stay. Almost.

My Jewish roots thirsted for sand, but I couldn't take the
heat. I was glad when the bronze sky became that Mediterranean azure blue, and the swishing rains came. My parched
skin drank it in like Nivea cream. My G-d friend shivered and
wore a parka in fifty-degree weather, while I pranced around
in shorts, T-shirts, no socks. G-d was amazed.

By the time the rains came and the ulpan ended, I had
been on the kibbutz for nearly a year, had hardly been off it.
I was getting restless. To relieve my cabin fever, I headed for
London, where I could be rained on continuously, abuse my
reason with gallons of Coke, eat meat. As a native New
Yorker, I needed greater doses of bright lights and promises
than even Tel Aviv could offer me.

I really meant to get back to Israel. That was five years ago.
I chose the Diaspora because it made no demands on me. I
need not serve in the army, speak Hebrew all the time, or
become a vegetarian. Nor do I get my exercise wrestling with
Goliath weeds in a cotton field. I have puny courage, ninety-
eight-pound moral muscles. I don't deserve Israeli sand in my
face.

Now, when the harvest rains swish against my New York
window pane, watering my Queens interior gardens, I remember how it felt, once, against my legs, when I lived in
Israel. The Diaspora needs Jews, too, I told myself, but I knew
I was lying.

So, I listen to the Israeli tapes my cousins gave me. My
favorite song title means "This Rain." I am writing, with my
life, my own desert song. As for G-d, well, she keeps sending
me menstrual cramps and letters in Hebrew asking me to
come back and help her build that pipe in the desert. Her
plea adds words to my lament.

Dina Elenbogen

The One Who Receives

A few years ago, while I was just beginning to study Kabbalah, I fell in love. A man in my Hebrew class, it turned out, took the same road to school. We lived one block apart in a run-down Chicago neighborhood on the edge of Lake Michigan. We had met before but always at the wrong time, the wrong place. Now we drove together. We both loved Hebrew but couldn't master the future tense. We both loved Israel but couldn't commit to living there. One night in class we were talking about religious Jews and arranged marriages. He said, "By the time we get married we have known so many people. They only know the one they marry—for life." I too envied the ideal of loving only one person. After he stopped speaking we looked at each other for a long time. Rain began to fall hard outside the classroom window. Everyone else seemed to vanish except for the two of us. I blushed and then told him in Hebrew, "The rain falls hard." He blushed and smiled. After he had finished talking about arranged marriages I knew that I could love him. This frightened me because he was living with another woman. Yet I looked at his face and imagined it next to me when I gave birth.

That spring I was on fire. Something awoke in me after a long, dormant winter of watching the Gulf War on TV and slipping on ice on my way home from teaching poetry. On Monday nights I sat in a room filled with Jews of all ages, conjugating Hebrew verbs, talking about the war. On Tuesdays I sat around a long table at the Chabad House where the rabbi spoke of Kabbalah. He described love as knowing G-d; he spoke of revelation and concealment. He said the thirty-nine scuds that had fallen on Israel and directly killed no one were the thirty-nine lashes that had been described in the Zohar as arriving just before the Messiah.

The rabbi's words followed me wherever I went; they gave me an energy I had not known before. Everything around me felt richer and deeper: colors, textures, the smell of the mint leaves I brought to the man in my Hebrew class. When I was alone I sang prayers and the new rock-and-roll songs my students taught me at the top of my lungs.

After a particular day of struggling with a poem about pomegranates I attended the rabbi's lecture on creativity. He said that sometimes we struggle with something—figuring out a problem, painting the perfect portrait—and we reach the highest rung in the ladders of our own minds. When we give up, something else takes over—a higher power—a deeper knowledge than ourselves—and we are able to finish our task. I listened in fascination because that is how my poems were being written that spring. My poems were spilling out red with pomegranates and mulberries. My poems were on fire.

Sometimes when the rabbi spoke I did not write down his words, I didn't exactly listen, but the rhythm of his voice would flow through me. My eyes wandered to the books on his shelves, the gold lettering of his Zohar, and I would see the deep brown eyes of the man in my Hebrew class, the eyes I had begun to long for.

The Monday after we had watched the rain it was his turn to drive to Hebrew class. I saw a car waiting outside ten minutes early. I thought he couldn't wait to see me either and as I ran down the steps of my apartment I shouted to the air—I love you too—. It was not him in the car. It was an-

other man waiting for another woman. He didn't show up
that night. He was in New Orleans, I found out later, and he
had left my number at home. My heart was broken. After that
we drove together every week. In the car, through the darkness of late March, we spoke about Israel and separation. We
did not speak of love.

I held this love in because I didn't know how it would be
received by him. I held this love in until I couldn't anymore,
until pieces of it spilled over like light emanating from a broken vessel. One night after class, after I parked my car and
we stood under the viaduct where we were to turn down
different roads—he to his girlfriend, me to my empty
apartment—we started leaning toward each other. I kissed
him first, quickly, then turned away. The light from the street
lamps spilled from our eyes. We hesitated, about to turn back
toward each other but instead we took our different paths.
When I got home I wrote in my journal: *Do we stop here
because we can go no further or because we begin to touch
something, which if ever lost, would prevent us from returning
to any knowable place.*

The next week he turned off his ignition when it was time
to drop me off. He spoke about his imminent breakup with
his girlfriend because of their religious differences and about
the peace conference we would both be attending in Jerusalem that summer. He asked me to join him in the desert.
When I told him I would not get involved with anyone again
until I knew it was "the one" he kissed me deeply. I threw
my Hebrew book and my keys on the floor of his car. I held
his face in my hands and we kissed and touched for a long
time. I kept smiling at him thinking how long it had been
since I told the truth.

The next Monday we did not go to class. He walked over
with his dog on a leash and we began kissing again before
he was in the door. I did not want to let go of him and when
I finally did, after we lay on the couch together for a long

time, I said, "I am afraid." When he asked me why, I had no words. When he left, we agreed to spend that next Sabbath together; his girlfriend would be out of town.

On Tuesday the rabbi read from the Zohar while the reflection of the late April sun sank into Lake Michigan. *"The mystery of the Sabbath, the Sabbath . . . that unites itself through the mystery of the One . . . And as they unite above, so also do they unite below in the mystery of oneness, in order that the oneness above be a reflection of the oneness below . . ."*

"You are so far away," he said sitting across a wide table from me at our first Sabbath together. In my apartment we blessed the candles, the wine and the bread. We spoke of the years we'd lived in Israel, about the land, the people we loved, the books we'd read. When I could not speak, the light radiating from his eyes flushed my skin, I cleared the table. He followed me into the corner of the kitchen looking deeply into my eyes; he captured me and held me in his kisses. We leaned against a wall and I felt the wall tumble down and I knew the only place I'd fall was into him; I let myself fall.

Afterward we spoke about love and G-d and showed each other the scars on our bodies. He carried me, naked, in front of my north window so the entire city could see us. "I am so tired of hiding," he said. For hours he had become the only one I had ever known. But he was not mine.

Over the days that followed the marks he had made on my neck faded from red to pink to mauve. I waited for him to receive the courage to break up with his girlfriend and then I waited for her to move out. I waited in vain for my fear to pass.

The day he finally broke up with her, a woman had arrived at his architect office with a four-volume set of the Zohar. She was of Moroccan descent and told him that if he did not buy it, there could be another Holocaust. He laughed at her, although he was reading Chaim Kaplin's *Warsaw Diary* and his girlfriend had accused him of being obsessed with the Holocaust. "How can I read the Zohar if I don't understand Aramaic?" he asked this strange visitor.

"Just point to any passage in the book and the words will seep into you."

"But I can't use the Zohar if I don't understand it."

"You don't know how an aspirin works and yet you still use it for your headache."

He shrugged his shoulders and convinced her to lend him the first volume so he could test it out before committing to buying the whole set. At the end of the day he carried it onto the El with him. He opened the book in the middle, pointed to a sentence and read the Hebrew letters of the Aramaic words—understanding nothing. He walked into his apartment where his girlfriend was sitting in front of the TV and told her that it was over. They had been fighting bitterly for weeks. She accused him of having a lover. He denied it. He told her they had no future.

He came to my apartment later that week with toothpaste still on his lips and the Zohar under his arm when he told me the story of their breakup. He said the book had instructed him to break the bond with her that moment. She began throwing pots of geraniums and vases out the window. All night glass broke in the alley between our two homes.

But something had broken in him. We hardly touched anymore. When she finally moved out and returned to Los Angeles, I knew from the pain in his voice that he still loved her. We decided not to share a room in Jerusalem. We both attended the peace conference.

I had wanted to reveal myself to him in the desert, to give him everything I still held back. And I knew he could love any number of people; he was afraid to be alone. We never entered the desert together. We stayed instead in the city of concealment where the June sun smoldered over Jerusalem stone, where the fire that burned in me took on the bitter taste of anger. I lost him in Israel to the gazes of unencumbered women.

How could someone I love leave me alone at the center of a desert? Martin Buber wrote about the crucial moment of connection, about losing that moment and losing something forever. Which was the crucial moment? When I shouted to the air I love you?

Susan Merson

Blood in the Sand

On the Upper West Side of Manhattan in the 1970s, the Vietnam War was raging. It raged in the rice paddies of Southeast Asia and in the beds and brains of the liberated, smart kids. There were boys and there were girls. There was the war and there was sex. There were Catholics who dove into the fray and fretted about morality and murder and there were a lot of Jews who talked about it.

At first, I chose a chosen boy. A med student, long, lean, bespectacled and sucking a pretentious meerschaum pipe. We talked about the war and its woundings. Or rather he talked and I crocheted yarmulkes for the Black Panthers. And when he was finished (and my yarmulkes sold to SDS), I was to be ready. I was to make the ultimate sacrifice for the Jews. To give or get out. I laughed. Such tzedakah could not come from the heart. He raged. I could not take my place as a dutiful daughter of Judah. I hadn't the proper humility, respect. I had no respect for the Jews. I fled. Feeling the shards of Kristallnacht hurled at me from my fellow inmate, leaping over chasms and past barricades, I ran and found myself far away from home and then, finally, at peace. Happy in my anonymity.

I hid from the Jews in the priestly robes of Manhattan. My

girlfriend had dallied at a monastery before she found her
real God and so her pals were the holy men who questioned
and wrestled with Yahweh on a daily basis. I was introduced.
The Jewess. I was a gift and they lifted their eyes to the heavens. My Jewish breasts were breasts that had erupted before
the Virgin and my Jewish eyes had seen the miracle of the
coming of the law. I was permission for flesh and spirit to
become one. I was valued.

While the Jews shouted and preened, the Catholics quietly
got it done. They poured blood over draft files. They resisted
the war with measured, consistent, civil disobedience. They
didn't need to howl their convictions or defecate in paper
bags on Seventh Avenue like Jerry Rubin and his pals. They
needed only to look to the example of Jesus and his disciples
and they resisted quietly. Firmly. Without sweat. With a lather
of holiness. It was irresistible.

I ministered to them—Matthew, Mark, John, and Bill. I met
them at the rallies. For the Harrisburg 8, the Camden 9, the
Baltimore 14. On trial for their obedience to a higher law.
Lost in their holy robes, their souls on the rack, their bodies
picked up the scent of my curiosity. We smiled in shy recognition and set about the task of making holy our desires.

These men were healing the earth's woes. They were fighting for farmworkers. And making soup in the Bronx before
the homeless had a name. And organizing tenants rights. And
forgetting their rosaries on the kitchen sinks. They stumbled
back to their rooms at night and then fought the wrath of the
bishop in a nightmare forced by their dreams. Christ did not
embrace them in his name. I did.

And soothed their woes. And spoke of Teilhard de Chardin
and Edith Stein and Simone Weil. The mystics of the flesh.
And wept over Merton's fate, the charged visionary volted
into heaven by an electric fan. And asked for wonder from
Heschel and forgiveness from the poetry of the Berrigans. We
shared our souls. They taught me their holiness and then, one
by one, I taught them mine.

First, Frederick. His member, flaccid at our encounter,

flapped in the wind, and he fled tearful from the collar. Forever erect, he flies planes at Newark, never to be earthbound again. Then, Conlan. He fancied boys, truly, and yet landed my pudding as a trampoline from which to vault into the gay political world that predated AIDS. And Billy-boy, the Irish drinker with rotten teeth, felt my lips next to his tongue, too, but chose a cat and an upstate parish and never again the feel of a woman's warm bottom. Next came Kenny, not yet promised to God, but tall and dumb and a heartthrob for the schoolgirls. And then Seth, who still rots his days away in a Mexican jail for leaving marijuana in his pocket when he went to prison to visit his sister. She was stuck with the senoritas for smuggling cocaine out of the country in a plastic bag thrust cozily into her vagina. I sought the holy ones but seeking does not always yield a find.

Until there was Jake, the clown. A fool for God. He traveled the world writing sound poems about Christ and folded origami for Indian children on reservations and ended up roadkill on an Arizona highway neither priest nor fool, just dead.

Jake christened me the goddess of his deliverance. He took my long chestnut hair and wrapped it around his body and danced with me on a waterbed with mirrors in an apartment where the cat litter needed changing and Corita's prints screamed deliverance to the faithful. He smoked the peace pipe of love with my ancient eyes and I opened before him like a flower.

His memory of woman was ancient and rusty. Eighteen years before he had fumbled in the balcony with Melody O'Connor. Now, at twice that time, he acted the puppy dog when it came to the actual dig and delve of it all. But, then, he sang praises of Hosanna! Wept ecstasies of devotion as the spirit moved from his body to mine! And we conjured Rebecca and Sara and Judith and Deborah and anyone else we felt could teach him the soft underside of God's art. He held me in his sway. "How goodly are thy tents, O Jacob?" As the sheets floated to the ceiling and the pillows exploded feather by feather both within and without.

And we returned to the college where the priests slept and ate and drank scotch and felt the eyeburn of the uninitiated and he thought of being a rabbi and I a sex slave for Christ.

"Oh Susanna," he called to me. "Let not the natives take you to their fires. Let your song be my song and we will lift our hearts to the skies."

Jake wanted me to travel his road with him. A Jewess in his caravan would make holy the celibate journey of his time. But I refused his plea. I was of the meadows, not the sand dunes, the river wild, not the stars. And he left, weeping pussy willows of despair that carefully led a trail that I could—would I?—follow for his good.

The tire tracks faded in the sand. I sat back and watched the Catholic boys adore my soft brown skin and the hair that swept and hid my secrets. I was fascinated with being the other, coming from a world in which I had always been desperately the same. I waited for them to come and lay their troth at my altar and then, feeling time slapping rudely at my buttocks, I deigned to dance with them less and less.

The years tumbled on. And life forced leather over soft places. And the womb began to feel like a sperm bank. And the skin lost its smoothness and became needles on toast.

I abandoned my goddess. Tucked her tired into the trundle beds of the Upper West Side. She sleeps there, comatose, still, while I, like the citrus fruit ripened, become harder and harder, still sporting the deceptive colors of youth.

I've gone to the nunnery for a stay with the Jews.

I think of Jake lying in the wind with the coyotes and now I rest only in the memory of the sandstorm, the memory of the blood and the riot of deliverance in which we once gave suck.

Otherwise, I wait for the pogrom.

Allegra Goodman

Onionskin

DR. FRIEDELL,

This is to apologize if I offended you in class a few weeks ago, though I realize you probably forgot the whole thing by now. I was the one who stood up and said Fuck Augustine. What I meant was I didn't take the class to read him, I took it to learn about religion—God, prayer, ritual, the Madonna mother-goddess figure, forgiveness, miracles, sin, abortion, death, the big moral concepts. Because obviously I am not eighteen and I work, so school is not an academic exercise for me, and not just me, as I'm sure you'd realize if you looked around the room one of these days and saw there are thirty and forty-year-olds and some a lot older than you are in the class—the point is, when you've been through marriage, kids, jobs, welfare, and the whole gamut and you come back to school you're ready for the real thing, and as far as I'm concerned Augustine's Conception of the Soul or whatever is not it. What is "it"? you're asking—well, that's what I came to find out, so you tell me. Obviously what you are paid for is to deal with the big religious issues and you are not dealing with them, which is what I was trying to point out when I made that remark in class, which I apologize for tone-wise but not for the feelings behind it.

232

My feelings still are that basically as a "mature student" I was supposed to feel grateful that the University of Hawaii let me in or gave me a second chance on life or whatever, like I am the lowly unwashed and I should come in the gates to be blessed by the big phallus. Or I am a housewife coming "back" to "school" driving my white Isuzu and eating my curds and whey. Look, I didn't come to salivate at your office door. You like to make distinctions, so you should make distinctions between you the employee and me the customer. You're the guy behind the counter. Can I take a guess at what you're thinking?—"Another crazed woman in my class anti the educational system." But I'm not, I'm putting everything I've got on the line for religion.

Because the thing is that after I walked out on your class I sat down by the sausage trees near Moore Hall and I started watching the undergrads walking by in their Bermuda shorts going to lunch without a thought in their heads. I felt bad because for some reason I sort of believed in the universe part of university, that it was all about Life and Time and God, and Freedom, and when I got back in it was just so male and linear and there wasn't any magic in the religion classes, it was all a construct—the angels were symbols and the miracles were just things in nature. So I got up and took all my books to the bookstore and sold them back (for less than half what I paid for them) and I went home—a room in a termite palace. As I was saying before, I felt really bad because I think you might have the wrong idea about me—you probably don't know how into school I really was. I originally dropped out of Simmons in 1974 for a lot of reasons, my father died for one thing, but basically because I didn't see myself in school at that time in my life. The only thing I could really see myself doing was folk dancing—I was in the original core Israeli folk-dancing group at MIT, which you probably have never even heard of, but it's actually nationally famous—it's almost like the model for all the other clubs in the country. I spent those "college" years living in Brighton and dancing. When I say dancing I'm talking about a way of life—I knew over two hundred dances and I also did Balkan. We would get over to MIT and dance straight from 8:30 to 11 P.M., steaming into Walker Gym straight from the snow to sweat like you would not believe. We stripped down every night from coats, sweaters, and boots to tank tops, gauze skirts, bare feet, and cutoffs, and when we left we were so hot we carried our parkas under our arms. I actually knew a lot of the key people in the folk scene and performed in New York at some of the big festivals. So that was kind of my "schooling." I was a secretary—actually for two years I temped, we were all menial slaves in the folk club, with a few graduate students and programmers sprinkled in. At the time I was in a relationship with one of them, which is how I ended up going to Hawaii—he had an upgrade deal. After a week he freaked out and took off for Fiji, and I was stranded at a fleabag joint in Waikiki with about twenty-two dollars to my name and the room bill.

When he took off I sold my return ticket and got a job busing tables at Zippy's, then I worked in the kitchen doing prep, then I worked in the find-a-pearl oyster stand in the International Marketplace, then I sold gold electroplated cockroaches when they were in, then I sold paraphernalia and sex toys in back where Oriental Imports used to be, behind The Stop Light and the bikini store on King Street, then after that place folded I got a job in Crack Seed World, then I landed a job in luggage at Shirokya, worked at Longs Drugs checkout, and did inventory at The Good Earth. I was thinking about going back to Boston. Thinking a lot, Dr. Friedell —it was happening at an underground level. I realize you aren't interested in what kind of thinking a student who walks out of Augustine is experiencing, because you can't think about anything that hasn't been totally hashed out already by geniuses—that's the impression you give me anyway, all that stuff about us living on the last mushroom of the dunghill of Romanticism and the pygmies on elephants and all you can do when you go back to school is learn how to use the library and document everything. Why do they make such a big deal

about plagiarism if it's all been said already? Not that I think
you're actually reading this, since it's written on onionskin in
ballpoint when you only accept typed stuff.

While I was working those different jobs I taught folk dancing at Kaimuki Y (once) and the Temple (five x). I went to a
Hebrew class at the Temple because I was teaching all these
dances to Israeli music and I didn't know Hebrew, but every
time we would get past the alphabet some new guy or some
kid would come into the class and we had to learn the alphabet again, so I never got beyond the letters. A total joke.
Rabbi Seigel up at the Temple used to go on these digres-
sions, so obviously we never got anywhere, and finally after
class I went up and said, "Rabbi, aren't we all just wasting
time in here?"

He looks at me under the fluorescent lights in the Learning
Center, which is all white linoleum and woodgrain tables and
green plastic chairs, and nailed up on the walls all the Old
World stuff, those ticky-tacky pictures of the bearded men,
and Rabbi Seigel in his suit with his silver tiepin. "Sharon,"
he says, "I'm sorry you feel that way."

"I want to learn Hebrew," I said. "Isn't that what we're here
for?"

"Sharon, I think you realize that in the end the words
are the least important aspect of what I'm trying to teach.
Come here," he says, pushing me into the sanctuary. He was
one of those big-time formal guys who wore black robes at
services and had like a whole set of hand signals for the
organist—I think he was a frustrated conductor or actor. We
go into the sanctuary and he flicks on the lights, floodlighting
the Temple ceiling, stained glass, etcetera. "Sharon," he says,
"Judaism is more than a few simple phrases. It's a culture,
one of music & art, poetry & light, it is the intimate & the
sublime, exalted &"—I forget the exact words. "Think of the
lyric music of the Psalms," he tells me. "While the Egyptians
were building tombs we were singing of life and love, while
the monuments of the ancients were crumbling to dust we
were treading over the ruins in a tradition that arced back

over the millennia and forward to the future. Our friends in class may never remember a word of Hebrew, but if they can sense something of the grandeur of our tradition the historic sweep of the epic blah blah blah chosen people."

I guess I sort of gave him a look, because this chosen-people crap was always one of my big problems with organized religion.

He heaves a big sigh, folds his arms over his belly. "I think you know how strongly I feel about that one," he says. "Each people is dear to God in its own way, and I often make the analogy to the different states of the Union." He was a great guy, Seigel, but when you asked him a question it was like throwing a bottle in the ocean and just watching it drift away over all his metaphors and comparisons plus the incidents it reminded him of. And as far as where I was coming from in the folk movement, he hadn't a clue because he was into "High" art, which goes back to what I was saying about the past. He used to say, "When I say the Bor'chu—'Bless ye the Lord'—I think how fitting a trumpet fanfare would be right there."

Meanwhile I was getting really alienated, not so much by him but by life in general, and by the kind of things I was doing, and I sort of disappeared for a while on Molokai with a guy I was having a relationship with at the time and grew pot out there on government land, and I really got into the Hawaiian way of life and just nature out there, the greenness and the livingness of the rain forest. It's just so pure out there where the hotel moguls don't have their greasy colonialist paws on it yet, with the chrome and glass and penned-in dolphins and chlorinated-swimming-pool bars and the hills paved over with Day-Glo golf courses and the electric patrol carts to ward off trespassers and the guys who have to comb the sand out with rakes every morning. We lived in an abandoned toolshed/bungalow thing that this botanist had originally built as a field station. The roaches bit, although you understand out there because they're hungry, too. You kind of got to understand the Jainists with their temples with the plank floors over the insects and just that basically every creature has just as much right to do whatever as you do. So anyway we lived out there maybe a couple of years and slowed way down, no telephone, newspaper, or any of that shit—shut out all the noise. The problem was, the government was trying to wipe us off the map—not that we were on the map, but the Feds were always looking—and we had to move a lot of times, plus there were naturally poachers and we had to set traps, and so of course we had to worry all the time some hiker would get killed walking the wrong way. We had to keep a gun out there too, which was a pain in the ass morally, because I've always been a complete pacifist. Looking back, we definitely would've gotten killed if we were any better at farming than we were, but we didn't grow much surplus—the marketing scene was something we were just not that into. I would compare what we did more to the 18th-century utopia "Make your garden grow."

As it turned out Kekui's (the guy I was living with's) father died, we heard through his sister Roslind. So we fly in to Honolulu for the funeral, a shock, let me tell you, coming in to Disneyland, with the high-school kids in aloha-print bathing suits with those plumeria leis on their arms or decapitated carnations strung together—"lei greeters" for the package tours and the Japanese honeymooners in their white white tennis whites. And in front of all of them is Mrs. Eldridge standing with her car keys in her red muu-muu and her hair piled up on her head with a red hibiscus at her ear—a big woman, not fat, big like an opera singer, big like photos of Princess Ruth when she sat at the Summer Palace on her throne.

We got to the funeral up in Makiki at the church there, I forget the name, and after the ceremony in the car she, meaning Mrs. Eldridge, turns to Kekui and me, who she hasn't said a word to all day, and she says, "KK, you're coming home."

"What?" he says.

"Roslind and her kids have the back room, Minnie and her kids are in front, Earl and Matthew have Minnie's room, Leilan and Mitchell are upstairs," she says.

"What?" he says.

"We cleaned out your room," she tells him.

"Excuse me?" I say.

"Keep quiet, girl," she says. We drive up to their house in Aina Hina with two plumeria trees in front, not a flower left —they picked them all off for the grandkids' May Day pageant. She had six of the eight kids living in the house and about five grandchildren. There were all these add-ons in back and a second story above the garage—Mr. Eldridge was a contractor. And there were something like seven cars in the driveway plus a boat and a tour van, just to give you an idea. We sit down inside, everyone depressed from the funeral, some of the babies crying. Mrs. Eldridge takes them on her knee, she looks around like she was ready to take everyone on her knee. For what? To rock us? To hit us? "KK," she says, "you've come back home to stay."

"Excuse me?" I say.

"Quiet, girl," she says.

"I have an application for you," she says. She brings out a bunch of forms. "West Oahu College," she says. "I brought up all my children to go to college. OK?"

KK looks down totally crushed with this heavy guilt—he never went to visit his parents or his father before he died, and this was probably some Oedipal thing with his father dying and him coming home to mother—the minister at the funeral gave a whole speech about obedience and duty to the parents in times of sorrow.

"Everyone in this family is a worker," she says. "You filling this out?" She gives him the application forms.

"Yeah," he says.

"Goddammit!" I get up off the floor. "You dickless idiot! Don't you care about me at all? You're going to leave me in Molokai so you can live with your mother?"

"Get your mouth out of my house," she declares, standing

up in her full dimensions. "Hippie girl, just 'cause you washed up here on Oahu you don't need to come invading my family. Go back to where you started—California, England, Holland, or whatever nationality you are. And don't you dare walk around taking the Lord's name in vain blaspheming my husband's funeral. Get your pakalolo face away or Earl'll get his badge out and arrest you!"

So the upshot was Kekui and I broke up and I ended up getting a job at Paradise Jeweller and actually picked up some Cantonese there and got kind of close with the family—went to a lot of the family functions and stuff like that. They were working on evangelizing me and we had some really interesting conversations—they were Pentecostalists—and I went to Church with them a couple of times out of my interest in religion. This is what I think you don't realize about me, Dr. Friedell, that this has been my lifelong interest—don't tell me I haven't thought about the concepts. So that's when I started at the University and took religion courses. And they were great experiences, let me make that clear—I never had a problem until you. I got an A in Discourse and Intercourse in Hindu Myth, I got an A in Jesus and Liberation, and only your course threw me for a loop—I mean, can I be honest? Religious Thinkers has been totally frustrating in that you keep sidestepping the issues and you are totally obsessed with detail—I mean were you raised a Pharisee?

So the point is I sat there in Moore Hall, I listened, I read these books you were assigning, but what you couldn't see was how much more Religion means to a person like myself who comes into a class like yours not with a lot of classical shit under my belt but with a whole life of experience and with these questions, the big ones I previously mentioned, and I knew when I walked out on you I had to find this stuff at the source, that I'd tried asking my questions to professors and rabbis and missionaries and lovers and to myself—sober, high, clean, dirty, unemployed, working, etc. In other words all states of consciousness, in other words I go for the em-

pirical method, which is maybe the one thing I get from my
father—he was an economist at BU which is beside the point,
because obviously I am anti-wealth, anti-capital—I wasn't on
speaking terms with him even when he was dying—and anyway I knew I had to go to the source of some of this religious
debate, as in a quest. Like the great poet Yeats when he
picked up and traveled to Byzantium—I picked up and took
all my money, bought a ticket, came here to Jerusalem.

So you're probably saying What the Hell is she going to do
in Jerusalem and what does she think she's going to live on
just out of the blue ending up in the Middle East without a
dime. Actually I have close friends here who are putting me
up—the guy I referred to earlier who I was in a relationship
with 12 years ago when I went out to Hawaii and he decided
to go to Fiji is currently in Jerusalem, now involved with the
Torah Or—which means Torah Light—institute. He had written me a lot and extended an open invitation ever since he
got here, and has basically become like what I have always
defined as a holy spirit. He was always this quiet kind of guy,
but the quietness just deepened in the last few years—I
barely recognized him when I saw him, he used to be such
a beer-swilling heavyset kind of guy and he's real pale now
and thin as wire. At the airport I walked right past him, naturally being out of it after 20 hours flying. So I sort of wander
off the plane into the Hebrew and all those guards. "Sharon,"
I hear. It's him, Gene, with this thin pale face, wearing a navy
suit jacket. We just stood there, looked at each other. We both
started to cry. It was mystical. "You've changed," he said,
which was the real shocker. I'd changed? I've had the same
hair style since '74, straight to the hips like Crystal Gayle, and
I was wearing my old folk-dancing skirt plus an original Boston Folk Festival T-shirt.

We drove off in the Torah Or hatchback Hyundai, started
ascending the hills. I was just staring the whole way as we
were driving up. It was such a spiritual odyssey—I said, "I
feel like this is the culmination of my whole life." I said, "This
is the ancient city of Jerusalem; I'm going to get some an-

swers." So the city rose up before us, made out of Jerusalem stone, naturally, and with the olive trees and even flocks on the hillsides—I felt like my whole spiritual experience was coming together like an epiphany. It was The Land.

Torah Or has its central office in the Old City right near The Wall, and the school is in Mea Shearim, where I've been the last two weeks. In the mornings I wake up—there's like a dormitory for students where we sleep—and I go to pray in the synagogue/cafeteria—it's kind of a small-scale school so they have to double up. There are about 25 women stu dents, something like 20 young ones on their junior year abroad from college, like Queens College, Brandeis, and a couple from Barnard, then there are a few of us older ones. The college girls just speed through the prayers and sit down for breakfast while we older ones are still standing there with our books. Then eventually these women start finishing up, but I'm still standing there, praying till the cows come home, just because my Hebrew is so bad I'm spelling out the words—it takes me around four hours to finish praying every morning. The Yemenite women come in, clear away break- fast, I'm still praying. They fold up the folding chairs, I'm still praying. They start hosing down the floor around my feet, they start squeegeeing the water, I'm still standing there like the rocks and the planets. There's one other woman who also takes a long time. I've noticed she keeps looking over at me to see what page I'm on. Then she turns back to her book, bobbing up and down like a maniac. After about a week I figured out this woman is into praying with feeling, which means for each word you have to move your lips, knit your eyebrows and shuffle around as much as you can, and so obviously the slower you go the more feeling you have, right? So she's like envious of me because I'm going slower than everyone else, so I must be the holiest one there, but she can't for the life of her figure out how to go as slow as I do —every morning I drive her up a wall, since I never told her I know hardly any Hebrew. She has to give up after about three hours. Stalks around glaring at me. There are some real lunatics in Jerusalem, these religious groupie types walking the streets. It kind of taints the atmosphere.

I mean I got here and I saw the city and had this sort of epiphany at the beginning, yet I still have all these major questions exploding in my head, but with the praying and seminars I have hardly any time to think, and also classes here are kind of low-level, focussed on these questions like What is a Jew? and What is Torah? I guess it's kind of over-centered on the ethnic stuff for me. I've done ethnic stuff all my life. I mean, when you've been in the folk movement you've kind of already paid your dues as far as ethnic. I want to go beyond that. I'm ready to go beyond. So today I went in to see my friend Gene, who mans the Old City office. "I'm ready for more," I said, standing there right in the light of his slide projector—he was organizing slides on the carrousel. "I want to talk about God," I said with this big projection of some Dead Sea Scroll across my arm.

"Sharon, by the way, you haven't paid the office," he mentioned, which totally pissed me off.

"You aren't hearing me," I said.

"I'm hearing you," he said, "but we're having a financial crisis. Without tuition payments the school is falling apart. Then what are we going to discuss?"

This was so materialistic I would have walked out, but the truth is Torah Or gave me hope I was getting somewhere, so I asked him, "How much do you need from me?"

"Three hundred dollars."

"What?" This just stunned me. I mean, three hundred dollars is all the money I have in the world right now. I mean, holy shit.

Then, after I took the bus back to the school I got a real blow—an actual telegram. It's my cat.

I have this cat I picked up when I got back from Molokai. It kept moaning and screaming outside the building and I took him in and named him Ugly, which he is—so he's kind of lived with me through all my moves and now I've got him staying with a friend from the University and he sends me this telegram. "Tests back; diagnosis positive." I look at this telegram. It's like I've been trying to run away from this thing and it caught up to me. My cat has feline AIDS. It's just a big blow to me—I mean Ugly and I were never demonstrative, he's kind of mean, he's from the street, he likes to go off alone for a few days—he gets kicked around and comes back—but we've been together a long time, maybe seven years.

I just took the piece of paper outside and I walked and walked with my bag slung over my shoulder. I walked through the narrow streets and the vegetable markets with the Mea Shearim kids with the black hats like black Panama hats on one block and then round-brimmed hats on the next block—these are like their school uniforms—and I walked past the shops with the silver candlesticks and olivewood stuff and little stinky alleyways between them with clothes hung out to dry. Shirts, shirts, shirts, little shirts, little fringes, and then this satin wedding gown hanging on the line, I swear to God. And I looked in the wig shops and I saw the kids buying beige twisted candles and feathers on the street corners. I walked all the way up the road, up the hill, and I got to this park in front of the Jerusalem Nature Conservation Office, and I am sitting here with this paper and pen, I am sitting on this huge stone from an olive press, which looks like stone money from Yap or Yip, I forget, lying on its side, and it's getting cold out because April is not that warm, and I am full of all these questions and just mainly, What is God? Where is s/he? and What should I do? and What is the earth here for?

I know you don't take this, coming from me, seriously, but I am serious—I feel like I could explode. I read but I don't understand. It's like with Hebrew—I can sound it out but I don't know the meanings. That's the metaphor of how I feel. I came to Jerusalem but I don't feel gathered up and I mean I came from far; Honolulu has to be one of the 4 corners of the earth. But where is the canopy spread over me—forget of peace—when I look up at the sky at night I'm afraid, it's

so dark you can drown in it, it's so black and they say the
stars up there aren't even the stars, they're just the ones that
used to be there and it takes so long for the light to get down
here the real ones have died already. So is it just dead bodies
up there? Are they messages from the past that we don't understand? Just words floating down but no one can read them?
I've seen those people writing messages and sticking them in
the Western Wall in between the stones like it's some kind of
goddam wishing well. They're writing these crazy things—
who's going to read them? They're writing to the wall. I'm
writing to you.

The light is white lavender gray blue and there are two
stars and the moon, I'm watching them, they aren't dead,
they're definitely alive. I believe they are alive. Ha. I believe.
What the Hell does that mean? Do you want to know the
truth? I believe in God without any reasons. That's the part
that drives me crazy—I know he exists but I'm not sure how
I figured it out. Maybe you're born with it, who knows—
maybe it's just basically because I've had a good life. I mean
maybe more like Coyote than Road Runner and with those
crackly bloodshot eyeballs once in a while and flattened like
a cat under a truck once in a while and mad as Hell most of
the time about these completely meaningless things like,
no offense, your lecture that time, but inside me somewhere
there's this person naïve and ready to do something totally
different—then boom, you get a telegram like this and you
just wonder all over again if it makes any sense. I guess I'm
basically an optimist with nagging metaphysical questions.
Why else would I clean out checking and savings and come
to Jerusalem?

And the thing that hurts most is that after getting here and
driving up and seeing the flocks and the ancient walls you
see that Jerusalem is just a place. It's just such a place. I
thought it was going to be so much more—I mean, not like
I thought I was actually going to see the valley of the shadow
of death, but I keep seeing plain hills and valleys and that's
it. Which has got to be me, right? I know it's what you bring,

I realize that. It makes me cry because I don't have it in me.
I just don't understand and I want to. I didn't understand
Augustine, which is one of the reasons I hate him, because I
read it and read it and it doesn't make sense to me. Satisfied?
And I can tell you I thought seeing this place would make
more sense but it doesn't, it doesn't at all. I feel ashamed of
myself sometimes, like I'm constantly sidetracking from the
bigger questions. There is this whole spiritual existence out
there and I can't get there. What do you need to do? How
many books? How many journeys? What are the words and
what kind of food? macro? micro? do roots feed the soul?
carrots, turnips, potatoes? or the ancient songs? I lift up my
voice in the wilderness, eyes to the hills, my timbrel and lyre
to the mouth of the sea from whence cometh my aid and
dance on the sand a song of praise with words I don't understand. What can you do with just an alphabet when you
don't know the constellations, just that ayin is an eye and a
well, but what's down the well? You live in this thin layer on
the crust and you can never delve down to the underground
rivers or get onto the other planets and get any perspective.
And they say you should climb to the top of the hill and cry
God is in this place! and lift up your voice along with your
eyes to whence cometh your help, but what if you do that
and afterward it wears off and you're just sitting there on the
hill back where you started? Where do you go from there?
Because I've had some real out-of-body experiences and you
always come down afterward. I want to go further. My spirit
has dancing feet. That's the one thing I guess that keeps me
moving, being a dancer. I can dance without shoes, without
music, without words, without partners. I look down at these
two feet, they keep each other company. I guess you have
to keep moving and dwell on the stars instead of the neg-
ative.

So I'll be back in Honolulu on May 1 to be there for Ugly,
and I was wondering if you could possibly take this as my
final paper for the course, since it basically summarizes some
of my current views and independent research into religion.

I realize it only touches on Augustine briefly, but since he was sort of the starting point of the research it was justified. I could type it up if you want—but the main thing is if you would give me full credit for it, because, obviously, your course is required. Thanks,

Sharon

Fern Kupfer

Sleepwalking Through Suburbia

When we moved from the Bronx to Plainview, Long Island, in 1956, I was ten years old and getting out of the city was something that parents wanted to do for their children—fresh air, grass, better schools. Long Island was, next to Israel, the Promised Land for my parents' generation.

In suburbia, in the fifties and early sixties, we had it good. Never before had American Jews so much financial and personal security. Look how far we had come from a tenement to a three-bedroom split-level with two-and-a-half baths. Look how far we were from the devastation of the Holocaust. How finally after assimilation, it was easy to be ourselves. From the shtetl to success. From pogroms to prosperity. That story.

But there was something else again; the opportunity after the great onslaught of the thirties and forties, depression, blatant anti-Semitism and genocide, a chance to coast a little, even sleepwalk. Certainly there's something dreamlike about my memories of it.

Suburbia seemed rural then. "Put your shoes on, Ma, we're going to town," I used to say when we picked up my father at the Long Island Railroad. Wives put on fresh lipstick and moved over to the passenger's seat when the men (all in dark suits, newspapers rolled up under their arms) emerged from the trains.

Plainview, Long Island. What used to be potato fields became a development of identical split-level homes with streets named "Deborah Drive" and "Judith Avenue"; Deborah and Judith were daughters of the builder Sam Hochman. One street in the development was named Hochman Boulevard until the homeowners rose in protest and renamed it "Shelter Hill Road."

I was afraid walking from school that I wouldn't be able to find my way home. All the streets looked alike. So did the houses. All the suburban mothers waited in their shiny, new kitchens. My mother actually wore an apron and had a snack ready for me. I suppose I could have walked into any kitchen and been similarly greeted.

My aunt Anna had moved up to the Catskills to work in the hotels, my grandmother had died, so my grandfather moved with us to our new house, having his own room in what other suburban families called the den. I remember my grandfather in his long, blue overcoat, taking walks, looking like some Old World Tevye lost himself in the maze of suburban streets. He used to meet me at school to carry my books home. "Luz mir truggin," he commanded in Yiddish. Give it here!

I begged my mother, "Can't you keep Papa in the house?" Apparently, she could not. I walked home from sixth grade with my friends, followed by a gaunt, eighty-year-old Jewish man carrying a pink loose-leaf notebook.

My grandfather had not come from a religious family even in the old country, but it was the plight of European Jewry during World War II that made him turn his back on religion entirely. He was unable to reconcile a God who allowed Hitler and permitted so much suffering. How can there be a God who could watch as children died in the ovens? he would ask.

Yet even in my nonreligious family there was a certain Jewish chauvinism. My grandfather always had books about famous Jews and Jews who *should* have been famous had they received the recognition they deserved from the gentile world of power. My grandfather had theories about who *really* invented the telephone and discovered America and cured diseases—every one a Jew. It was implied in my family that there were certain ways of behaving. Jewish children didn't get bad grades in school, Jewish women didn't keep sloppy homes, Jewish husbands didn't go to bars or hit their wives. People who were not good with money had "Goyisher kops." Jews respected bookishness and were clearly unenamored of the American fascination with football, guns, and motorcycles.

When I was in junior high school, my mother got a job selling real estate. (My father said she could work only if dinner was still on the table every night at six.) In December there was always a flurry of activity, people from the city shopping around for houses. They came to see which Plainview neighborhoods had Christmas lights strung up—and which didn't. The dark houses, of course, were Jewish.

For some of my friends, the sixteenth-birthday present of choice was a nose job. There was the sweet-sixteen luncheon at a fancy restaurant followed by a brief hospitalization over spring break for the operation. Then the girls would come back to school black-eyed and bobbed. It was before Barbra Streisand made having a "Jewish nose" acceptable. I don't remember anyone ever questioning the necessity (or the political implications) of such an operation. We just assumed that a cute shiksa nose was a standard of beauty.

Like many suburban teenagers, my friends and I complained a lot about the homogeneity of our lives; the fact that there was "nothing to do" in Plainview. It was the early sixties—before drugs and sanctioned teenage sex—and Plainview was a safe place to be bored. All my high school friends (I believed at the time) were virgins. No one's parents were divorced. Everyone was going to college. Being Jewish seemed a small, unremarkable part of who we were. It wasn't something that you *choose* any more than you choose left-handedness or curly hair. For me, being Jewish had less to do with religion—I didn't go to synagogue or Hebrew Schools—than with a complicated mix of genetic inheritance and family narratives.

But there was more diversity in our community than might be believed. I had an Italian boyfriend—an athlete, not one of the Italian "hoody" kids who hung around their cars after school, collars up, huge combs in their pockets, cigarettes dangling provocatively from their lips. There was something seductive and dangerous about them; an allure because of their otherness. They seemed older, more like men than the overprotected Jewish boys. But none of the Jewish girls I knew ever went out with one of the "hoods." Still, my parents were considered "progressive" because they never put pressure on me to date only Jewish boys—a necessary requirement for many of my girlfriends.

And one of my best friends was Italian. I loved going to Rosemary's house because her mother always had "sauce" cooking on the stove, sausage, crusty bread. Her family used to leave presents for me under their tree at Christmas and I'd sleep over and go to midnight mass with them. But Rosemary had a boyfriend named Phil Goldberg, and there was a turning point when she chose to hang out with the Jewish girls rather than with her Italian friends from junior high. This was only natural: Rosemary was in honors classes—filled disproportionately with Jewish kids. The school was divided into tracks: there was the beauty school crowd and the "commercial" class, being trained for jobs rather than college. A Jewish kid who played ball generally hung around with the Irish and Italian athletes. And an Italian who made honor society was likely to have many Jewish friends. So how and what you did in school determined how those ethnic lines were crossed.

I graduated from Plainview High School in 1964 and, as expected for smart girls in 1964, headed for a state college where I was going to major in English and get a teaching degree. My mother said teaching was a wonderful profession for a woman because I could be home in time to have supper ready for my husband. I knew that I would do what was expected of me: get a degree, marry, have children. I could never have thought that I would end up living in Iowa, become a writer, lose a child, get divorced.

My grandfather died when I was a freshman in college. For years afterward, I had a recurring dream that I was riding a train and saw my grandfather in his long, dark coat walking up the aisle; sometimes he would be sitting by a window, reading his Jewish newspaper. "Papa?" I would say, surprised and delighted to see him. "What are you doing here?"

He would only nod in recognition. "Go," he'd tell me, waving me away with his hand. "Gai avek." Strange, but the dismissal did not seem unkind. Go away. And go on with your life. I awoke missing him, missing the part of my history that he represented.

Now I've lived half my life in Iowa where I write and teach. *Iowa!* A more gentile state would be hard to imagine. Here the students I teach drive pickup trucks and hunt deer; they are big and blond and unrelentingly polite. I am here in Iowa, but my voice will always echo the nasal twang from the borough of my birth.

My parents have moved to Florida and live in a retirement condominium community that is almost all Jewish. In fact, most of their friends from New York live near them, old friends who share their roots, who remember the way it used to be. The spirit of my grandparents hovers amid the palm trees. Oh, what a strange tribal migration: from Białystok to the Bronx to Boca Raton!

Looking back, I know there was a certain flatness of the emotional landscape of my suburban childhood. Long Island was not the Promised Land, but there was a sense of community that was remarkable only for its lack of consciousness and self-reflection. Oh, nostalgia. Some say it ain't what it used to be. What do I remember through the filter of memory?

I see an adolescent girl happy with her friends and family, her pink bedroom with the ruffled curtains, the phone that is ringing—usually for her. She is safe, but slightly bored, looking dreamily beyond the horizon of the next shopping center, and waiting for her real life to begin.

Erica Jong

Needlepoint

Mothers & daughters . . .
something sharp
catches in my throat
as I watch my mother
nervous before flight,
do needlepoint—
blue irises & yellow daffodils
against a stippled woolen sky.

She pushes the needle
in & out
as she once pushed me:
sharp needle to the canvas of her life—
embroidering her faults
in prose & poetry,
writing the fiction
of my bitterness,
the poems of my need.

"You hate me," she accuses,
needle poised,
"why not admit it?"

I shake my head.
The air is thick
with love gone bad,
the odor of old blood.

If I were small enough
I would suck your breast. . . .
but I say nothing,
big mouth,
filled with poems.

Whatever love is made of—
wool, blood, Sunday lamb,
books of verse
with violets crushed
between the pages,
tea with herbs,
lemon juice for hair,
portraits sketched of me asleep
at nine months old—
this twisted skein
of multicolored wool,
this dappled canvas
or this page of print
joins us
like the twisted purple cord
through which we first pulsed poems.

Mother, what I feel for you
is more
& less
than love.

Joan Lipkin

Silent Night

I have this melancholy that kicks in like the flu around Christmas and lingers the year 'round. It's when I watch everybody around me behaving like a Hallmark card and I'm nowhere near the frame. I know in my heart that not everybody's that happy. Maybe the guy in the Santa Claus hat hits his wife. Or the kids in their matching red flocked ice-skating outfits go home to an empty house. But it looks like everyone is celebrating a Kodak moment. Everyone but me.

So you might say that I was doomed before I even met Jim. Tall. Blond. Irish Catholic. And Male. Everything that I'm not. Besides, the boys where I was from had names like Sam. Ira. Howard. How could I go out with them? They had names like my father. They were my father.

It was the fall of my senior year, in between borrowing the car and choosing a direction for my own life. My father was so pleased that I had been selected to speak at graduation. At dinner, he used to sit at the head of our heavy oak table, looking drained and angry, daring us to rouse him from his exhaustion with our brilliance.

"What did the president know and when did he know it? Quick. Quick."

Like knowing the day's events would erase the tattoo on my second cousin's forearm.

The memory of the Holocaust hung heavy as furniture wax in our house. Maybe it was about leaving home, but that summer the nightmares came back as I imagined they were coming for me. After all, didn't I look just like my grandma Hannah? Everybody said so.

My father's answer was for us to be smarter. Quicker. More verbal.

"I expect my children to be exceptional," he said.

But I didn't want to be exceptional. I wanted to eat Chef Boyardee from cans instead of my mother's carefully planned meals. To call my father Pops like they did on the *Patty Duke Show* and loll about on the floor like a dumb teenager. To disappear into a crowd of average.

What if I said the wrong thing? I asked him silently, wrapping my hair tightly in orange juice cans to look like the girls who lived safely within the pages of *Seventeen* magazine. What then?

With Jim, I began to plan my escape. Maybe I could have a life different from the one I had been handed. Hey, this is America. Isn't that why my mother braved the long boat ride from Poland? So there could be a choice?

The day of the Christmas party, I lied to my mother and said we were going to a concert.

"But it's the first night of Hanukkah," she protested, trying not to look hurt.

"Look, we've had these tickets for weeks," I said. "And it's not like we don't have all those other nights."

She let it drop, and turned her attention to polishing the already gleaming menorah. We were careful around each other for the rest of the day, neither one sure what the etiquette of betrayal and rejection should be like.

As I walked into the party, the wreath on the door seemed to wink at me. Maybe I could pull this thing off. Always a good student, I had studied well, trading my usual tie-dyed

T-shirt and jeans for a navy blue calf-length dress. From a distance, it would be hard to pick me out in a lineup.

Jim smiled and handed me a glass of spiked eggnog. My eyes buzzed. "You don't think I can get through this family scene without a little help," he said, gesturing at a sea of similar faces.

I thought of my younger sister curled up in front of the television doing her algebra homework and my father, who was probably squinting over the financial page and figuring out how to pay for three unexpected sets of braces.

"Merry Christmas," someone said. "Merry Christmas," I said back, tasting the words that I had heard so often but had never said. Someone else called me Kathleen. Jim's previous girlfriend.

"She doesn't look anything like Kathleen," he snapped. "What does Kathleen look like?" I asked. "Oh, you know . . . different." I drank another glass. Questions always made me thirsty. So did the nut-studded cheeseball. I thought he said there would be dinner.

Someone—I think it was Jim's cousin Betsy—asked how long I have known him. Someone—I think it was Jim's brother Hank—asked where I go to school. Someone—I'm sure it was his mother—asked where my family lived.

"Hey," Jim said, coming to my rescue. "What's with the third degree?"

"It's okay," I said, teetering in my new high heels as I backed up into the tree. The hot ring of lights felt like barbed wire. "They don't know me."

Then the singing began and they turned toward each other. I checked my hair in the mirror over the highboy in the front hallway. It was starting to frizz.

> Silent Night
> Holy night
> All is calm
> All is bright

Jim squeezed my hand the way he had squeezed my breast three hours earlier in the front seat of his sky blue Ford Pinto.

"Did I forget to tell you? Everybody gets to solo," he whispered in my ear. "It's kind of corny, I know, but my dad likes to show off. You don't mind, do you?"

> Round yon virgin
> Mother and child
> Holy infant so tender and mild

Mind? I had waited my whole life to sing this song. I gazed into the large crackling fire and tried not to think of my family gathered around their tiny flame.

> Sleep in heavenly peace
> Sleep in heavenly peace

Surely I knew the words. They had been piped into every elevator and shopping mall and radio station since I could remember. My mother had even taken us for a holiday breakfast downtown at Saks one time until she realized it meant pancakes and sausages and sitting on Santa's lap. My beautiful, curly-haired mother, who was home right now, watching Walter Cronkite on the nightly news while she made a holiday dinner that I wouldn't be there to eat.

> Silent night
> Holy night
> Shepherds quake
> at the sight

I leaned in toward the singing blond circle, where everything seemed easy and casual because they took for granted their right to be there. And as the solo shifted from Jim's sister Mary to his brother Hank, I wondered, were these the secret passwords?

Glory streams from heaven above
Heavenly hosts sing alleluia!

But as I began to sing, my tongue suddenly felt thick as pickled herring, my eyes filled with salt. "Go for it, babe," Jim whispered. "Then we can get out of here and have some, you know, real fun."

Christ our savior is born
Christ our savior is born.

As everyone smiled expectantly at me, I sat in horror at the eternal silence a few seconds can hold. Then, slowly, from somewhere came a voice that sounded like my own.

Bo-ruch at-ta a-do-nai
e-lo-hey-nu me-lech ha-olam
a-sher ki-d'sho-nu b'mits-vo-tov

As I sang, first softly, then louder, my hands flew out of my lap, like birds released from their cage. I watched them, as I had watched myself enter the room in my new blue dress. No, this was not Kathleen. It was my mother. My grandmother. My aunt Sadie who was married to a pattern cutter on the Lower East Side of New York.

v'tsi-vo-nu
l'had-leek neyr
shel Hanukkah.

I dropped my punch glass. The crystal cup that had been in this country longer than my family.

"It's all right, dear," Jim's mother said, dabbing at the pale spreading stain. "These things happen." Jim's brother Hank snickered. Jim stood looking puzzled, as he rubbed one foot against the other.

"No, it's not," I said. "I'm sorry. And I want to go home." And as I mouthed the words of that ancient prayer, I knew I was home.

Letty Cottin Pogrebin

I Don't Like to Write About My Father

During more than twenty years as a writer, I've poured out thousands of words about my mother, but my father, who lived until 1982, has earned only a sentence here or there. I've written extensively about my husband, my children, my colleagues, my friends, but I don't like to write about my father.

I'm afraid to read what I have to say.

I would have to start with the good things: He looked like Clark Gable and dressed like a movie star too. He carried his bills in a gold money clip shaped like a dollar sign. He wore cream-colored trousers and cashmere coats, breast-pocket handkerchiefs, white-on-white shirts, initialed gold cuff links, and a pinky ring with an onyx eye.

"Real snappy," he'd say, smoothing the brim of his fedora as he passed the hallway mirror. "Real snappy."

As a child, even more than watching my mother dress, I loved to watch my father perform his toilette. I remember the way he tapped a little mound of Pepsodent tooth powder on his palm, dipped his toothbrush into his hand, and then brushed methodically, uppers, lowers, left and right. I marveled at the way his straight, light-brown hair turned dark as he smoothed it down with pomade, making his hair sleek

and close to his head like the men in *The Great Gatsby*. But
the main event was his shaving ritual: I loved watching him
slap the straight razor, thwack-thwack, back and forth over
the razor strop until the blade glistened, then swirl his bone-
handled shaving brush against a cake of soap in a wooden
bowl where it foamed like whipped cream. Sometimes he let
me lather my face as well. Then both of us "shaved" together
in front of the mirror, he with the straight razor making trail-
blazing paths down his cheeks, and I zigzagging through my
soapy beard with an empty chrome safety razor.

"Great job, Bunny," he'd say approvingly, his praise show-
ering me with self-respect as we drizzled ourselves with Men-
nen aftershave lotion and a light dusting of talc. He had
nicknamed me Bunny at birth, but when I was especially
adorable, he called me Sugar Pie, or Ketzele (pussycat), or
Kepele. To be told I had a good kepele, a smart head, was
the ultimate compliment; brains were all that mattered and if
my father said you had a good head, you might as well be
Einstein.

My father knew everything. First of all, as I've said, he was
an all-American boy in a generation of greenhorns. Although
his parents had barely arrived from Russia, he was born with
the century on Valentine's Day, 1900, in New Haven, Connecticut, which made him, as he put it, "a regular Yankee
Doodle Dandy."

Secondly, he had credentials. He graduated from Town-
send Harris, a high school for gifted boys, entered City
College at sixteen, whizzed through NYU Law School with
honors. And now, while all the other fathers were furriers,
cloak-and-suiters, or men who "went to business," my daddy
was a lawyer.

Third, he really knew his history, classics, Torah, Talmud,
Hebrew, Yiddish, French, carpentry, plumbing, electricity,
sailing, fishing, baseball, you name it, so you can just imagine
how he could talk. And he didn't just talk, he pronounced,
like a sage. And he was a great teacher, though far from easy-
going. I loved it when he taught me things no one else in

the family had mastered, like chess, diving, Ping-Pong, or my haftorah (the reading from the Prophets recited by the child who is being bar or bat mitzvahed).

Preparing me for my bat mitzvah was perhaps his finest hour. He was well equipped for the task, having learned Hebrew at age six from his paternal grandmother ("a most unusual woman," he would say) and studied Talmud with his father, a man so erudite that rabbis came to him with questions. At ten, my father was reading the Torah for his synagogue congregation, reading it with perfect cantillation, the singsong litany that makes Torah reading unmistakably its own art. He attended Uptown Talmud Torah after school, then transferred to a yeshiva on the Lower East Side, continuing his study with his father on Saturday afternoons after he moved on to high school. While attending college and law school, he taught Hebrew School for twenty hours a week and took four boys per year for bar mitzvah training at $150 each, a princely sum in 1920.

No wonder my father brought so much facility and fervor to my bat mitzvah lessons. He was in his element. He put me through my paces as if he were a rabbi, which he could have been, and as if I were a boy, which I should have been to please him although he never said it. I adored him for treating me like a son and taking me seriously. He drilled and polished my Hebrew recitation until I was the kind of virtuoso performer that synagogue legends were made of back in 1952, when girls, as a rule, did not do that sort of thing. But I did whatever my father valued. More than anything, I wanted his approval because he was my mentor and I saw myself as his intellectual heir. There was no son to make that claim. Betty was long out of the house with kids of her own, and the mysterious Rena had yet to turn up in his life. Clearly, his legacy was mine if I proved myself worthy of it.

Even when I was very young, he made me feel important just by talking to me. He spoke didactically but never condescendingly the way he sometimes addressed my mother and aunts. He talked to me as if I could be trusted to get it on first hearing. He was an intelligent man but not a patient one.

I was in heaven when he talked law or Judaism, explaining the convolutions of an ongoing case, the outcome of a lawsuit, the rationale for a particular Jewish ceremony, some intricate point of Mishnah or Gemara. I asked him a million questions and he answered them; for smart questions, he was patient.

"Daddy, why is the Mishnah called the Oral Law if it's written down?"

"Because the rabbis wanted to prevent any confusion between the Torah, which was God's law given to Moses and never to be changed, and subsequent case law, which was meant to be flexible and subject to new insights and interpretations."

"Daddy, why does the Mishnah demand twice the penalty for a slap in the face as for a punch in the stomach?"

"Because an insult is twice as destructive as an ordinary injury. A punch in the belly hurts, but a blow to the face humiliates and degrades a person."

"Daddy, why does the Talmud say judges can't sentence criminals on the same day as their trial?"

"Because if you're going to condemn someone to death, the least you can do is sleep on your decision."

I knew that if I could get him started explicating a text, he would smoke one Lucky Strike after another, meandering from midrash to midrash long after I was supposed to go to bed. I became adept at engaging him in conversations that piqued his interest while he fed me the information I needed in order to grow up and be like him.

My father's life was so much more exciting than my mother's that I thought it only logical to make him my model and my hero. He was the hero of others in our family as well. For instance, his sister Esther, college-educated and married to a lawyer herself, always held up my father as the example of man-at-his-best, putting her own husband and sons under pressure to match my father's style and accomplishments. Esther's younger son, Simon, who is a musician and was always a very studious child, recalls that when my father asked him what he wanted for his bar mitzvah (that fateful weekend in Winthrop), he requested a baseball mitt. Simon didn't care about sports at all, he just wanted to impress my father.

Beyond the family, my daddy seemed to be other people's hero too, judging by how many groups elected him their leader: the United Jewish Appeal, B'nai B'rith, the Zionist Organization of America, State of Israel Bonds, to mention just a few. At the Jamaica Jewish Center, where we went for services every Shabbat and holiday, my father was president of the shul. He did the Torah reading, sat up on the bimah (raised platform), or busied himself in the congregation, giving out kipot (skullcaps) and talitot (prayer shawls), helping people find their place in the siddur (prayer book), all the while davening (chanting the prayers) by heart with the loudest voice in the sanctuary.

There were distinct advantages to being Small-Daughter-of-the-Big Macher (Big Shot). I could sit in the front row at services, set the table for the Men's Club bagel breakfast, use Jamaica Jewish Center stationery, or help operate the switchboard with its octopus cords, switches, and plugs. Best of all were the special times when my father took me along wherever he was going. I've never forgotten when we went to the Jewish War Veterans' convention at Grossinger's Hotel in the Catskills. I was five or six. My father was J.W.V. County Commander, so he sat up on the dais and I sat on his lap. Next to us was a withered old man who seemed lost inside his uniform. My father introduced him as a veteran of the Civil War; he was ninety-eight years old, the most ancient person I had ever met. As the old vet took my hand in his bony grip, he said, "Bunny, you must always remember me because you just shook the hand that shook the hand of Abraham Lincoln."

I don't like to write about my father because I don't want to have to give him credit for that memorable encounter or for any of the other special events of my childhood. He didn't go out of his way to make them happen; he never went out of his way for anyone. He got credit for so much because he himself seemed so important that just being with him made you feel important.

Somehow I learned how to be fathered by this man. I understood that if I wanted to have him at all I had to enter his world and do things his way. I learned that I was adored when I was smart and cute, but never when I was inconvenient. In my early years, I didn't notice that he wasn't around much, except when my mother cried and begged him to stay home from his endless meetings and accused him of giving more of himself to his organizations than to his wife and child. For me, it was enough to be his well-behaved little pet, his mascot, his creation.

I don't like to write about my father because I would have to describe the good memories, as I just have, and he would sound like a better father than he was. And then, I would have to set the record straight. I would have to explain what it took me years to absorb: that he gave to me, not so that I would have, but in order to show the world what he had to give. Even the bat mitzvah was ultimately for him. Lauded as an extraordinary lay teacher, he claimed the triumph long after it was mine. The patriarch of the Jewish community had shown that he could teach his Yentl Torah.

I would have to point out that the reason I remember everything my father did with me is because he did so little.

He read two books to me at bedtime. One was Charles and Mary Lamb's narrative, *Tales from Shakespeare*. The second was a series of stories by Arthur Train about the adventures of Mr. Tutt, an old-fashioned country lawyer who wore a stovepipe hat and smoked a pipe. I must have been seven or eight at the time.

My father administered a couple of alcohol rubs when I had a fever. I remember once during the night, I woke up sick to my stomach and he helped support my head over the toilet while I vomited. I also remember feeling ashamed that he had to see me that way.

Most of the time when I was sick my mother nursed me back to health. She read me hundreds of stories, not two. She taught me to make Alexander Calder–type sculptures from the wires that were wrapped around the caps of the glass milk bottles that were delivered to our house by Holland Farms Dairy. Together, she and I made cutout paper people, and set up my toys amongst my bedclothes in what Robert Louis Stevenson described as "the pleasant land of counterpane." She brought me magazines, puzzles, and other "sick girl presents," cups of tea and bowls of soup and toast that she'd shaped with cookie cutters to look like stars and gingerbread men. Her constant care blurs into the maternal mists while his few alcohol rubs are as memorable as if they were anointments by a prophet.

He taught me how to swim when I was five. Soon after that, he took me horseback riding and made sure I learned how to post and canter. A year or two later we went to the Bronx Zoo. In a snapshot taken that day, I am wearing a leopard-skin coat that my Uncle Herman the furrier made for me. I remember my father joking that I might be mistaken for a baby leopard and claimed by a leopard family as one of their own, and he would have to climb into the cage and rescue me.

Back then, I believed he could.

I remember a summer evening in Coney Island where we rode the bumper cars and ate hot dogs for supper; and a winter outing to some park with a frozen pond where he and I went ice-skating for about an hour while my mother sat on a bench in the snow, watching us. Two or three times, he took me along with my Uncle Ralph and my cousin Danny to watch the Brooklyn Dodgers play in Ebbets Field.

My father was proud that I understood the game, but it was no thanks to him that I did. My baseball mentor was my cousin Danny, who was six years older than I and lived next door. Danny kept track of the Dodgers in bulging scrapbooks he fashioned out of black composition notebooks with spidery white designs on the cover, the kind I filled with arithmetic problems and geography homework. It was my job to paste in newspaper stories about Jackie Robinson, Pee Wee Reese, Billy Herman, and Dixie Walker; that's how I knew their names and positions. As we listened to the play-by-play on the radio (neither of us had a television in those days), Danny explained the rules of the game and taught me how to record the action on an official scorecard. He let me hang around when he and his friends played stickball in the street, and when the planets were in perfect alignment, I even had a turn at bat. To this day, I have Danny to thank for the excitement I feel when I first enter a baseball stadium. My father didn't give me that.

But Daddy did give me a feeling for Ferris wheels the one time he took me to Coney Island. On the first turn of the huge wheel, my stomach dropped, my mouth went dry, and I began to cry. I wasn't sure if I was going to faint or die, but I became so terrified that I begged him to make the operator stop the motor and let me off. Daddy wouldn't hear of it. Instead, he put his arm around my shoulders and instructed me to chant one phrase over and over again to myself until the ride was over: "Uuuuup and dowwwwwn, round and round; uuuuup and dowwwwwn, round and round," he intoned in the singsong voice I knew from his synagogue davening. Focusing on his litany of calm, I did as he said and amazed myself by not only taming my fear but enjoying the ride so much that I decided to go around again. Many times since then I've used my father's mantra to cope with anxious situations. But he never again took me to Coney Island.

That's it. Those are my memories of life with father from birth to age fifteen. If I'm lucky the good days add up to a month all told. Maybe I don't like to write about my father because I'm afraid I'd discover that they don't even amount to a month's worth. Then I would have to move on to the rest of the memories which would reveal this brilliant, dashing man to be another kind of father altogether.

One man, two fathers. Daddy and the Other Father. Maybe

I've been afraid that if I were to examine the Other Father more closely I would forever destroy the mythic Daddy, the man I once thought perfect. But as long as I did not write about him at all, I could keep the two images separate—grouse about the man I came to know from age fifteen onward, and keep Bunny's Daddy, the mentor Daddy, the Jewish sage, safe in the bell jar of childhood.

The Other Father was another story. I came to know him, and to be disappointed by him, during the year of my mother's illness and then all the years after she was gone. Without her there to cover for him, to run interference, to neutralize his absences with her luminous presence, and his selfishness with her love—without her there as our go-between, my father's Russian doll broke open and little by little, layer by layer, I saw the real person inside.

Even before she died, there were a few previews of the Other Father, thanks to a strange family reunion.

Spring 1954. It is an unseasonably warm afternoon. I answer the doorbell and there on the doorstep is a young woman wearing glasses and a long braid. "Hello," she says, extending her hand. "I'm Rena."

That is how I meet my father's third daughter, my other sister, who has finally come to life from the family tree in the sand. Given the drama of the moment, the twenty-seven-year-old Rena seems subdued though not at all unpleasant. Her mission is a practical one, she says, with a directness I would soon recognize as typical. She has come for "our" father's help. She wants to move out of the apartment where she has been living with her deranged mother, whose violence has escalated so alarmingly that it is not even safe for her to go back alone to pack up her things. She needs Daddy to get a court order so that she can return in the presence of a marshal or a police officer.

After a reunion with our father that can only be described as sedate, and after a dinner during which my mother seems to be trying extra hard to make her feel welcome, Rena spends the next several days with us sleeping in our attic bedroom. I rush home from school every day to spend time with her, as if she is a visiting mermaid who might disappear with the next wave. One evening, she tells me almost dispassionately how her mother hears voices, hallucinates, beats her mercilessly. Once the woman nearly blinded Rena with a blow to her eyes that broke her glasses; several times her mother attempted to strangle her, and once she dangled her out of a window, bragging, "I gave birth to you, so I can kill you."

"Why did you stay?" I ask, incredulous.

She says she stayed because there was nowhere else to go, no one else to support her mother, and no one to protect her half-sister Ellen, who is about my age. But now it has become too dangerous to remain. "If I get killed myself, I can't protect Ellen any better than I can by leaving," she says. "And if I stay, I know I will be killed."

Daddy obtains the court order and helps Rena secure her belongings. She moves into an apartment of her own, but continues her regular visits, saying she wants to get to know me better. Sometimes she sleeps over for a few days at a time. Neighbors have noticed. Friends are asking questions. Mommy and Daddy tell Rena they want to acknowledge her in the community, but rather than disentangle everyone's complicated relationships at this late date, they ask if she would mind being introduced as a cousin.

To be disowned not once but twice, to be rejected after being rediscovered, to find her father more interested in the judgments of his community than the feelings of his daughter—how that must hurt. But Rena just nods and says cousin is fine.

I notice that whenever Daddy is around, Rena's voice assumes a flat, formal tone, whereas in Mommy's presence, she is chatty and relaxed. As Mommy's illness sets in and her condition worsens, Rena is helpful and solicitous, in the manner of one who has a lot of experience putting herself last. I am confused by her alternating kindness and coldness, her eagerness to visit and then her airs of detachment once she is here.

The hours I spend with her away from the house confirm that this new sister of mine is a true eccentric. She keeps her entire wardrobe piled up on her ironing board. A Bohemian-style nonconformist, she wears a long braid and no makeup when the most admired woman in America is Mamie Eisenhower. She makes obscure references to the principles of cybernetics or physiometry, and enjoys correcting people's pronunciations. ("When you hide something, you secrete it," she intones, though the word sounds like oozing to me.) Her arcane vocabulary sends me rushing to the dictionary after every visit to look up words like *tautology* and *anima*, which she sprinkles throughout ordinary conversation—and which I will gleefully encounter months later on the College Boards exam.

"Her I.Q. is 180," says my father by way of explanation one evening after she has left. He seems proud and proprietary, as if her intelligence were entirely of his making.

Rena is an anthropologist specializing in Gypsy cultures. She has a Ph.D. She speaks twenty Romani dialects. As she reveals more and more about herself, I begin to feel like an apprentice rather than a baby sister. She brings me with her to visit with the Gypsies who live in upper Manhattan among whom she did her doctoral fieldwork. I meet the king of the tribe and learn that he has adopted Rena as his honorary daughter. I do not miss the irony of this: my father, our father, adopted Betty, who had wandered like a gypsy child in search of a family, while his daughter Rena found her family in a Gypsy tribe.

I realize "all of a sudden" that I am the sister of a certifiable prodigy and a Romani princess. As delighted as I am with Rena, I am still mystified by her emotional restraint. Even though Daddy did not feel able to acknowledge their relationship publicly, I cannot understand why she isn't happier to be back with her long-lost father after all these years.

"I came to him because I had no place else to go for help,"

she says, when I ask about her intractable coolness. "Now, my interest is in developing a compensatory relationship with you, not with him. He could live without me for fourteen years. I can live without him now."

"But he wanted to keep seeing you," I insist, repeating the story as I heard it on the beach three years before. "It's just that your mother threatened to harm you if he tried to get in touch or fight for you in court, so he stopped trying."

"My mother harmed me anyway," she says bitterly. "And he knew she would because she was always violent. No, that's not what happened. His court-ordered visitation rights were contingent on his paying child support. When you were born, he stopped paying, so my mother stopped the visits. He never fought for me. He didn't want me. He left me alone with her and I never heard from him again."

I think of Rena, twelve years old, waiting every Saturday morning for a father who just stopped showing up. I must have seemed like her replacement, her father's new toy. I think about the next fourteen years without a word, a phone call, a letter; fourteen years trapped with a demented woman; fourteen years of beatings. I cannot believe that the father who abandoned his daughter to that abuse is the same man I call Daddy. I cannot believe my father could do such a thing. Therefore, I cannot believe Rena. Soon, I will discover him for myself.

February 3, 1955. It is an ordinary school night except that my mother is not home; she is in the hospital. After supper, my father takes me into his study, closes the door, and offers me one of his Luckies. He flicks his Zippo lighter for both of us to draw from the flame. I know something terrible is coming. Until now, I had only smoked behind his back. His gesture tells me I am about to be addressed as an adult.

"Your mother has cancer," he says.

There is no preamble. He prides himself on going straight to the point. "The doctors say she has less than six months to live. You'll have to be very helpful and very brave."

That's it. And that matter-of-fact attitude marks his behavior after we bring Mommy home from the hospital to die slowly and painfully in their bedroom. During the whole ordeal, he takes care of things in his no-nonsense, efficient way. There are treatments and medications, doctors to consult, a housekeeper and nurse to hire. No time for reflection. No room for feelings, or ceremony, or despair.

"We all die sometime," he says.

But not my mommy. Not this wonderful, giving woman who sacrifices for everyone else. Not my mother.

"No use complaining about what we can't help. But you can help me get through this. Talk to me. Hug me.

"The best thing we can do is to go on with our lives." And he does.

April 20, 1955. She dies during the night. There are tears in my father's eyes when he awakens me. I won't say he cries but they are, to my knowledge, his first tears. He says I can go into their room and kiss my mother good-bye. Then he shifts into his lawyerly mode, making phone calls, giving out assignments, complaining about how much detail work is required by death and dying. Even the modest requirements of a Jewish burial, he says, are too elaborate.

"Don't do any of this for me, I just want to be cremated." (Twenty-seven years later, he is cremated, according to his wishes, and contrary to Jewish law.)

Our week at home sitting shiva (the seven days of mourning) is interminable for him. He is impatient with the daytime inactivity, the constant flow of visitors, and the mountains of food accumulating on the kitchen counter. During the evening memorial service, however, he comes into his own. He leads the prayers.

One night, about twenty people are milling about the house but by Jewish computation, there are only nine Jews in our living room. This is because only nine men have shown up for the memorial service. A minyan, the quorum required for Jewish communal prayer, calls for ten men.

"I know the Hebrew," I say. "You can count me, Daddy."

I meant, I want to count. I meant, don't count me out just because I am a girl.

"You know it's not allowed," he replies, frowning.

"For my own mother's Kaddish I can be counted in the minyan. For God's sake, it's your house! It's your minyan, Daddy."

"Not allowed!" says my father.

He calls the synagogue and asks them to send us a tenth man.

May 1955. My father gives away my mother's things. Barely out of childhood, grieving, I do not think to petition for a hope chest of her clothes, or her paintings, or the books, china, or costume jewelry that were precious to her. Unmindful that I might someday have a home of my own and wish to own concrete mementos of my mother's life, my father lets the relatives pick through her closets and drawers like scavengers at a flea market. He lets them load their arms and pack their cars and take away her history.

Summer 1956. I find out that my father has sold our house and most of our furniture. He never asks me how I feel about it. He never gives me the chance to say what objects have special meaning to me. It does not occur to him that I might think of the contents of our house as mine and hers, as well as his.

Everything is sold before I know it. At first, I do not understand. And then I understand. He is getting married. He gets married. His new wife is a Southern belle with an exaggerated drawl, Jewish but unschooled in Judaism and unobservant, fifty-four years old but relentlessly girlish and charming, and self-centered to a fault. She is given to dramatic color-coordinated outfits and dyed black hair styled sleek as patent leather into a chignon at the top of her head. I am in my peasant-blouse-and-black-stockings Bohemian phase. She and I have nothing in common but our mutual distrust. Her Southern baby talk is insufferable. She manipulates my father who dotes on her, serves her, tolerates her domestic ineptitude, seems enchanted by her glamour and helplessness. She is to my mother as polyester is to pure silk. She is a phony. I hate my father's wife. It does not occur to me to hate him for choosing her.

They rent an apartment. The apartment has one bedroom. There is a daybed for me in the foyer. I am a freshman in college. I don't need a whole bedroom just for school vacations, do I? It is clear the new wife doesn't want me around. What my father wants is not at all clear to me anymore.

November 1958. I am a senior in college. I call my father at the office and tell him I must see him. I will leave after my last class and will arrive in New York around seven P.M. Where can we meet?

Since I've never before asked for a scheduled appointment and since I will be driving for four hours from Massachusetts on a weekday night, I expect he will deduce that my business with him is urgent. In a wild moment, I even imagine he might ask me to have dinner with him. But that night, as always, he has a meeting. He tells me to come straight to the Rego Park Jewish Center on Queens Boulevard, and fetch him out of his meeting. We'll have our talk in one of the empty Hebrew School classrooms and when we're done, he will return to his meeting.

I leave Brandeis at three P.M., drive for four hours, and locate him in a smoke-filled room. He excuses himself and we find some privacy in a classroom with low kindergarten tables and little chairs. I sit in a little chair. He sits on the table. I tell him I am pregnant. My life will be ruined if I don't have an abortion, but I don't have the money. (Abortion was then illegal and expensive.) I don't know where to find a doctor. I am paralyzed with fear. He assures me that he will make the necessary arrangements. No moralizing. No scolding. But also no comfort. Straight to the practical issues: who, when, where, and how much. Then he returns to his meeting and I get back into my car and drive back to school.

Late one night, a few weeks later, I go to a darkened doctor's office accompanied by my father and his new wife. I hate having her along but my father insists we may need a woman in case there are complications. She acts as if we are asking her to rob a bank. Then she plays the martyred accomplice. There are no complications. The abortion costs my father $350 but I pay him back.

It takes me five years, but I pay him every penny.

I needn't dredge up other such recollections. You get the point. That's the Other Father, the one I have to reconcile with the good Daddy before I can fully understand myself and, most particularly, my relationship to Judaism.

In the years after my mother died, incident after incident left me feeling confused and betrayed. At first, I excused my father's behavior, blaming his maleness for his mindless insensitivities, blaming his new wife for everything else. Gradually, it became clear to me that "his behavior" was who he was. I lowered my expectations. It didn't help. I began to feel the emotions that Rena had acted out during her visits with him. I withdrew. I closed up. I stopped hoping. This might have been a manageable psychological problem if it had not become an untenable spiritual one.

Somehow, father and faith had gotten all mixed up; I could not separate them. I couldn't mark where one began and the other ended. Both were male-gendered sources of rewarding power. My religion was personified by my daddy, and I was socially enmeshed in a Jewish world controlled by Jewish men. Whatever honors I had been given or denied were granted or withheld by Jewish men. The creators of historical consciousness and the guardians of privilege were Jewish men like my father, often my father himself. When it suited his needs, Daddy had taken me into his realms; I was his little scholar, his Bat Mitzvah girl. But when it mattered to me to be included, he had exercised his masculine right to shut me out.

In a matter of months, this man who was once my adored mentor had revealed himself to be self-centered, unfeeling— almost a stranger. Because father and faith had been so intertwined, it was only logical that when I broke away from the enchantment of my father, I also cut off my formal affiliation with Judaism. Merge the Jewish patriarch with patriarchal Judaism and when you leave one, you leave them both.

For years, I stayed away from organized Judaism, from the institutionalized Judaism of my father. I married a Jewish man who had never been bar mitzvahed. I raised a Jewish son and two Jewish daughters but did not have a bar or bat mitzvah for any of them. I suppose I did not want those I loved to be covenanted in the faith of the father who betrayed me, the faith that left me out.

Over time, I reconnected to Jewish life in a process that I shall describe another day. But I have yet to deal with Daddy. The Other Father keeps getting in my way.

cynthia morse

legacy

when i return
and rustle the dust
peel away the shrouds of
ancient and precious things
stored away for a long passage
assembling the truth of
happenings and remembrance
what will be my measure?
where will i set them as a guide?

i have journeyed the way
on my own
reaching for a path to my history
veiled from the icons
cast precisely around my feet

i will voyage my self
alone
and where will you be
that i might call to you?
how shall i cry out
across the fog and muddied plain?

what will you answer?
will i know it and respond?

how shall i incant you
summon up the torn and ravished
wanderings of
our tribe?
and then piece our covenant back together
lovingly
but blind?

Marlene Adler Marks

Macaroni and Cheese

Proust had his madeleines, the buttery cakes that conjured up his childhood. And Laura Esquivel (*Like Water for Chocolate*) has her quail with rose petals. But I have macaroni and cheese, eternally evoking for me postwar suburban family life before the advent of takeout.

When I say that I had a macaroni-and-cheese kind of childhood, I'm not talking about the gourmet "pasta and four-cheese" concoctions we see these days. No, I come from the world of Kraft, "good food and good food ideas," as Ed Herlihy used to say on *The Children's Hour*, which the company sponsored. My mother was a disciple of the home efficiency movement of the Eisenhower era. An excellent cook by nature, and a born skeptic, she nevertheless accepted as gospel that Minute Rice, Potato Buds and "boil in the bag" vegetables were inherently faster and tastier, not to mention cheaper, than their unprocessed ancestors. Once, when I was already married, I challenged her to a "rice-off": a cooking competition pitting her Minute Rice against my full grain. She turned me down, lest she lose her faith.

And faith was important. Through these convenience foods, families like mine made their passage out of the ghetto and into the heart of America. The journey from knishes to

Potato Buds was a leap of both consciousness and belief. At the dining room table, we children and grandchildren of immigrants were making not only culinary but political assumptions, learning to identify ourselves not with Warsaw, Berlin or Kiev, the war-ravaged places left behind not so long ago, but with Kellogg's of Battle Creek.

And so it was that fictional cooks like Betty Crocker became the culinary equivalent of Andy Hardy, welcomed into our homes as helpful ambassadors to a new land. And behind them were scores of anonymous chefs from test kitchens all across America, dreaming up classy dishes like Chicken a La King, which my brother and I regarded as "boss" and which were available to everyone via the label of Campbell's Cream of Mushroom Soup. Gourmet democracy in action.

And, of course, there was Wonder Bread—in every particular, from its spongy white center to its grainless, seedless crust, a rejection of European rye. Wonder Bread was not only everything that it took to be an American—why else must a bread build strong bodies twelve ways?—but everything that a would-be American was expected to give up: taste, specific culture, grit. The Wonder Bread factory was right across the river and every New York City school child visited there as a school trip, peering into the vats filled with yeasty dough, bringing home gifts of tiny spongy loaves wrapped in red-yellow-and-blue-ballooned bags. How could we not feel safe in this breadbasket America?

Because what, really, was the alternative? Those who today shake their heads at the immigrant generation's rush to cut off their roots have forgotten one crucial fact: Life in the old country was hell.

I used to ask my grandfather, "Please, tell me something of the Way It Was."

"What's to tell?" he would say. Plenty, actually. Statutes covering thousands of pages of discriminatory laws against Jews. Pogroms. Fear. It was no Paradise Lost; even the potato knishes are better here.

My mother loved those Sputnik-era foods, and all these

many years later, I can see why. In their very efficiency they gave tacit approval to her (and much of American woman-hood's) fondest wish: to get out of the kitchen and get down to business! The very packaging for the frozen carrots and peas that were our family's staple (the carrots cut into tiny quarter-inch cubes, cutting preparation time to seconds) said so all but explicitly: there's more to life than what you've got.

And indeed there was. The contributions of American women during the last thirty years are immeasurable for a simple reason: a woman finally freed from household drudg-ery lives not only for herself, but for every woman before or yet to come who lives in chains. She forms committees, reads to children, organizes her community, works to pass national health care legislation. All because some home economist thought to cut a carrot into cubes.

I learned to make macaroni and cheese as part of the Mon-day and Thursday regimen of "dairy meals" by which my mother ordered her week. (Tuesday and Wednesday were lambchops and meatballs; Friday chicken; Saturday and Sun-day were, respectively, cold cuts and Chinese food.) When I got home from school on dairy days, I'd take the fleshy white flounder out of the refrigerator, dip a piece first into egg, then into flour, and leave it ready for my mother to fry when she came home from work.

Then I'd open the blue-and-gold box that cost seventeen cents and fed a family of four. The water was in the pot, ready for boiling the noodles. I did as the package directed: Melt three tablespoons of butter or margarine. Add three table-spoons of milk. Stir in package of "cheese sauce mix."

During the seven minutes I stood there stirring the amber-colored gloop, I imagined little girls across the country doing the same thing. We were part of a great historical stream, from the farmer with his cow, to the scientists who turned cheese into powder, to me with my spoon. On and on to greatness. Ah! Macaroni and cheese. How America loved me!

Contributors

Karen E. Bender grew up in Los Angeles and now lives in New York. Her fiction has appeared in *Response, The Iowa Review and the Kenyon Review* and won the 1993 Pushcart Prize. "Inside the Ark" is from a novel in progress.

Dinah Berland's poetry has appeared in *The Antioch Review, Ploughshares, The Iowa Review, New Letters, Stand-up Poetry Anthology,* and other publications.

Jane Bernstein is the author of a novel, *Departures,* and a memoir, *Loving Rachel.* Her work has appeared in the "Hers" section of *The New York Times.* She teaches in the writing program at Carnegie Mellon University.

Amy Bloom is a short story writer and practicing psychotherapist whose first collection, *Come to Me,* was nominated for the National Book Award.

Hindi Brooks has had plays and TV scripts produced and published in America and abroad. She teaches playwrighting at UCLA and is a member of The Dramatists Guild and the Writers Guild of America.

Belinda Cooper is a lawyer, journalist, and translator who has just returned from seven years in Berlin.

Laura Cunningham is a playwright, novelist *(Sleeping Arrangements, Sweet Nothings,* and *Third Parties),* and journalist. Her plays have been produced at Steppenwolf Theatre. She is the recipient of a National Endowment for the Arts award and a New York Foundation for the Arts fellowship. Her pieces have appeared in *The New Yorker, The Atlantic, Esquire,* and *The New York Times.* Laura Cunningham lives in New York City.

Carol V. Davis is a poet living in Los Angeles.

Shira Dicker is a freelance writer who has written for a variety of publications, including *The New York Times, The Forward, Tikkun,* and the *Jerusalem Report.* "The New Girl" is excerpted from her unpublished novel, *Revelations of a Rabbi's Daughter.*

Dina Elenbogen's poems have appeared in *Calyx, Prairie Schooner,* and Poet Lore, as well as such anthologies as the recent *Rage Before Pardon: Poets Bear Witness to the Holocaust.*

Marcia Falk's recent books include *The Song of Songs: A New Translation and Interpretation* (Harper San Francisco, 1990) and a translation of Yiddish poetry, *With Teeth in the Earth: Selected Poems of Malka Heifetz Tussman* (Wayne State Univ. Press, 1992). Her latest book is *The Book of Blessings: New Jewish Prayers and Rituals for Daily Life, the Sabbath, and the New Moon Festival* (Harper San Francisco, 1996).

Shirley Polinsky Fein, storyteller and writer, lives with her husband Arnold on an island off the west coast of Florida. She is completing a family memoir, *Dear Nathan: Family Matters.*

Jyl Lynn Felman is a writer and critic whose work has been published in *Her Face in the Mirror* (Beacon 1994), as well as in *Tikkun, The Forward, Jewish Currents,* and *Bridges.* Her first collection of short fiction, *Hot Chicken Wings,* was a 1993 Lambda Literary Award Finalist. She teaches in the Women's Studies Program at Brandeis University.

Jane Schulzinger Fox's short fiction has been published in the *ORT Reporter, Reconstructionist, Toronto Jewish Dialogue, Western People,* and elsewhere. She spends most of her days wrestling with computer networks and databases at the University of Wisconsin and usually she wins.

Jennifer Futernick is a poet and writer in San Francisco. She has been published in the *San Francisco Examiner* and *A Small Box of Poets.*

Miriyam Glazer is associate professor of literature and chair of the literature department at Lee College of the University of Judaism. She is the author of many scholarly articles, most recently on Jewish-American women writers. She edited *Burning Air and a Clear Mind: Contemporary Israeli Women Poets* and is editing a new book, *Contemporary Israeli Women Writers: Poetry and Prose* (SUNY Press).

Karen Golden is a Los Angeles-based storyteller, musician, and writer specializing in Jewish, multicultural, personal, and historical stories. She has been featured in the *L.A. Times,* on NPR and in 1993 released her audio tape *Tales and Scales: Stores of Jewish Wisdom.* Her work appears in *Chosen Tales: Stories Told by Jewish Storytellers* and *Life Cycles, Vol. 3.*

Allegra Goodman's stories, originally published in *The New Yorker* and *Commentary* while she was a student at Harvard, are collected in *Total Immersion.* Now completing a Ph.D. in Renaissance Literature as a Mellon Fellow at Stanford University, her new story collection is *The Family Markowitz* (Farrar, Straus & Giroux, 1996).

Vivian Gornick's essays on literature and feminism have appeared in the *Village Voice*, *The New York Times*, and *The Nation*. She is co-editor of *Woman in Sexist Society* and author of *Women in Science, In Search of Ali Mahmoud: An American Woman in Egypt*, and *Fierce Attachments*.

Kathryn Hellerstein teaches Yiddish literature and language at the University of Pennsylvania. She translated and edited the Yiddish poems of Moyshe-Leyb Halpern, *In New York: A Selection* (Jewish Publication Society, 1982). Her poems, translations, and essays have appeared in *Poetry, Partisan Review, Tikkun, The New York Times Book Review*, and other journals and anthologies. She has just completed *The Selected Poems of Kadya Molodowsky*.

Erica Jong is the author of six novels and memoirs including *Fear of Flying, Fear of Fifty* and *How to Save Your Own Life* as well as five volumes of poetry, a children's book, and a classic book about witches.

Persis Knobbe, who writes in Marin County, California, is working on a collection tentatively titled *The Morris Stories*. Two stories have been published, in *American Fiction III* and in *The Best of Writers at Work, 1994*.

Fern Kupfer is the author of three novels including her latest *Love Lies* and a memoir, *Before and After Zachariah*. She teaches creative writing at Iowa State University.

Joan Lipkin is a playwright and director of That Uppity Theatre Company in St. Louis, Missouri. Her plays include *Some of My Best Friends Are, Small Domestic Acts* and *He's Having Her Baby*.

Marlene Adler Marks is a writer, speaker, and award-winning nationally syndicated columnist for Jewish newspapers and the *Los Angeles Times*. She is managing editor of *The Jewish Journal of Greater Los Angeles*.

Susan Merson is an actor and director in Los Angeles, whose writing includes her own one-woman play, *Reflections of a China Doll*.

cynthia morse is a poet who lives in Los Angeles.

Sara Nuss-Galles has written for such publications as *Lilith*, *Ort Report* and *Na'Amat Woman*. She lives in New Jersey.

Grace Paley's classic short stories have appeared in many volumes including *The Little Disturbances of Man* (1959), *Enormous Changes at the Last Minutes* (1974), *Later That Same Day* (1985) and *Grace Paley: The Collected Stories* (1994). She is also the author of two books of poetry and one volume of poems and prose pieces.

Letty Cottin Pogrebin is an activist, essayist, and author of six books including *Among Friends*, *Family Politics*, and *Deborah, Golda and Me*. She is a founding editor of *Ms.* magazine and co-developer, with Marlo Thomas, of the "Free to Be" series.

Sharon Pomerantz is a freelance writer who lives in Manhattan. Her essays and features have appeared in the *Village Voice*, *New York Newsday*, *Hadassah Magazine*, and *The Jewish Week*.

Jori Ranhand is a poet, writer, and critic who teaches English in New York. Her articles have appeared in *Parting Gifts*, *The Plowman*, *Scrivener* and *Arizona Mandala Magazine*.

Carolyn A. Rogers lives in Los Angeles, where she writes essays and short stories. She teaches the Great Books course at the University of Judaism.

L. Schimel's work has appeared in 45 anthologies, including *Daughters of Darkness II: More Lesbian Vampire Stories*; *The Random House Treasury of Light Verse*; *Weird Tales from Shakespeare, Tales of the Knights Templar*. Her work has been published in Dutch, Finnish, German, Mandarin, and Polish. This piece originally appeared in the literary magazine *Rosebud*.

Sheila Schwartz was a Stegner Fellow at Stanford, has received grants from the Illinois and Ohio arts councils, and is currently working on a novel.

Enid Shomer is a poet and writer who has been published in *The New Yorker, Atlantic, Paris Review, Tikkun*, and others. Her books include *Imaginary Men*, winner of the Iowa Short Fiction Award, and *This Close to the Earth*.

Ilana Girard Singer is a columnist for the *East Bay Journal*. A different version of this article appeared in *Lilith*.

Susan Terris is a poet and critic whose work has appeared in *The Antioch Review, Poetry Northwest, Poet & Critic, Tikkun, Spoon River Poetry Review, Pudding Review*, and other publications. She is the author of *Killing in the Comfort Zone, Author! Author*, and *Nell's Quilt*.

tova is a poet whose work has appeared in such anthologies as *Sinister Wisdom, Common Lives/Lesbian Lives, The Raven Chronicles, Songs of Our Voice: Award Winning Poetry on the Jewish Experience and Lesbian Bedtime Stories*. She has won the Anna Davidson Rosenberg award for poems on the Jewish Experience and in 1994 was a judge for that contest.

Judith Ungar is an attorney and writer in New Jersey whose stories have appeared in *Tikkun* and *The New York Times*.

Alexandra J. Wall is a writer in New York. This is her first published story.

Theresa Weisberg began as a dancer on the Jewish stage, then worked at the VA in Illinois and as a butter agent at the Dept. of Agriculture, ending up in the Chemical Warfare procurement office part of the Lend-Lease Program for Russia. She ran political campaigns and sat on the first Illinois commission for the status of women. Her daughter, Ruth Weisberg, is a nationally acclaimed artist whose shows have been featured at the Jewish Museum in New York, among many others.

Carolyn White, a professional storyteller living in Michigan, writes adult and children's fiction encorporating folklore. Her stories have appeared in such publications as *Parabola*, *Magical Blend*, and *Green's Magazine*; her poems have been published in *Michigan Quarterly Review*, *The Book of Contemporary Myth*, and *Dreamworks*. This poem appeared in the anthology *Bubbe Meisehs by Shayneh Maidelehs*, edited by Leslea Newman.

S. L. Wisenberg's stories have appeared in *Common Bonds: Stories about Modern Texas Women, Ploughshares, Tikkun* and *Word of Mouth 2* (Crossing Press).

Jane Yolen is the author of over 150 books for children and adults including *The Devil's Arithmetic* (winner of the Jewish Book Award) and *Briar Rose*. "Names" was published in her anthology *Tales of Wonder* (Schocken Books, 1983).

Permissions

"Needlepoint," from *Loveroot*, by Erica Jong, first published in *Ms.* magazine, ©1968, 1969, 1973, 1974, 1975 by Erica Mann Jong, reprinted by permission of Henry Holt and Co., Inc.

"The Nose-Fixer," by Persis Knobbe, used by permission of the author.

"Sleepwalking Through Suburbia," by Fern Kupfer, used by permission of the author.

"Silent Night," by Joan Lipkin, used by permission of the author.

"Macaroni and Cheese," by Marlene Adler Marks, used by permission of the author.

"Blood in the Sand," by Susan Merson, used by permission of the author.

"legacy," by cynthia morse, used by permission of the author.

"Schmutz" by Sara Nuss-Galles, used by permission of the author.

"In This Country, But in Another Language, My Aunt Refuses to Marry the Men Everyone Wants Her To," from *Later The Same Day* by Grace Paley, ©1985, by Grace Paley, reprinted by permission of Farrar, Straus & Giroux, Inc.

"I Don't Like to Write About My Father," by Letty Cottin Pogrebin, from *Deborah, Golda And Me*, ©1991 by Letty Cottin Pogrebin, reprinted by permission of Crown Publishers, Inc.

"Grinder," by Sharon Pomerantz, used by permission of the author.

"Desert Song," by Jori Ranhand, used by permission of the author. This piece appeared in the Baltimore Jewish Times.

"The Get" by Carolyn A. Rogers, used by permission of the author.

"Kiddush Cup," by L. Schimel, used by permission of the author.

"Mutatis Mutandis," by Sheila Schwartz, ©1991 by Sheila Schwartz reprinted by permission of Pushcart Press, P.O. Box 380, Wainscott, NY 11975. Telephone (516) 324-9300.

"My Father's *Kichel*," by Enid Shomer, used by permission of the author.

"The Secret," by Ilana Girard Singer, used by permission of the author.

"Baba," by Susan Terris, used by permission of the author.

"the mourner," by tova, used by permission of the author.

"Prayers," by Judith Ungar, used by permission of the author.

"The Way 'We' Were," by Alexandra J. Wall, used by permission of the author.

"Theresa Weisberg's Wedding," as told to her daughter, Ruth Weisberg, used by permission of the author.

"My Grandma Had a Lover," by Carolyn White, used by permission of the author. It originally appeared in *Bubba Meisehs for Sheyna Meidels*, edited by Leslea Newmann (HerBooks, P.O. Box 7467, Santa Cruz, CA 95061).

"Shema, The First Prayer You Learn," used by permission of the author. It was first published in *Belles Lettres, Winter 93/94*.

"Names," by Jane Yolen, ©1983 by Jane Yolen, reprinted by permission of Curtis Brown Ltd. First appeared in *Tales of Wonder*, published by Schocken.